WALTER TULL, 1888–1918 OFFICER, FOOTBALLER

All the guns in France couldn't wake me.

Phil Vasili

Raw Press

This book is dedicated to Cindy Creasey,
and the Finlayson, Humphrey and Coombe families

First published in Great Britain by
Raw Press, 285 Commonside East, Mitcham, Surrey, CR4 1HD

Book production by The Running Head Limited, 13 Tredgold Lane,
Napier Street, Cambridge CB1 1HN, www.therunninghead.com
Printed in Great Britain by the MPG Books Group,
Bodmin and King's Lynn

A catalogue record for this book is available from the British Library

ISBN 978-0-9563954-1-2 (hbk)
ISBN 978-0-9563954-0-5 (pbk)

Photographs 1, 6, 7, 9, 15–19 and 25 by kind permission of the Finlayson
Family Collection, © 2010; photographs 4 and 5 courtesy of Action for
Children, © 2010; photograph 14 courtesy of Imperial War Museum, © 2010

Other books by Phil Vasili:
The First Black Footballer: Arthur Wharton 1865–1930. An Absence of Memory
Colouring over the White Line: The History of Black Footballers in Britain

Contents

Acknowledgements 9

1 Finding the Tulls *11*

2 A mixed-heritage family in 19th-century Folkestone *27*

3 Tull, the 'many' and the 'few' *36*

4 The Children's Home and Orphanage *54*

5 Football *75*

6 Other pioneer Black footballers in the UK, 1872–1918 *110*

7 Bloods, sweat and fears: other Black sports people *127*

8 War *138*

9 'Not of pure European descent' *187*

10 Here and now *216*

Notes *231*

Bibliography *245*

Index *251*

Acknowledgements

There are many people to thank for their help and encouragement in ensuring this book is available to those that are interested in Walter. The descendants of his brothers Edward and William, the Finlayson and Humphrey families, have been nothing but helpful, kind and supportive as has Stephen Coombe, a cousin of Walter's from his mother's family. Maggie Stephenson of the Dover War Memorial project kindly put me in touch with Stephen.

Professor David Killingray and Marika Sherwood encouraged me at the beginning of my research in 1993. David took the time and effort to read a draft of the manuscript in 2008, providing invaluable comments and suggestions.

Thanks also go to Andrew Riddoch who agreed to read, edit and offer observations on early chapters covering Walter's military career.

There are many altruistic individuals who have volunteered information about Walter, most notably Northampton historian Paul Bingham. Also from that town and county has come an incredible amount of interest in, and support for, bringing this story back into the public domain. Other Northamptonians who have selflessly given their time, energy and assistance include Sean Donovan, Brian Lomax and Tony Clark of Northampton Town FC, Nikki Taylor of the Northampton Black History Association and Northampton South MP Brian Binley. Friends and colleagues have had to suffer moans, listen to my excitement, witness my setbacks and still they remain friends. You have been magnificent in your patience, advice and loyalty: Alan Harman, Eddie Shevlin, Tony Whelan, Colin Yates, David Thacker and Eric Burnett are unlucky enough to be identified. There were many more.

ACKNOWLEDGEMENTS

I met David Thacker, Tony Whelan and Colin Yates through my research and I've had the pleasure and enjoyable experience of working with them on Walter Tull related projects. Colin's beautiful portrayal of Walter can be found on the cover.

I have gathered useful and enlightening insights from Sarah Metcalfe, who prompted me to consider Walter's poignant and revealing statement, written from the Western Front, as the title of the book (and is surely destined for a great career as documentary filmmaker); also Peter Daniel and Camilla Webb of Westminster Archives with whom I had the humbling experience of bringing Walter's inspiring story to hundreds of school pupils around the country. Their enthusiasm for facilitating a greater knowledge of Walter among primary school pupils added a sensitivity to his narrative that I hope has helped me communicate his story more accessibly than I would have done.

A belated thank you to Ambalavaner Sivanandan, Liz Fekete and all at the Institute of Race Relations for publishing the early research findings. Your confidence in the story provided the adrenalin and energy for what followed.

To Manley, Daphne and Teresa Thomas, thank you for your assistance, help and hard work.

To Paul Thomas of Raw Press, you are a valued friend and mentor.

To David Williams and Carole Drummond of The Running Head, your expertise has been invaluable.

Finally, much love and gratitude goes to my partner Cindy and my children, Andrea, Fionnulla, Alex and Louisa. They, as much as the man himself, have helped me in more ways than I can list to understand Walter's preoccupations and concerns and in doing so to understand a little more about myself.

1

Finding the Tulls

A problem with having a second-rate memory is that you lose confidence in what you know. You forget that you have that piece of information, detail, reference stored somewhere in the darker, more inaccessible corridors of the brain. Before starting to write I went back to my files, re-reading everything I had on 2nd Lieutenant Walter Tull and his wider family. It wasn't insubstantial. A consequence of diminished memory is that you carry with you *always* a faint feeling that you do not have enough information, or that you have not exhausted every line of research, confidently to embark on writing a narrative that will do justice to your subject. Despite the slowed momentum caused by these niggling doubts, the upside of returning to my files and folders was relearning Walter and the tale of his discovery.

At a Black and Asian Studies Association (BASA) conference in Nottingham in October 1993, David Killingray, a historian of Blacks in the British armed forces, among other topics, asked if, while researching the history of Black footballers in Britain, I had come across Walter Tull. I had, briefly, in Maurice Golesworthy's *Encyclopaedia of Association Football* under 'Coloured Players'. He is listed as 'D. Tull, forward with Northampton Town (then Southern League), Tottenham Hotspur, 1908–1914'. Another member of BASA, Marika Sherwood – this is probably the first time Marika has been described as 'another member' – had sent me a note mentioning Walter Tull and his older brother Edward, encountered while she was perusing the *League of Coloured Peoples Newsletter* from 1940. Edward was correcting his friend Harold Moody's assertion that his son Charles Arundel Moody had recently become the first Black infantry officer, reminding readers that Walter had achieved that status some 23 years earlier.

Neither Killingray nor Sherwood were pursuing Walter but they wondered if I was. I hadn't been with any great effort, until these casual enquiries. Close by dense, green Sherwood Forest, I was beginning to see the wood for the trees. Probing, poking and delving it appeared there had been no previous research into his life. Yet his status as a footballer and officer suggested a much more significant figure in Black and working-class British history than Golesworthy's few lines indicated.

Disappearing from my young family for a couple of weeks, I indulged myself by wading through Edwardian match reports at the British Library Newspaper Library in Colindale in north-west London. Searching blind, I soon realised that Golesworthy's information and chronological order of clubs – Northampton Town then Tottenham, between 1908 and 1914 – was inaccurate because nothing was turning up in the sports pages of the various newspapers from north London and the East Midlands' shoe and boot capital of Britain.

Dispirited but not defeated, I then hit the books, requesting any and every early 20th-century football book, annual and player biography at Cambridge University Library. This investigation reversed Golesworthy's order of clubs – Spurs, not Northampton, was his first professional club – and threw up another name, Clapton FC. However, in hindsight the most crucial piece of information unearthed was not about Walter but about his brother Edward, who had been a dentist.

Returning to my leaky shed-cum-study, using what little further information I'd uncovered, I sent out letters to academics and the three football clubs, begging for any scrap of information on this elusive and increasingly captivating figure. Impatient in my wait for replies I soon hit the road, scanning the microfiche records of the General Dental Council (GDC). This gave me Edward's last address before he died in 1950: 6 Marchall Street, Edinburgh, a detail of time and place that provided a useful marker; a research base camp.

Armed with a little more knowledge I wrote more letters, this time to free newspapers, appealing to readers for information about Mr Tull-Warnock, as Edward was known in his GDC records, and his immediate family. The *Edinburgh Herald and Post* phoned saying they would run an article containing the gist of my request, arguing it would give this intriguing story a few more column inches, attracting greater attention.

I don't know if it worked in that particular paper but I did receive some warm letters from former patients and acquaintances of Edward's. Mr A. C. Loudon of Glasgow wrote of his earliest memory of Mr Tull-Warnock, in 1925 as a 10-year-old boy, recalling the dentist living and practising at 419 St Vincent's Street, Glasgow. 'My parents were caretakers and I lived there. He was indeed a gentleman.' But the generous senior citizen provided no information on living relatives.

Isobel McDonald of Aberdeen wrote that Edward was her family's dentist in Glasgow.

> The last time I remember an appointment at Mr Tull-Warnock's is 1948. I was expecting my first daughter so the treatment was free. Until my husband left for Aberdeen in 1954, a Mr Godfrey had taken over the practice. I can remember the daughter's wedding photo in the waiting room, if I remember correctly, the groom was a minister.

The National Health Service was introduced in 1948, providing free dental treatment in circumstances such as those mentioned. I later found that the wedding photo is of Edward's only child, daughter Jean, marrying Duncan Finlayson. I saw it in June 2008 and was struck by Edward's proud, satisfied demeanour as he stood on the church steps, straight backed, arm-in-arm with his beloved child immediately after he had welcomed his son-in-law, who was pursuing a career as a minister in the Church of Scotland, into the family. Edward was known for speaking his feelings. He certainly wore his heart on his sleeve that day.

Isobel McDonald's letter delivered evocative detail in just a few sentences, yet frustratingly there was still no clue as to the whereabouts of living relatives, if indeed there were any. Another letter, from a Mr James M. Jack, told of Edward's practice in the Ayrshire coastal town, Girvan, where he treated patients on Saturdays and Wednesdays. On these days in the winter he would travel from Glasgow, said the writer from Troon, while in summer he stayed over. The house, he thought, belonged to a relative. 'I am sure he told me he played for Glasgow Rangers . . .'

Thirteen years after these details were thrust through my letterbox, I now know it wasn't Edward that played for Rangers; the address of the house-cum-practice was 5 Daisy Bank, Henrietta Street; and the relative was his eldest sister Cecilia – Cissie – Tull, who lived there permanently for some years, acting as caretaker, housekeeper, dental assistant and company for her younger brother.

While it was a thrill to open James Jack's envelope and read the contents, refolding his handwritten note I felt, guiltily, yet another tinge of disappointment in not finding an address, phone number or any contact detail for the Tulls and Tull-Warnocks. Interestingly and admirably, none of these letters writers mentioned Edward's ethnicity.

The frustration didn't last, extinguished with the arrival of two letters revealing the name and address of the Reverend Duncan Finlayson, a retired Church of Scotland minister, and his wife Jean, née Tull-Warnock. Bingo! Bullseye! Yeeha! They were from Mrs L. Wilson of Ayr and the Reverend Donald B. Rennie, respectively. Both, uncannily, mid-page, indented the Finlaysons' address in order to make it clear and emphatic. While the former did not elaborate on her connection to the Finlaysons, Rennie had taken the time and trouble to phone his close friends and associates before writing.

I've not been able to personally repay the kindness of these people. Some, such as Mr A. C. Loudon, 80 years old in January 1995, may not even be alive. All I can offer is acknowledgement of their generosity, which has continued to ferment and prosper. Their thoughtfulness helped set me on a path which has as yet no end, rather a series of destinations, some known, that have yielded more surprises, bounty, battles and meanderings, offering a quality to my life that I could not have imagined, hoped for or envisaged when Walter Tull first entered my world.

After reading the Rennie and Wilson letters I fired off a desperate plea to the Finlaysons: please tell me all you know about Walter. Came back the swift reply, we never met him! But we will meet you if you can find your way to North Shian, Appin, Argyll. The journey was more fruitful than I dared expect and I'm still en route, my days now, in 2008, taken over with the telling of the Tull story. Catching the West Highland Line train from Glasgow Central to Oban I was excited at meeting Walter Tull's living relatives and nervous that they would find my interest in their family an invasion of privacy. Though apprehensive, as the geography surrounding the train got more dramatic, the natural beauty of the landscape calmed me. After leaving Dumbarton, crossing the River Leven at Craigendoran, we met the West Highland Line proper. From this point the hills became bigger and the lochs more numerous. Gare Loch was the first, its blue-grey expanse supporting numerous colourful sailing boats.

Once out of Garelochhead station, we soon found Loch Long, which is an apt description of this slither of water. Here the hills push further into the sky and become mountains. As they enlarged so did the size of the lochs, with Ben Lomond and Loch Lomond dwarfing the train which, in comparison, resembled a toy on a miniature track. According to folklore the renowned Rob Roy MacGregor once robbed the rich to help the poor in these parts. I felt like I'd assumed a similar identity, that of the socially aware kleptomaniac, coming to steal the secret treasure of the Finlayson family vault.

We passed about five more lochs, all backdropped with imposing mountain terrain, before reaching the station of Oban, a port town, where I was met by the Reverend Finlayson. The village of North Shian, in Appin, Argyll, where Duncan and Jean lived, is some 23 miles north. Driving along the A828, following the contour of Loch Creran, listening to Duncan breaking the ice with tales chosen to amuse and relax, I soon realised my mischievous, charming host was no straight-laced minister of the Church of Scotland.

Taking a narrow track left we arrived at Rhugarbh Cottage, a caber-toss from the loch shore. Jean Finlayson welcomed me into their bungalow in this beautifully quiet village as if I was a long-standing and valued friend.

The Finlaysons had boxes and boxes of precious memorabilia relating to 'Uncle Walter', a wealth of family treasure her father had kept and protected since his brother's death and to which Jean and Duncan added their own reminiscences. These primary sources not only provided flesh for Walter's bones but also an abattoir of meat for all the other skeletons rattled by their rediscovery in west Scotland by a nosey interloper from southern England.

In front of me in these boxes, files and note books was so much of interest: letters from the orphanage where Walter was raised, letters from Argentina, letters from the Front, postcards of Walter playing for Spurs, team photographs of Spurs and Clapton, a citation for gallantry, a gold medal he won with Clapton, spoils of war sent from France; photo albums and more. I didn't know where to start.

After hours of indulgent scanning, note taking and referencing I taped an interview with Jean and Duncan in the hope that their recollections would help me better understand these artefacts. I hoped also that their memories would suggest a suitable starting point for further exploration of Walter's life.

Like all daughters who love their fathers, Jean wanted to talk about Edward as much as her uncle, who had died two years before she was born. She joked that football must have been in the Tull genes because, before practising as a dentist, her father had played football for Ayr Parkhouse and Girvan Athletic. During this time Edward had met Jimmy Bowie, who became a lifelong friend and golfing partner. While Bowie was a player for Rangers FC he encouraged the club to sign Walter. Edward had not been passive in the coaxing and capture, he had longed for his younger brother to live in Glasgow. He liked having his family close, said Jean, who, on Saturday afternoons during her adolescence, would travel by subway to Ibrox Park from their home in Randolph Road to watch Rangers from their seats in the directors' box, tickets courtesy of Mr Bowie. (After playing, Bowie became president of the club.)

Septuagenarian Jean's memories of her childhood were ingrained with fond nostalgia for her first home at 419 St Vincent's Street, the family home until 1926. Children remember scale, and her recollection was framed by the largeness of their ground floor flat in central Glasgow. It doubled as the dental practice, established by James Warnock, Edward's adoptive father and unqualified practitioner. Their dining room, used only on Sundays, was the patients' waiting room for the remainder of the week. Their sitting room looked out upon the yard, 'a vast grassless rubbish filled space surrounded on four sides by tenements'.[1] In the basement was the kitchen, maid's bedroom and a workshop in which dentures were made and repaired. The workshop mechanic was 'Wee Ferguson', whom Duncan remembers as having a wry, Glaswegian humour. Just after the Second World War posters offering 'twenty pounds a week with all found' for police work in troubled Palestine were scattered about Glasgow. 'Nae bloody likely, twenty poonds a week and nae foond' was the dental mechanic's response, conjuring an image of missing expatriate policemen dotted secretly around the Holy Land.

In her memoir Jean stresses that maid Bella, from Port Charlotte, Islay – with its sister islands Colonsay and Jura, off the west coast of Scotland – 'was very much part of the household and my confidante'. The young Gael even tried to teach the younger Glaswegian her language, without success.

Bella stayed with the Tull-Warnocks most of her life, living-in until she married in 1939, thereafter working as a daily helper. Yet she still 'had to fight for an increase in wages from £3 to £4 per month'[2] for a six-day week, commented Jean, just a touch sacrilegiously. Bella's work would begin at 6.30 am with the preparation of Edward and his wife Elizabeth's morning tea, after which breakfast would have to be ready before 8 am in order for Jean to be ready for school, the dentist for his practice. While having a maid was not what Edward had been used to in childhood, his wife had been raised in a domestic environment of servants, chauffeurs and relative affluence in Aberdeen.

Jean felt also she had had a privileged existence. Not only as a middle-class girl attending the fee-paying Glasgow High School for Girls but also as the only child of the extended Tull family patriarch. Though her father was a workaholic, she had had a stable, loving upbringing surrounded by concerned, active relatives and close family friends: 'I had a very happy childhood, very spoiled.'[3] Her recollection gave the impression her pigment-ation had not been an issue, which of course, in inter- and post-war Britain, it was. Indeed, that was why Edward paid for her education. As Duncan explained when I interviewed him again in 2008, Jean's father did not want her to suffer any more than she had to. Though proud of his mixed origins – a member of the League of Coloured Peoples, an admirer of Paul Robeson, a committed socialist, a singer of Negro spirituals – he was determined to use all powers and resources at his disposal to protect his daughter from casual racism. And, if this meant going against his col-lectivist principles and paying for her to attend an academic institution where there might be less overt prejudice, so be it.

> By my blood my daughter will have problems of the kind that I have had and if I can do anything to give her confidence and a bit of status, I know it's wrong but I am going to do it.[4]

Duncan mentioned an instance of bigotry that had seared Edward's con-sciousness with its brutal denial of human sensitivity: on graduating with a degree in dentistry – LDS – from the Royal Faculty of Physicians and Surgeons, Glasgow, in 1910 Edward's first job as an assistant dentist was in Birmingham. He had been appointed by post, having applied by letter, voluntarily enclosing a photograph making clear his ethnicity. Travelling south by train, arriving the evening before he was due to commence, new suited and clean booted, gold watch and chain adorning his waistcoat – a present from his proud, adoptive father – the expectant novice tapped on the door of the practice. What met him clawed the shine from Edward's beginner's enthusiasm. With an expression of uncomfortable surprise, bordering on shock, the dentist spluttered, 'My God, you're coloured, you'll destroy my practice in 24 hours!' before, without ceremony, sending him away. Edward did not want such emotive grenades landing at the feet of his prospective son-in-law. When Duncan asked for Jean's hand he forewarned: 'I can see there is no question of colour matters affecting you. You do realise your children may be Black . . . They may be blacker than me. And don't underestimate what that means'.[5]

Some thought Jean to be Mediterranean – Maltese was the most common assumption. Edward's prophecy did not take long to materialise. Walking the hallway of the hotel to the breakfast room on the first morning of their honeymoon at Bridge of Orchy, they were blasted with the outpourings of an anonymous diner telling his companions in a loud, emphatic voice that, on hearing the news that a friend had married a 'nigger', promised there would be 'no tar in his family'.[6] On entering the dining room, Duncan, an ex-boxer, wanted to silence the whitewasher with his knuckles but was persuaded otherwise by his resilient, thicker-skinned wife.

Edward's willingness to sacrifice political principle for personal circumstance is not unique. In 2003 Diane Abbott, the Labour MP for Hackney North and Stoke Newington, was criticised for sending her son to a fee-paying school in order that he should escape the supposedly irrepressible allure of gang culture within state schools. Her opponents mockingly noted her hypocrisy in earlier condemning other MPs from her party, such as Harriet Harman and Tony Blair, for sending their children to selective schools, in contravention of Labour Party policy of equality for all in 'education, education, education'.

Jean's father had a more relaxed approach to such matters because of his experience as a pupil at Allen Glen's, an elite (but not elitist) fee-paying school that emphasised sport and science as essential pillars of education. The ethos of their curriculum is summarised in the maxim 'healthy body, healthy mind'. The mature Edward, a practitioner of medical science and keen amateur sportsman, was living proof of the efficacy of his school's philosophy. As its embodiment it is no surprise that he was asked to be president of the Old Boys' Association. If this science and sport academy concentrated and focussed Edward's intellectual and physical predilections, a nod must also be given to the discipline required for single-minded success, a legacy forged during his 33 months' boarding at Bonner Road orphanage: Jean remembered her father taking a cold bath each morning and when off duty doing household chores, habits instilled while living in the Sister-run family houses of the Children's Home.

Allen Glen's innovative headmaster, John Guthrie Kerr, on taking over in 1890 transformed the learning environment from one of dour academic effort to the pursuit of intellectual and physical excellence through rigorous endeavour. He believed the formula nine parts perspiration plus one part inspiration equalled success.

> No obstacle – no progress; no fight, no joy of conflict . . . It is in personal effort and a sense of contest, in the things of the mind or the muscles, that youth will best attain to intellectual manhood, moral courage and physical fitness, and so promote efficiency for service to the world.[7]

For a period in the early 1900s Allen Glen's sports days were grand social events held at Hampden Park. It is said Edward 'played [football] with distinction'[8] for his school, which in all probability meant a few games on the hallowed turf of Scottish football. Later he turned out for Scottish League second division Ayr Parkhouse, local club Girvan Athletic and junior club Ballantrae. Characterised as 'a tricky inside forward and a menace in the goal area'[9] he was also a member of Turnberry Golf Club. In one season walking the greens he won three trophies, including the Glasgow Dental Cup which he retained for three consecutive years. Given the notorious exclusivity of golf clubs at this time – coloured clothing that stings your eyes, yes please; people of colour, no thanks – how Edward managed to bypass regulation and tradition and become a swinger at Turnberry would have had a lot to do with his cultural assets: his profession, education and religious beliefs and the friends and contacts made and fostered in those overlapping universes, such as Jimmy Bowie and Colonel Fred Reed, the latter raised in the slum tenements of William Street, Glasgow, who became a friend of Hugh Gaitskell and head of the General Post Office.

Edward eventually got a post as a probationer sometime around 1911, in Aberdeen, where, attending the Methodist Church, he met Elizabeth Hutchison. The knockback from Birmingham was serendipitous. He fell in love and, on 28 September 1918, Edward and Elizabeth married at

Crown Terrace Methodist Church, Aberdeen. Unfortunately the mood of the occasion was sombre, Edward still mourning the death of Walter, six months earlier. James Warnock had also passed away a few years previously, with Cissie coming up from England to look after 'mater' Jean Warnock.

Elizabeth – Betty – came from a family of well-known Aberdeen bakers, her father, Alexander Burnett Hutchison, using his business success and acumen to further his local political power and status by becoming Senior Baillie of the city. Jean felt her grandfather's illegitimate origin, down-to-earth nature and Methodist convictions helped him willingly accept Edward. Did Alexander see those qualities – 'outgoing, cheek of the devil, a fixer and joker, obstinate and forthright'[10] – considered by Duncan as residing in his father-in-law, reflected in himself?

Jean thought her mother Elizabeth ('a dear, good and faithful person'), as a wife, got a very good deal: Edward would lovingly present her with an armful of sweetpeas once a week when in season, other flowers when not. He 'did everything for her. She never bought a railway ticket in her life', she chuckled.[11]

Edward eventually registered as a fully qualified practising dentist in 1912. On the death of his adoptive father before the end of that decade he left Aberdeen, taking over the Warnock surgery in St Vincent Street. The Glasgow flat was the newly-weds' first home.

During the First World War Edward invited sisters Cissie, Elsie and Miriam, stepmother Clara and her second husband, Bill Beer, to Girvan. For the Beers he arranged the rental of another house and a job for Bill at a local horticultural nursery. He felt his Kent family would be safer away from the coast, always susceptible to invasion in time of war.

In Edward's role as head of the extended Tull family perhaps an explanation can be found for Bella's battle to increase her wage. With his move to a family house in Randolph Road in Glasgow's West End in 1926, Edward was financially responsible for three properties and households. Jean commented that in both hours worked and money spent he lived up to his limits, such as travelling by taxi and first-class train. Yet there is no doubt he was generous. He treated poor patients for free and Jean recalls his give-away days where she played 'Lady Bountiful' in distributing her unwanted toys and outgrown clothes to their impoverished working-class neighbours in Richard Street, 'a dreadful tenement with 100 folk to one stair. At the appointed hour they descended and quite overwhelmed my well-meaning parents'.[12] And, in Bella's case, actions spoke louder than words. She stayed with the family.

Paul Robeson influenced Edward. The African-American communist inspired him on a number of levels. Politically, Robeson's willingness to voice the concerns, anger, preoccupations, dreams and hopes of Black people galvanised the adopted Glaswegian's local vocalising on similar themes (Duncan fondly remembers attending, with his father-in-law, a Robeson concert and rally at Kelvin Hall at which the latter's singing mesmerised his audience comprised of many hard-bitten, hard-nosed, hard-drinking Glaswegian working men). Culturally, Robeson had an international profile and acclaim as a ground-breaking actor and singer of Negro spirituals, a musical genre proudly emulated by Edward. And in sport, as an excellent (American) footballer suffering at the feet and hands of White opponents, often brutally, Robeson refused to be bullied, eventually winning representative honours. This is commented upon in an undated talk about him written by Edward, 'He was battered in every scrimmage but he fought on'.[13]

Robeson's passionate affection for the UK – 'in England I have found perfect freedom and peace',[14] in contrast to his experience of overt racism in the USA – was conditioned by his socialist outlook.

> In England, Robeson gradually developed a political sensibility from his identification with the labouring and working classes. The mutual plight of oppressed communities, beyond the strictures of race, struck him profoundly. He forged a close relationship with English workers, seeing in their condition of neglect a similarity with the exploited black Americans. Of particular importance was the hospitality of the English towards him, which bore a striking contrast to the United States.[15]

In order to for me to go to the country of my great-grandmother's birth, in the future it should be stressed that Robeson had a deep affection for, and close relationship with, the mining communities of south Wales. In the UK-produced film *The Proud Valley*, set in a Welsh pit village, he played a heroic collier with a name, David Goliath, which encapsulated the movie's theme. Giving his life to save his colleagues, his character illuminates the liberating potential of class solidarity and the ultimate irrelevance of colour difference. Goliath is a Black hero, a role unavailable in the Hollywood of the 1940s, with its strict ethnic stereotyping and formulaic narratives.

Edward's adulation of Robeson seeped into his daughter's consciousness, with Jean writing letters to, and receiving replies from, the giant African-American. Yet under their noses, in their family, was a Black British hero! Duncan met Jean while they were both students at the University of Glasgow. He first saw her in the university chapel and decided there and then that this olive-skinned beauty, who accentuated her looks with poise and elegance, was going to be his bride.

In their cottage on the loch shore Jean and Duncan set me on the trail of her uncle William's family over half a thousand miles away in Kent. As the only Tull child working, Walter and Edward's eldest brother had remained in Folkestone when his brothers left for the orphanage. On a family tree on the dining table they traced the geometric line to Rita Humphrey, William's granddaughter, living in Maidstone. Still alive was Mildred, William's daughter, the sole surviving family member to have known personally her footballing uncle.

The Finlayson's genealogical map showed William Stephen Palmer Tull was born on 7 April 1882, at Allendale Road, Folkestone, just under fourteen months after the birth of Bertha Susannah, first child of Daniel and Alice Tull, who died in infancy. Alice and Daniel gave their first son the middle names Stephen Palmer, after Alice's father.

Writing to Rita led to contact with her son Graham Humphrey. In appearance they embody the ethnic mixture of the Tulls: Rita looking like her grandfather and Walter; Graham, blond haired and light skinned. Since, it has been Graham who has been my practical link with the Kent branch of the family, providing documents, details, phone numbers and addresses of the various families dotted around Maidstone. He has subsequently investigated his grandfather's biography, located his grave and searched for him in the censuses.

It has been my fortunate privilege as researcher/writer that once Walter's ball started rolling again and others become interested, the accumulation of material became easier and faster. Family, friends and other interested people sent their findings as a matter of courtesy, for corroboration or simply to help.

Soon after William's brothers were relocated to the East End, stepmother

Clara married, in 1899, William 'Bill' Beer, a farm waggoner half a dozen years her junior. They settled in Coldred, Dover.

Unsettled by yet another parental figure in his life – however benign Bill's impact may have been – William, missing his brothers, decided upon a nomadic journey, skirting the edges of south London, east and west. The same year his stepmother remarried, aged 17 he moved to 10 Thanet Road, Erith, Kent, nearer London. A few months later he rented lodgings at 99 Gresham Road, Brixton, south-west London (then in the county of Surrey), less than 10 miles from the Children's Home and Orphanage (CHO) in Bethnal Green, east London. While at these addresses he often wrote to the Home asking to see his brothers and also requesting they visit him for holidays which, sometimes, they were allowed to do. On two occasions in 1899 and 1900 they stayed with William at 53 Medara Road, Brixton, and sang in his local church where a collection was afterwards taken for the CHO. His desire to have them for two weeks in August 1900 was turned down because they were on a choir trip. Yet setbacks such as this must have seemed easier to suffer now William was living on the south side of the river, nearer to his beloved younger brothers.

It wasn't until July 2008, when I looked again at the correspondence between William Tull and the CHO, that it hit home how much he missed Walter and Edward. As William remained, initially, with the family in Folkestone the assumption was he did not suffer as much as his younger brothers. Yet, on a second reading of his letters, it is clear that he was hurt. The rejection of some of his requests to see Edward and Walter must have cut deep. On one occasion, as we saw above, it was due to a choir trip; on another, because the date suggested conflicted with school time; on yet another, because they didn't want to allow the visit. On first reflection it seems cruel to deny all three contact. Maybe the Home felt William's persistent need was stunting his brothers' independence, an emotion they would need to develop as a survival tool? His letters are not detailed, fluent, expositions of his feelings but brief, inarticulate pleas for contact with two people he was missing deeply. I believe this is why he moved to London, so he could be near. While Walter's most troubled years were after Edward left the Home in November 1900, William's began on 24 February 1898.

Yet by June 1900 William was back in Folkestone, living at 11 Park Road. This was a walk away from eldest sister Cecilia, now in service at Mrs Broadbank's house, 47 Broadmead Road. In his wanderings, wherever he lay down his cap for the night, it was not far from one or more of his siblings.

The 1901 Census records him lodging at 37 Oswald Road, Dover, the home of a widow and her two infant children, in the ecclesiastical parish of Buckland, St Andrew. This is close to Clara and Bill Beer's cottage at Little Singledge, Coldred, Dover, the home of his youngest sisters, Elsie and Miriam.

His marriage to a local White woman, Gertrude Mary Boxer, a few years later did not extinguish William's wanderlust. After the birth of Mildred in 1906, their second daughter, Gladys Muriel, was born in Nottingham in 1908. Why they were in the city isn't known. By the start of the war, in August 1914, William and Gertrude had returned south, the journeyman joiner a member of a team constructing accommodation huts for Kitchener's new army at Sandling, near Folkestone.

Coincidentally, while researching the Watford Police Court appearances of Eddie Cother, an Anglo-Indian footballer for Watford in the last decade of the 19th century, I came across a William Tull, convicted in 1911 of poaching and fined £1 3s 6d (£1.18). A hard-up William looking after the needs of his family?

If William had arrived back in Folkestone by August 1913, he might have been impelled to walk down to the harbour with Gertrude and daughters Mildred, Doris and Gladys to watch world heavyweight champion boxer, African-American Jack Johnson, come ashore. He could later read about this proud, famous Black sportsman, who also had the cheek to marry a Caucasian, in his local paper, the *Folkestone Express*: 'The prize fighter . . . came from Paris on his way to London. When the steamer came alongside the darkey was seen seated in a handsome motor car which stood on the main deck. His white wife was with him'.[16] Having a celebrity such as Johnson, however controversial, ethnically mirror his own marital status would have reassured William; a positive reference to another 'big brother' in the same situation.

After making contact with the Humphreys in 1995, I realised my next port of call should be spinster Mildred, approaching her 90th year, in the hope that she could recall unwritten hidden detail of Uncle Walter. She was now in a Home for frail senior citizens, needing daily care and attention. It was suggested I write to her close friend, Nina Daniel, who saw her a couple of times a week. We corresponded during the summer, discussing a potential visit to Folkestone to record an interview. Tragically, Mildred, one remove from Walter, died before we could meet. She had outlasted her father William by 75 years. He died at 59 Greenfield Road, Folkestone, of pulmonary tuberculosis on 12 March 1920, his lungs fatally damaged by gas during the war. He had been Sapper 7313 in the Royal Engineers. Gertrude also passed away at this address in 1952, aged 70.

William's war-induced illness ravaged his body insidiously and slowly. Not having died during the conflict, his name does not appear on any war memorials. His headstone in Cheriton Cemetery, Folkestone, while military in make and design, is situated away from the designated ground for war graves, with just one other casualty of the 1914–18 conflict close by. He is typical of many thousands of war casualties not recorded as such. Their deaths after the Armistice of 11 November 1918, from the effects of their involvement, deny them a place in the official memory of the First World War, such as casualty statistics and physical memorials in workplaces, village squares, town and city halls. While brother Walter is remembered with an inscription in five locations – Arras, Glasgow, Folkestone, Dover and River (Kent) – William does not even have a resting place among other fallen comrades. The poignant irony of this enduring omission is that William may have been instrumental in ensuring Walter's name was included on the Folkestone War Memorial, sited at the peak of the Road of Remembrance.

It is a platitude to say the war affected whole generations. Some historians argue it shaped the direction and momentum of the 20th century. While its influence was undoubtedly profound, unless the impact is explained from the bottom up, given meaning in the form of personal detail, the opening sentence of this paragraph is a blunt, vague truism.

Within the extended Tull family, in particular Walter's mother's side, the Palmers, yet more evidence is provided of the sustained capacity of silenced guns to wreak death. A key figure in the Dover War Memorial project, Maggie Stephenson-Knight, became interested in Walter Tull sometime in 2006. She felt his deeds as a man of Kent were not fully recognised in the county and beyond. Researching local records, she told her story of rediscovering the Palmer family in an article in the *Dover Express*, 12 October 2006. A reader, Stephen Coombe, contacted her saying he was a relative of Walter's.

Sometime later, after Maggie had interviewed him and sent me detail of the family connection, I visited Stephen at his home high up on the cliff road, just outside Folkestone in Capel-le-Ferne. He was very tolerant of me: I had turned up a day early! Stephen's grandfather, John Alexander Palmer, and Alice Tull, Walter's natural mother, had been brother and sister. Also, Walter's stepmother Clara was cousin to Stephen's mother, also called Clara. But it is John Alexander's biography that is particularly relevant in the context of the present discussion of the damaging legacy of war. Named on the Dover War Memorial are two of John Alexander's sons, George Thomas Palmer and Stephen John Alexander Palmer. George, 24, a Private in the 8th Buffs (Royal East Kent Regiment), was killed on the Somme on 19 August 1916; Stephen, 22, a Lance Sergeant in the 7th Battalion Royal West Surrey, at Passchendaele on 19 July 1917. Neither was found. George is remembered on the Thiepval Memorial in France, Stephen on the Menin Gate, Ypres, Belgium. Two more of John's boys served in the war: William, a Private in the Royal Regiment of Artillery, and Ernest, a Private in the 1st Buffs. John had already lost his sister, Alice, in 1895. It is not known if her son, Walter, who was also fighting on the Western Front at the same time, crossed paths with his cousins Stephen and George before they died. Given the closeness of the Palmers and Tulls, it would have been highly likely that the cousins would have sought each other out had their battalions been in the same sector.

In January 1921, a body was found with its throat cut in a ditch in St Radigund's Road, Dover. It was John Alexander Palmer. His family believe he committed suicide to escape the unbearable grief over the loss of his two sons. His unemployment and the spectre of the workhouse gave him the desperate energy needed to execute his desire. His wife Harriet was left with an enormous emotional chasm for her remaining 30 years of life. To help her cope she fashioned a brooch from the brass button of a uniform, ensconcing close to her heart photographic miniatures of Stephen and George.

Tragically, the possibility of suicide hangs over the death of another of John and Harriet's war-veteran sons, Walter Henry Palmer, a railway worker, found in Shepherdswell rail tunnel, Dover, in 1931.

If tragedy haunted the lives of many of the post-war generations, Walter's sister Elsie's 30 years' stint as a tea-lady at St Bartholomew's Hospital, Rochester, recognised with an MBE in 1976, provides a reassuring counterpoint upon which to conclude this chapter.

2

A mixed-heritage family in 19th-century Folkestone

Walter Tull's father, Daniel, was born in 1856 on the Clifton Estate, St Thomas' Parish, Barbados, the son of William and Anna Tull, who had both been born into plantation slavery. Anna (née Lashley) and William were married at Clifton Hill, 8 December 1838. William had been known as William Criss. He and Anna had three children, one of whom was Daniel.[1]

Around 1861, the family – Anna, William, Daniel, his brother and sister – moved to St Michael's Parish, My Lord's Hill, where the children attended a Moravian school. Education was important for the Barbados Tulls. In Daniel's journal, begun on 10 October 1877, soon after he arrived in England, he informs us that his cousin Henry Simmons 'has the title of BA.'[2]

Leaving school Daniel was found an apprenticeship with a journeyman builder called Mr Giddens. Eight months later he began training as a carpenter with Joseph Massiah, the husband of his cousin. 'Then did my trials commence', Daniel comments with melancholy in his journal. Massiah was 'a good workman but a cruel man to his apprentices', suggesting not many stayed around and that he, Daniel, may have made a mistake in leaving Giddens.

> When a boy first goes to work or goes apprentice some master generally ask the boy what are we going to make of you A Man, A Mule or A Monkey. But he did not give me the chance to know the Rabit plane from the jack plane before he had a flogging on me they was scarcely a week pass over my head but for what I did not have a thrashing from him.[3]

Daniel stuck with his cruel master, the beatings mercifully decreasing in proportion to the increase in his skill and proficiency as a carpenter. How times have changed. My son Alex is an apprentice carpenter and he thinks his boss, Giuliano, is sound because he starts after 8.30 am and some days lets him off early, before 5 o'clock!

After three testing years Daniel, fed up with his pay of 6d per week, left Massiah to work for 'one of his [Massiah's] mates'. Unfortunately, his troubles continued, the new master often not paying when Saturday came around.

> I was only a lad then but I went to his house with a determination to get my money or else give him a thrashing man as he was. I called at his house but could not see him & made several abuses. My father being a Godly man was very much put out about this and so was I but he sided with these oppressors . . . and never took my part but gave me a thrashing.[4]

Feeling hurt, betrayed and angry, Daniel informed his mother he would be leaving the island. Anna may have thought this was the impetuous anger of a teenager, expecting his frustration to diminish as the days passed. But Daniel was true to his word, sailing for St Lucia in 1873. In so doing, he revealed a stubborn trait that was a constant in his life and was noticed in Walter at an early age.

For young Bajan men, migrating to find work wasn't uncommon. Wages were often higher on other islands such as Trinidad, British Guiana and St Lucia, as much as four times the average Barbadian day rate.[5]

A law passed by the Barbados legislature of planters and slave owners in 1676 criminalised the introduction of Christianity to Blacks for fear of spreading ideas about collective equality and self-improvement that, put into practice, would undermine their privilege. Necessity is the mother of invention. Slaves and former slaves wanted to be literate because it was a gateway to personal, social and political progress.

Religious communities in the colonies competed in a marketplace for hearts and minds. Those souls tossed aside by the elitist Church of England planters were tempted by less established and smaller sects. Nonconformist Christian groups – notably Quakers, Methodists and Moravians – actively proselytised among the brown-skinned population, seeking to convert and educate. Although Barbados had more schools per square mile in 1834 than any other British colony, only five accepted Blacks.[6]

Having been educated at Moravian schools, Daniel had the portable skills of literacy and carpentry that could be utilised elsewhere. Like 16,000 other Bajans before him who had emigrated between 1838 (the abolition of slavery) and 1870, Daniel left the rigid ethnic hierarchy of his native island to try his luck in St Lucia.[7]

During the summer of 1876, after spending three years on the island, he worked his way as a ship's carpenter to Folkestone. There he found work, a place to worship and a woman to love. After five years in the thriving coastal resort and port, he married Alice Palmer. They met at the Grace Hill Wesleyan Chapel, Folkestone. Alice, 'a tender plant',[8] had been born at Elms Farm, Hougham, near Dover in 1853, the only daughter of Sarah-Anne (née Taylor) and agricultural labourer Stephen Palmer. Daniel's colour represented 'negative equity' in a society where the political and social elites propagated the notion of a hierarchy between 'races'. The cultural capital he had managed to acquire through his training as a carpenter, his literacy and his nonconformist belief signified upward social mobility for Alice in the eyes of her working-class family.

Sarah-Ann Palmer, to her future son-in-law in January 1880, writes an affectionate, thoughtful commentary on the meaning of marriage. Throughout, she refers to Walter's father as 'Dan'; 'dearest child'; 'my intended son'. It is a refreshingly open-minded welcome note from the Palmer family to a prospective new member, with an absence of Victorian 'common-sense' stereotypes and prejudices. It speaks of an alternative, egalitarian vision of the world where acceptance and rejection of people and persons is premised upon the quality of their behaviour.

> You have asked me for my only daughter . . . there are two things I must beg of you and the first is of the most importance that you will be kind to her for she is a tender plant . . . the other is that you will never take her out of England whilst I am alive. Do not think Dan in raising these two things that I doubt your love for her on that point I am perfectly satisfied your actions have shown that and your respect for the family . . . sharing in one another's joys and sorrows you will find the path at times very rough and uneven but you must bear with one another's weaknesses and try and help

one another . . . kindest and best love to your dear self . . . dearest child. [9]

Daniel and Alice were married at the Grace Hill Wesleyan Chapel a month later on 25 February. Their address given in the 1881 Census is 8 Garden Street, Hythe, Folkestone. Bertha, their first child, born just under a year later, survived a mere five weeks. Daniel may have wondered, in those dark days of March 1881, if the description of Alice by her mother as a 'tender plant' also inferred weak offspring. Though 'tragic, Bertha's descent into an infant grave wasn't an unusual occurrence in working-class communities. Child mortality rates were much higher than present and parents harboured inherited fear – expectation even – of premature loss. The birth of William Stephen Palmer on 7 April 1882, therefore, was celebrated with great joy by the Tulls, including those in Barbados. In her letter dated 25 March 1883, Anna writes 'We are very glad to hear that your wife has had a safe delivery with a son you must give him a dozen kisses from us'.[10]

It is clear from surviving letters written to Daniel by his mother and stepmother that he was surrounded by loving families. Neither the Kent Palmers nor the Bajan Tulls were prosperous. In the Agreement that formalised Walter and Edward's entry into Reverend Dr Stephenson's Children's Home and Orphanage, Bethnal Green, the wages of Alice's brothers, William and Robert Palmer, are recorded as 14 shillings per week, low even for agricultural labourers. Yet what they lacked in material resources, the Palmers, in particular, more than made up for in love and support. Daniel reciprocated this love through doing his best to provide for his family. His mother's letters suggest he was also aware of his historic duty and burden as an economic migrant to his family back in Barbados. In 1878 Anna replies to her son: 'Most humble thanks for your gift . . . it was very acceptable I do assure you . . . our little hut wanted great repairs, so it came in grand'.[11] She also thanks him for a photo portrait of himself he included while also explaining that 4 shillings of the pound (of 20 shillings) he sent had to pay for the excess weight of his letter. This seems a punishingly high charge to pay for inadequate postage.

In the letter of 25 March 1883, Anna acknowledges the receipt of 10 shillings that Daniel has sent and assures him it was needed 'in the time of their adversity'.[12] He also sent her over a piece of his wedding cake. 'I assure it was amazing and also strange to think that it would have last so long',[13] wrote Anna. While undertaking new obligations as a husband and father, he was not forgetting his duties as a son.

The emotional, psychological and physical support provided by their extended families would be much needed in the relatively short but fertile marriage of Daniel and Alice. Between February 1881 and November 1891, the latter gave birth to six children, a pregnancy period of 54 months. After Bertha and William, Cecilia Sarah Ann was born on 14 March 1884, Edward James Alexander on 28 June 1886, Walter Daniel John on 28 April 1888 and Elsie Alice Elizabeth on 7 November 1891. It was a strenuous decade for the 'tender plant'. The 1891 Census lists the Tulls at 51 Walton Road, Folkestone, a small terraced house in a working-class neighbourhood.[14] They had moved there sometime after Walter's birth at 16 Allendale Street, Folkestone.

All three addresses traceable to Daniel and Alice are in the Hythe district of Folkestone and very close to one another, all connecting to Black Bull Road, the address of North Board School – now Mundella Primary School – which the Tull children attended. Moving to different addresses in the same neighbourhood was common practice. Failure to pay rent through unemployment, the need for more bedrooms after birth and cheaper rent were some common reasons for loading up the handcart and pitching up five minutes away.

The arrival of the South Eastern Railway in Folkestone in 1843, using the port as its railhead for services to France, revived the ancient town in such spectacular fashion that by the end of the century the population had grown by a factor of 10 to 40,000, the town having developed a reputation as a fashionable resort with its fast links to London.

The speed of this expansion is even more remarkable when considered alongside the population growth from the Domesday Book figure of 600 in 1086. In the 757 years to 1843 it rose only by a factor of seven. 'On Bank Holidays', observed *Blackwood's Edinburgh Magazine*, 'it is *swamped in excursionists*'[15] (code for loud-mouthed, working-class Londoners!). The discreet monthly journal also noted extreme differences in the physical qualities of a disproportionate number of its residents, there being large numbers of elderly and soldiers. The former coming for the sea air and the vivifying ingredients of its spring water; the latter stationed at Dover, Hythe and Shorncliffe barracks. There was also a military hospital at Sandgate. 'On the seafront, amid the khaki and the bathchairs', continued

Blackwood's, 'there are German bands but few nigger melodists in gaudy raiment',[16] implying Folkestone wasn't downmarket enough for the showy Blacks to earn a living from entertaining the promenaders. It was not like Margate, Ramsgate or Hastings, but superior to them all.

A less elitist, local view is presented in the *Folkestone, Sandgate and Hythe Pictorial* of 1890 which talked of a variety of entertainment on offer, from military bands that 'discourse sweet music to itinerant companies of minstrels and harmonious brothers' that performed at the Exhibition Building and Pier Pavilion. Folkestone in the 1890s was growing, attractive to outsiders, relatively prosperous and a gateway to the continent. It was a place where Walter would almost certainly have seen other people of colour outside his family. In the letter written to Daniel dated March 1883, his brother in Barbados identifies a Bajan whom Daniel had met in Folkestone

> The gentleman whom you were in conversation with from Barbados to the railway station as you mentioned in your letter Mr Jones his name is, his business is well known by the caracter [*sic*] of J. B. Barrow & Co., Roebuck St, Bridgetown. He is my employer a very good gentleman I believe he would have done you any favour withy perfection.[17]

('Favour' in this context implies he could be trusted to deliver letters, presents, documents, etc., between the UK and Barbados.)

Mr Jones may well have been an expatriate White Briton with business interests in Barbados, rather than an African-Caribbean with whom Daniel could share common cultural experiences. However, the latter did meet him in the UK, and by chance. The British ruling class was, in the 1880s, in the last major phase of its imperial expansion. As guns and goods left, labour passed in the opposite direction. The UK was an increasingly cosmopolitan society. Indeed, another family of African-Caribbean, White and mixed heritage was living in Kent before Daniel arrived in Folkestone, headed by Thomas Brown, a Guianan petty officer in the Royal Navy. Brown's son Donald married suffragette Eliza Adelaide Knight. Their daughter, Winifred Langton, has written a biography of her parents.

Living at 51 Walton Road, Folkestone, the Tull children attended the North Board School in Black Bull Road. The school was at the top of their road, the playground and classrooms visible from their front windows. The school gates one minute's slow walk away, they were near enough to troop home for dinner, siesta and return for more monitor-supervised rote learning in the afternoon.

Daniel seems to have been in constant employment. This conclusion is supported by his remittances back to Barbados, and by information given in the application form to the CHO by Clara stating her deceased husband worked for local magistrate Mr Holden, then later his son and subsequently a Mr Webster of 6 Claremont Place, Folkestone.

The other constants of Walter's life were the proximity of his school, the love and support of the extended Palmer family, the spiritual sustenance and communal solidarity of Methodism and the camaraderie of his brothers and sisters – the environment in which he spent his most formative years appears to have been secure, stable, protective and 'happy', a description used by Edward in his talk 'The Film that Will Never Be Screened', written around 1937. In late Victorian Britain, asserts the successful Glasgow dentist,

> outside pleasure for the working-classes were [sic] negligible. [My] family found its whole life centred in its Church and being a happy family there was no need for compulsion to attend church services or to take part in the Church's activities. The children had their Sunday School and the parents their Church and for them the Sunday was the day of the week.[18]

Sometime in the autumn of 1893, Alice was diagnosed with breast cancer and the brightness of 51 Walton Road suddenly, unexpectedly, dimmed. Her treatment over the next 17 months at best slowed her painful decline. The ever-darkening shadow enveloped the Tulls completely on 14 April 1895, exactly a week after William's thirteenth birthday and a fortnight before Walter's seventh. Alice's death marked, for the latter, the first of a series of cataclysmic traumas that would become a feature of his life.

Daniel, mourning his wife of 14 years and responsible for five children under 14, looked to the Palmer family for help. Consistent with their history of support, they did not fail him. Twenty-six-year-old Clara Alice Susanna Palmer, the niece of Alice, daughter of her brother William and his wife Sarah Ann, married Daniel at the Grace Hill Wesleyan Chapel on

17 October 1896, 'largely to mother the children'.[19] Like her Aunt Alice, Clara was born at Elms Farm, Hougham, Dover. While imposing such an all-embracing familial obligation was practical, given her single status, and socially acceptable, given the norms and values of the period, it was none-theless burdensome. On marriage this young, unworldly woman became stepmother to five children. Yet it also reaffirms the close ties that existed between the Tull and the Palmer families. The birth of Miriam Victoria, on 11 October 1897, provided a physical refutation of the inference that the union of Daniel and Clara was *wholly* one of practical convenience; the ad-ditional responsibility of an extra mouth to feed, if it did not cause worry at the time of birth, certainly would just two months later.

While the gradual withering away of Alice had been torturous for both families, the sudden death of Daniel from heart disease on 10 December 1897, so soon after the birth of his fourth daughter, must have been crush-ing for 27-year-old Clara. Thrust by misfortune into the all-consuming role of single parent, she was now head of a family of six, yet only just over a decade older than William, her eldest stepson.

Daniel had paid into a life insurance policy with the Prudential Assur-ance Company from which Clara had received £16. By the time of the application to the CHO in January 1898, most had been spent on medical and funeral expenses. Whether this was the case absolutely is questionable. It was a relatively large sum of money, equivalent to six months' wages for an agricultural labourer like her father William, the uncle of her step-children and grandfather to Miriam. In fact, one hopes Clara did have some cash under her mattress for emergencies. In such a situation – poor, female, young, with five dependants – it would have made rational eco-nomic sense to lie through your front teeth about your circumstances.

The ability of the extended Palmer families to assist further was spent: they had neither financial nor physical spare resources to offer. Getting by on farm labourers' wages meant poverty was always a foreboding vista on the horizon. William, 15, earning 7 shillings a week as an apprentice car-penter, was the only member of the Tull family in employment. The rent at Walton Road was 6 shillings a week. In the absence of a widow's pension, Clara had no option but to beg for parish relief from the Guardians of the Elham Union, a recourse usually taken only in the most desperate of situations. Turning to the taxpayers of her community for money to live would entail a demeaning scrutiny of person and home by local worthies ultra-sensitive to their obligation of keeping the rate burden upon the propertied classes to a minimum. Inspecting applicants in the misery and discomfort of their home, the guardians would distinguish *deserving* poor – God-fearing and sycophantic – from *undeserving* – non-churchgoing and/or class conscious. If categorised as the latter and marked for indoor relief, families would be fragmented, scattered to the dreaded workhouse, a harsh, regimented, emotionally cruel institution, sub-divided by gender and generation – a prison of the poor.

Possibly in light of their attendance at chapel and Daniel's proud record of providing for his own, on these shores and beyond, the Tulls were considered deserving poor and allowed outdoor relief of 5s 10d per week. Though a meagre sum, for the time being it meant they could continue living as a family at Walton Road. The donation from parish funds contributed toward a total weekly income of 12s 10d. However, after rent, 6s 10d was left for food, fuel and clothing for seven, one of whom was baby Miriam. Unsurprisingly, the figures did not add up. Despite this financial help, the family could not make ends meet. In desperation, Clara sought help from her last remaining port of call, the Methodist community. The resident minister of Grace Hill, the Reverend George Adcock, took pastoral control of Clara's plight and recommended Walter and his elder brother Edward to the Children's Home and Orphanage, personally sponsoring their application.

3

Tull, the 'many' and the 'few'

Introduction

The feeling of being alone, and that situation having permanence, is probably one of the least comforting human emotions. During our time on this planet we have evolved together, from small extended family units to larger communities based upon geographical proximity. In the more privileged parts of the world, it is only in this century that the choice of living independently has been available to a majority of the population. In Western societies we are encouraged to believe that the pursuit of life-enhancing aims and objectives through independent effort – individualism – is the way despite this notion flying in the face of history.

A year or so ago, at a bus stop on a cold, bright morning, I got into conversation with an energetic, opinionated and, as it turned out, remarkable, senior citizen. We soon lapsed into moans about the cost of things, how everyone seemed to be in debt, how we have to pay through the nose for everything – the usual Winter's Tale.

'You know,' she said, 'it's credit cards that have stopped people being interested in politics.'

I threw back a puzzled expression. It isn't unusual that conversations with strangers throw up random verbal grenades that come out of nowhere – that's part of the attraction of chatting to unknowns – but I was curious to hear the logic behind her statement.

'I worked in a factory, as many women as men,' she continued, picking up on my confusion. 'Of course, we were always gossiping, whingeing, joking around, winding each other up. We knew each other, there were no secrets

– or at least I don't think there were – and that included our wages and personal details like that. I knew what Marj paid for her rent, she knew what I paid for my shoes, Bill was open about what he gave his wife as housekeeping – well, he had to be, she was my cribbage partner! – so, it soon became obvious if we faced a common problem. And what's the most common problem people face?

'For me it's never having enough money, but I'm pretty useless when it comes to pounds and pence.'

The bus arrived. We sat together. I was keen to find out where she was going with this, not least because my dad had worked as a stores labourer in an electronics factory in the 1960s and 1970s and, while we had the latest compact transistor radio in every room of the house, we seemed always as a family to be a bit short of available cash for life's little luxuries, like a summer holiday. Perhaps her workplace was the real-life equivalent of Charlie's Chocolate Factory, in every wage packet there was a golden wrapper, a voucher that made your dreams come true?

'That's it, paying the bills!' she exclaimed. 'But do you say how much you wanna pay for your rent, electricity, gas, water and such like? No! They are set by the council and the companies.'

Now I was getting the drift. I was homing into her zone.

'Well, all of us knew if the cost of things was getting out of control because we were all in the same boat. That meant we sank or swam together. What stop are you getting off at, my love?

'Don't worry, I've got about five to go.'

'I was shop steward. Nineteen years old and representing my mates on the factory floor! That's what they were, mates. We relied on each other. If the bosses tried to introduce new things, like extra work without extra money, we would all object because we knew it could be us next. We had to be honest and open with each other. That way we were strong. So, if Millie said, "we're two weeks behind on our rent" and Janie said "I've had to cut down on the meat these last few weeks" and Linda couldn't afford some new shoes for her son, we knew our wages weren't covering our living expenses. That's when I came in for it!' she chuckled, with a cheeky glint in her eyes. "Right, Florrie, what are we gonna do about it?" So, we'd have a meeting and I'd be sent to the bosses to negotiate a wage rise.'

'But didn't you have set wage talks once a year? I know at my dad's place that's what they did.'

'Oh yes, but usually, and I'm talking about the 1950s now . . .'

'The fifties? You don't look old enough!'

'Oh shut up, don't you start flirting, I'm old enough to be your mum, listen where was I? See, now you've put me off . . . Yes, what I was going to say was prices didn't go up so fast as they did in the seventies say, so the company would often say, "look, inflation is 2 per cent, our order books are low" – we made hairdryers, that kind of thing – "so there won't be a rise this year." So, if we found we were getting worse off, we'd ask them for more money.'

'Yeah, but how does that have anything to do with credit cards and activity in politics?

'How many more stops have you got?'

'I'm all right for a couple of minutes.'

'Nowadays, people get their bills and sit at home worrying about them, I know my daughter does. Then, when she's spent out she pays her bills with her credit card. I said join a union, go and see your boss. "We don't have bosses anymore mum, they're called managers, and all our union seems to be worried about is getting your subscription and getting you deals for private health care." "You are the union," I told her, "if you don't like what they're doing, get together and change it. You're too bloody polite," I said, "we didn't call our guvnors managers, that's the last thing we called 'em. Anyway, whatever you call 'em, go and ask for a rise if you can't manage." But they don't do they? No, they all live in their own little worlds, worrying about their separate lives, getting deeper into debt and more pissed off . . . excuse my language!'

'You've deeply offended me and I couldn't possibly excuse you', I said with a straight face.

'Good, because you young ones have lost it.'

I smiled. I hadn't been called young for a few years.

'When I went to the boss as shop steward that was politics, real politics, sorting out our daily bread, for all of us, together. Is this your stop, darling?'

It was. 'Bye, Florrie.'

'Get together!' she said, as I stood. 'Don't take it lying down.'

I understood what she meant and was disappointed at having to get off the bus. Thinking about her – and I have thought about that conversation many, many times – it crossed my mind that it was because she fought for, and alongside, her workmates that she was still fighting. She could see the benefits of collective action. It also got me comparing her situation as a worker with Walter Tull's. Many of the problems he faced were difficult to share with his (White) workmates. This is not to argue that the discrimination faced by people of colour in a White society is completely separate to economic discrimination such as that faced by Florrie and her mates at the hairdryer factory. Her employers sought to extract the greatest profit from their workforce. To do this, a system of divide and rule is necessary, both in terms of relations on the factory floor between workers, and in the differential pay packets they receive. A hierarchy is as important for employers inside the workplace as it is for the Establishment outside the workplace. But by sticking together on the factory floor, those above hadn't managed to divide Florrie, this elderly Black woman, from her White workmates.

Politics

The unequal distribution of economic resources in society produces, and is the consequence of, class: the 'few' get more; the 'many'[1] get less. Gender and ethnicity are also used as instruments of division. This separation of people by class, gender and ethnicity is not a coincidence. It has a purpose: to divide the 'many', allowing the 'few' to rule. Yet we have evolved to the 21st century by, generally, co-operating with each other. Because the strong have looked after the weak, the young the old, the wise the ignorant, the hunters their community, the parents their children we have survived and evolved as homo sapiens over hundreds of thousands of years. Illogically, the 'few' would have us believe the opposite: that we have developed as humans in a perpetual state of competition and war; and that this state of affairs is immutable, a natural law, a fact of our humanity and therefore cannot be altered.

Yet my reading of Walter Tull's story suggests the human condition has co-operation as a primary characteristic. It is an instinct, a reflexive action and a major reason why Tull survived, achieved and prospered in his short, dramatic life. It wasn't until a senseless carnage of unique and unprecedented proportions was unleashed by the ruling classes – the 'few' – of Europe upon its populations that his life was unnaturally terminated.

The First World War that stole Walter's life, along with millions of others, was a phenomenon hitherto unseen in human history for the scale of its industrial killing. Over 20 million people had their lives extinguished in the conflict, most of them peasants or working-class men. Those who survived, if they also lived through the pan-European flu epidemic of 1918–19 which killed even more, went back home to poor quality housing, job insecurity, a lengthy and debilitating working week, low wages, periodic unemployment; and for the Black soldier, racism. However, what the war did was to increase the momentum for economic, social and political change among individuals and movements in the UK and abroad, particularly in the colonies.

In Britain the suffragettes, by the war's end, had in large part achieved their goal of votes for women. In 1918 women over 30 voted in a General Election for the first time. (It wasn't until 1928 that women achieved parity with men when their voting age was lowered to 21.)

In Italy, Caribbean troops mutinied, beginning in December 1918 and continuing through into 1919, a result of raised consciousness and delayed demobilisation. When they did settle back in the West Indies, as veterans, workers, political activists and unemployed, many participated in the growing militancy against colonial rule.

These suffragettes and the Black veterans of the First World War played their part in an historical tradition of bottom-up protest, revolt and revolution to which Toussaint L'Ouverture, Olaudah Equiano, Robert Wedderburn, the Cato Street Conspirators and the Chartists were earlier contributors.

Walter Tull, in not accepting his allotted place as a 'Negro' in an overwhelmingly White society – an ascribed status denying him human dignity and the White dimension of his ethnicity – was also part of this seminal drama enacted by the 'many', called 'fighting back'. As a mixed-heritage boy in Folkestone, adolescent in the Children's Home and Orphanage in Bethnal Green, young adult footballer at Clapton, Spurs and Northampton Town and 20s-something soldier in France and Italy, there were many times when Tull was seemingly alone and isolated. Not just physically, as a Black Briton, but emotionally also, in the sense of having no one close by who could empathise with his uncommon predicament.

How did he communicate to his White friends, such as Vivian Woodward, an experience they had not encountered without appearing oversensitive and/or paranoid? That the look in their friend's eyes spoke of contempt? That their relative's body language articulated hostility? In many hostile situations encountered by Tull, supportive words, gestures, acknowledgement would have been appreciated but were sadly absent.

Yet, in keeping with what seems to have been his philosophy of seeing the glass half full rather than half empty, his singularity strengthened his resolve. He would not be beaten down. And, in this stance he had the support of many close friends who could see the quality of his character and supported his efforts to live and let live.

While the places in which he grew up, Folkestone and London, were overwhelmingly monochrome, both were relatively cosmopolitan. The Kent town was a fashionable holiday destination and coastal port serving holidaymakers and sailors, while the capital of the British Empire was at the height of its modernity as the world's biggest metropolis. Writing from London in 1899, African-American rights activist Booker T. Washington observed:

> Nowhere can one get such a good idea of what is transpiring in all parts of the world as in London [because] the English colonial system brings every year hundreds of representatives of all races and colours from every part of the world to London.[2]

London was the political and commercial heart of the British ruling class's imperial project, providing a temporary or permanent home to many who came from elsewhere to study, train and settle. Movement, change, migration were the metronomic keywords that characterised a capital in transformation, constantly re-inventing itself. It assimilated, metamorphosed and moved on, constantly repeating the cycle. During the 19th century the population rose from one million to five. Some of these were people of colour. Certain parts of the capital, such as Shadwell, Whitechapel, Westminster and Canning Town, were being settled by people of African and Asian descent. By the last decade of the 19th century 'an average of 500 Asiatics came into the docks every week, and more than 10,000 Asiatics and Africans . . . visit London in the course of a year'.[3]

When Tull moved to Northampton in 1911, he left behind seven million Londoners in a schizophrenic megalopolis that was being compared to the great cities and civilisations of antiquity – Rome, Athens and Egypt – for its enormity, intensity, grandeur and power, while also decried as a hostile, insensitive *wilderness* where 'a man may be as easily starved in Leadenhall Market as in the deserts of Arabia'.[4]

For people of colour London has been: welcoming, to those jumping ship from 18th- and 19th-century slavery in the USA; frightening, to those subjected to communal assaults, such as the Notting Hill riots in 1958; and expedient, to delegates comprising the world's first gathering dedicated to challenging colonialism and imperialism, the Pan-African Conference at Westminster City Hall, July 1900.

This turn-of-the-century meeting of people of African, Asian, Caribbean and European heritage contributed to a tradition and legacy that has helped create today's London, one of the world's most tolerant and cosmopolitan cities. Black and White, trade unionists, socialists, progressives, Christians, Muslims, Marxists and others, conference participants were continuing a culture of collective resistance among all ethnicities that had been a feature of political life in Britain for generations.

Acceptance or intolerance of people of colour in the UK has long been demarcated by class. Elizabeth I felt there were too many Blacks in 1596: 'There are of late diverse blackamoores brought into these realms, of which kind there are already here too manie'.[5] Her complaint, a call to the nobility and urban bourgeoisie for action, fell on deaf ears. The aristocracy and wealthy merchants continued to buy in Blacks as slaves, domestic servants, entertainers, musicians and curiosities, and built their trade in slaves until it reached industrial proportions providing unimaginable wealth from which banks, baronetcies, pseudo-science and empire were built. This treatment of, and attitude toward, people of colour as implements through which ease and abundance were accumulated by a small elite was not a million miles from that meted out to the rural peasantry and urban working class. It is not surprising, then, that class solidarity, albeit inarticulate, imperfect and fragile, developed among dispossessed Britons. It can be seen in political actions against the Establishment, the 'few'.

In these revolts by the 'many' can be found the modern origins of Black radicalism, emerging during the anti-Catholic Gordon Riots in London during June 1780, when around 285–300 protestors were killed by the militia. For nearly a week normal relations between Londoners and their rulers broke down. Prisons were broken into and inmates freed. Subsequently, for their insubordination, 326 rioters were charged, including three Black participants, Benjamin Bowfrey, John Glover and Charlotte

Gardiner. All three were found guilty of capital crimes, yet only Gardiner was hanged (along with 20 others one of whom, McDonald, may also have been a person of colour). Little is known about Gardiner, Glover, Bowfrey and McDonald. Were they British subjects? Former American slaves? From the Caribbean? West Africa?

The confidence of Blacks Gardner, Glover and Bowfrey (and maybe McDonald) to participate in what some felt was the biggest revolt in the UK since the Monmouth Rebellion of 1685, when an attempt was made to overthrow James II, may have arisen from the Somerset case judgement of 1772 when Lord Chief Justice Mansfield ruled that sending slaves out of England against their will was illegal. London's Black community, estimated by the *Gentleman's Magazine* in 1764 to be 20,000, celebrated their joy. A few days after the court case, around a couple of hundred people, the majority of distinct African heritage, got together at a Westminster tavern and danced the night away. (However, as Killingray has noted, in a poignant and ironic display of serendipity, Mansfield's house was sacked in the rioting and his papers on the Somerset judgement lost, stolen and destroyed.)

The last quarter of the 18th century was a period of rapid change heralding potential political and legal emancipation for millions: the American Revolution began in 1776, the French in 1789, the Haitian, led by ex-slave Toussaint L'Ouverture, in the 1790s. Many of the ideas inspiring and cohering these revolutionary surges came from *Rights of Man* by Thomas Paine of Norfolk, a county where, over 200 years earlier, in 1549, Robert Kett led a rebellion of more than 15,000 against the 'few' enclosing common lands. They captured the second most populous city of England, Norwich, and held it for several weeks. Beating back the first attempt by the crown to regain the city, Kett's 'many' were eventually defeated by a militia led by John Dudley, the Earl of Warwick.

Paine's ideas, and those of the Enlightenment generally, contributed to the tide of fury against the mass trade in slaves. A leading activist in the Abolitionist Movement in the UK was ex-slave and radical Christian, Olaudah Equiano, also known as Gustava Vassa. He came to prominence highlighting the 1783 high-seas massacre of 130 sick slaves whom Luke Collingwood, captain of the Liverpool slave ship *Zong*, forced overboard so their loss as 'commodities' could be claimed from the underwriters. Had they been left to die from their illnesses aboard, Collingwood and the ship's owners – including banker and slave trader William Gregson – would have had to compensate the slaves' owners. Only after another court case in 1796 were slaves on English ships given the legal status of humans rather than mere cargo.

Equiano married a farming woman from the Fens, Susanna Cullen, at Soham, Cambridgeshire, in 1792. The Cullen family had land in Ely. One of Susanna's close kin was transported to Botany Bay. This fact, and Susanna's marriage to an African, suggests an obstinate vein of free thinking coursed through the family! Daniel Tull's marriage to the daughter of a farm labourer from rural Kent has a symmetry with Equiano. Both unions suggest that rural communities in 18th- and 19th-century England were not simple, ignorant backwaters populated by folk who cleared ditches left and right with their bare hands while standing in the middle of the one-cart wide dirt track.

After bearing two children, Anna Maria Vassa and Joanna Vassa, Sussanah died in 1796. By the close of 1797, of the Vassa family, only Joanna survived, her father dying in March, her elder sister in July. An epitaph, on the outside wall of St Andrew's Church in Chesterton, Cambridge, left of the main entrance, anonymously written with passion, empathy and poetry, bears witness to Anna Maria's short life:

> Should simple village rhymes attract thine eye,
> Stranger, as thoughtfully thou passest by,
> Know that there lies beside this humble stone
> A child of colour haply not thine own.
> Her father born of Afric's sun-burnt race,
> Torn from his native field, ah foul disgrace:
> Through various toils, at length to Britain came
> Espoused, so Heaven ordain'd, an English dame,
> And follow'd Christ; their hope two infants dear.
> But one, a hapless orphan, slumbers here.
> To bury her the village children came.
> And dropp'd choice flowers, and lisp'd her early fame;
> And some that lov'd her most, as if unblest,
> Bedew'd with tears the white wreath on their breast;
> But she is gone and dwells in that abode,
> Where some of every clime shall joy in God. [6]

Papers relating to the will of Equiano in the Cambridgeshire Records Office detail income, savings, land and possessions. In addition to generating a large income from the sale of his autobiography the length and breadth of the country, he also received an annuity from Dr James Parkinson – of Parkinson's disease fame – of £26 13s 8d (just over 10 shillings [50p] a week). In fact, when he died, Equiano was receiving, in annuities, a total of £184 16s 4d (£3 10s [£3.50] per week). A rough guide to ascertain today's values is to multiply by 170.) Raised in Cambridge by the executor of her father's will, John Audley, in April 1816, on reaching 21, Joanna received her inheritance of over £950 – worth about £160,000 today – and a silver watch. Another resident of Cambridge, Edward Jud, who died in 1808, had also been named as an executor. Joanna's status as a Black British middle-class woman of independent means and good connections was unusual, if not unique. Unfortunately, discovered records, documents and artefacts relating to her amount to no more than a few milestones marking out key moments of her adult life: in 1821 she married the Reverend Henry Bromley, a Congregational minister from Appledore, Devon, at Clerkenwell, London; they lived in Clavering, Essex, Harwich and De Beauvoir Town, east London; Joanna died in London in 1857 and is buried at Abney Park Cemetery, Stoke Newington.

A friend of her father was shoemaker Thomas Hardy, founding member of the London Corresponding Society (LCS), established in 1792. The LCS began campaigning for an end to high food prices and poverty but soon focussed its efforts on parliamentary reform: adult male suffrage, annual parliaments and the redistribution of seats. While adopting this political agenda, the Society also recognised that liberty for working-class Whites could not be separated from the struggle of dispossessed, displaced, enslaved Blacks. Those forces that made their fortune from the slave trade, Hardy argued, were the same that passed restrictive and draconian laws against the aims and activities of trade unions and working-class organisations in general.

Other Black members of the LCS were William Davidson and Robert Wedderburn, both revolutionary socialists. Davidson, secretary of the Shoemakers' Union in 1820, aged 34, was hung then beheaded for his part in the Cato Street Conspiracy to assassinate all 14 members of the Cabinet, including the prime minister. The son of Jamaica's English Attorney General and an African-Caribbean woman, he protested to the end his innocence of any crime, other than fighting for social and political justice.[7]

Printer Robert Wedderburn, like Davidson born in Jamaica to a White slave owner and a woman of African descent, had radicalism branded into his psyche watching, as a young boy, his pregnant mother and grand-mother flogged on the plantation. While the physical wounds of his mother eventually healed they seared deep into Wedderburn's memory and emotions, fatefully determining his rebellious trajectory.

> My heart glows with revenge and cannot forgive. Repent ye Chris-tians, for flogging my aged grandmother before my face, when she was accused of witchcraft by a silly European. O Boswell, ought not your colour and countrymen to be visited with wrath, for flogging my mother before my face at the time when she was far advanced in pregnancy. What was her crime?[8]

Wedderburn wrote essays, an autobiography *The Horrors of Slavery*, edited journals and pamphlets. A powerful orator, preaching rebellion, equality and freedom at his small Hopkins Street Chapel in Soho, he was impris-oned in solitary confinement for two years for blasphemy in 1820.

For his activism in the 1830s and 1840s, tailor William Cuffay – like Tull born in Kent – was transported to the other side of the world. Sacked by his employer in 1834 for going on strike, the injustice inspired him to join the National Charter Association, a nationwide working-class organisation dedicated to political reform. Their name derived from their charter of six aims: universal suffrage for all men over 21; equal electoral constituencies; secret ballots; abolition of the property qualification for parliamentary candidates; paid MPs; and annual parliaments. They had two factions, those that believed in non-violent action and the force of persuasion; and those advocating muscle and weapons to achieve their objectives, on the premise that their opponents would concede nothing without a fight. Em-bedding himself within the latter wing, building respect for himself and support for the movement, eight years later he was elected to the five-man national executive. In 1845 *The Times* described these London-based physi-cal force Chartists as 'the black man and his party'.[9]

Three years later, in the midst of revolution in Europe, on 10 April, close to 100,000 Chartists massed at Kennington Common in south London. By procession to Parliament they planned to deliver a mammoth petition of over five million signatures calling for their six aims. The government, acutely conscious of the February Revolution over the Channel in Paris, closed bridges across the Thames, and guarded them with 4,000 police. The young Queen Victoria was sent to the Isle of Wight. London's propertied 'few' armed against the imminent revolt of the 'many'.

In fact, after much argument, discussion and debate, the Chartists dispersed peacefully without the petition being delivered. Using spies and agents provocateurs the government ensnared Cuffay and other leaders of the movement, accusing them of attempting an armed uprising.

In court the diminutive London tailor defiantly demanded to be tried by his peers, jurors of the same class, as designated in the Magna Carta.

> I say you have no right to sentence me . . . It has not been a fair trial, and my request to have a fair trial – to be tried by my equals – has not been complied with. Everything has been done to raise a prejudice against me, and the press of this country – and I believe of other countries too – has done all in its power to smother me with ridicule. I ask no pity. I ask no mercy. I expected to be convicted, and I did not think anything else . . . After what I have endured this week, I feel that I could bear any punishment proudly, even to the scaffold.

Convicted, banished to Tasmania, Cuffay continued to promote political equality on an island in which other brown-skinned people like him – the indigenous population – were being killed, imprisoned, enclosed and exiled. The Chartist leader died in poverty, in the workhouse, in July 1870; the last native Tasmanian, Truganini, died in 1876.

Two other Black Chartists, David Anthony Duffy and Benjamin Prophitt, were also arrested in 1848 and transported. In parliamentary politics there has been representation by people of colour since 1892 when Dadabhai Naoroji was elected to the House of Commons as the Liberal MP for Finsbury, London, despite prime minister Lord Salisbury in 1886 declaring

> however great the progress of mankind has been, and however far we have advanced in overcoming prejudices, I doubt if we have yet got to that point of view where a British constituency would elect a black man.[10]

As if to ram the prediction down Salisbury's throat, six years later not only was Naoroji elected but three years later in 1895 Londoners returned Sir Mancherje Merwnajee Bhownagree as Conservative MP for Bethnal Green North-East; he remained their parliamentary representative until 1906, by which time one of his non-voting constituents was Tull. Another Indian-born man, Shapurji Saklatvala, was elected in 1922 for North Battersea, the first communist MP. His election agent, Black Briton John Archer, was mayor of Battersea in 1913.

The arts

During the 19th century, in that dimension of cultural life popularly known as the arts, there were numerous people of colour. On stage, the most prominent Black actor of the mid-Victorian era was New York-born Ira Aldridge. His career in the UK was characterised by performances simultaneously eulogised in the provincial press while lambasted by metropolitan newspapers. This national/regional dichotomy is noticeable also in the reporting of Black footballers, especially Arthur Wharton. In both domains of cultural life, sport and the arts the national, London-based press were finely attuned to their responsibility of adhering to an Establishment political agenda which included promoting the idea of a hierarchy of 'races'. Aldridge's youngest daughter, Luranah, studied at the Royal College of Music, her home in west London later becoming a popular watering-hole for bourgeois people of colour visiting the capital.

Composer and musician, London-born Samuel Coleridge-Taylor is usually recalled with puzzlement. He also attended the Royal College of Music, winning a scholarship in 1890, three years after Luranah Aldridge had graduated. His talent was recognised nationally after his most memorable composition, *Hiawatha's Wedding Feast*, inspired by Henry Wadsworth Longfellow's poem *Songs of Hiawatha*, was performed in public in 1899 to very positive reviews.

An outspoken advocate of Black emancipation, Coleridge-Taylor organised the music programme for the Pan-African Conference of 1900. The following year he wrote the concert overture *Toussaint L'Ouverture* in celebration of the leader of the slave rebellion in San Domingo. He also sat on the executive committee of the Pan-African Association.

The mixed-heritage composer died of pneumonia, aged just 37, on 1 September 1912. His funeral in Croydon, south London, attracted a large gathering of mourners, including many people of colour, and received press coverage nationwide. Whether Tull, a working-class orphan, would have identified with Coleridge-Taylor, an exponent of the 'high' art of classical music, is not known but there is a good, profound reason why he may have done so: Coleridge-Taylor was a Black Briton who had accomplished excellence in his profession. Also a lone navigator, Tull would have understood how difficult the route was that Coleridge-Taylor had travelled. With his classical training and revered status, the south London composer and conductor was following in the tradition of another Black musician, violinist George Augustus Polgreen Bridgetower, a sometime friend of and co-performer with Beethoven. Elected to the Royal Society of Musicians in 1807, he became a Bachelor of Music, University of Cambridge, in 1811. Bridgetower also performed with the Royal Philharmonic Society orchestra.

A century after Bridgetower and a couple of years after Coleridge-Taylor's death, another Black Briton, Mabel Mercer, was taking her first tentative steps as a popular singer. Her mother Emily Wadham was a White music hall artist, her father a no-show Black jazz musician. Touring with her aunt in vaudeville and music shows around Europe, Mabel Mercer achieved respect and fame in Paris and, eventually, the USA. Her admirers included Ernest Hemingway, Cole Porter and Frank Sinatra . . . and maybe, while in France between 1915 and 1918, a young soldier in the Footballers' Battalions of the Middlesex Regiment? Like Jesse Owens seven years before her, she was awarded the USA's highest civilian honour, the Presidential Medal of Freedom, in 1983.

While Mercer made her name as a singer in the USA and France during the inter-war years, Edwardian Londoners would have seen passing and permanent Black entertainers in all genres of popular culture: theatre, music hall, vaudeville, circus, sport and street. Some of these entertainers achieved distinction in more than one dimension of their lives, Tull being a notable example, Egyptian-born actor, playwright, newspaper editor and political activist, Duse Mohamed, another. Coming to notice on the Hull stage, Mohamed soon had London audiences gossiping of his talent: 'Mohamed is the only coloured actor and dramatic author in the world. If this fact is realised by managers there can be no question of the success of Mohamed as a novel draw'.[11]

Also touring Britain when Mohamed was making his name was African-American actor Belle Davis, appearing in 1905 in the West End at the Palace Theatre with compatriot Abbie Mitchell. Further north, on the bill at the Royal Hippodrome in Salford, was the singing, dancing double act of Connie and Augustus Smith, known as Smith and Johnson. The duo weren't the only Black entertainers in Cottonopolis in this year of the first Russian Revolution. Singer, impresario and boxing promoter Billy McClain, another African-American, the self-proclaimed patriarch of Black popular entertainers in Britain, was also in the city. While the UK was no haven for Black men, McClain felt the opportunity to be judged on the content of his character was greater than in his homeland.

> There are a good many colored performers in England, some doing well and others not . . . There is just as much prejudice here in England as in America and you will find it out if you stay long enough but . . . an Englishman believes in fair play and an American doesn't.[12]

This eastwards traffic of African-American entertainers to Britain, from Ira Aldridge on, only slowed after the First World War with the growth of the cinema industry in Hollywood and the decline of the music hall and vaudeville in Britain.

Perhaps the most popular and well-remembered show featuring Black entertainers was *In Dahomey, a Negro Musical Comedy* set in the United States and Africa, starring Bert Williams and George Walker. It opened at the West End's Shaftesbury Theatre in the spring of 1903, playing until January the following year, after which it toured the north of England, Edinburgh and Glasgow. A box office success with Black and White audiences, it confirmed the 'common-sense' image of the 'Negro' as simplistic, rhythmic, joyful, musical, comic and, most importantly, unthreatening. It wasn't overtly political and didn't challenge received prejudices. With its treasure-seeking plot, vibrant ragtime score and cakewalk dance routines, it was reassuringly self-deprecating. Revived in 1999 with a redrafted script, it even had a Broadway run.

Tull was 15 when *In Dahomey* had its original West End production. He might have seen it; other Black Londoners certainly did. While a stage wholly populated by people of colour would have been exciting and compelling, the stylised, stereotypical characterisation would have left many Black theatre-goers with an after-show feeling of frustration.

If Tull did not see *In Dahomey*, the odds on him watching a West End show would have shortened once he had signed for Spurs. With afternoons free and notes from the Bank of England in his wallet he would have been exactly the kind of punter matinée shows were aimed at. Walking from Shaftesbury Avenue to Aldwych to catch the number 11 bus toward his home in Bethnal Green, Tull may have been driven by fellow Black Briton Joe Clough who worked the route from 1908. Clough was not the only Black driver on London's public transport system: tramdriver Lewis Bruce operated the Kingston–Tolworth–Surbiton line in 1906.

Increasingly people of colour were populating British literary culture as imaginative creations of the writer. Sir Arthur Conan Doyle created Black Peter Carey and Ravi; the *Marvel* comic for children had three fictional characters Jack, Sam and Peter, the Black ventriloquist.

Meanwhile 'real' people of African descent were making an impact in Britain as editors and writers. Samuel Jules Celestine Edwards edited *Lux*, a weekly newspaper aimed at Christians, while at weekends standing on his soap-box in Bethnal Green's Victoria Park. In 1913 Duse Mohamed published and edited the monthly political journal *African Times and Orient Review* written for and aimed at London's brown-skinned people. An earlier Pan-Africanist Edward Wilmot Blyden, from Sierrra Leone, also tackled matters of the soul with *Christianity, Islam and the Negro* published in London in 1880. He penned 13 books in total but his credibility among some anti-colonialists was undermined by his hostility to people of mixed heritage. A contemporary of Blyden's, James Africanus Horton, one of the first medical officers in the British Army, also pursued the cause of liberation through his writings, most notably his 1868 publication *West African Country and Peoples*. Theophilus Scholes was a prolific turn-of-the-century writer who, perhaps, detailed the social condition of people of colour in Britain more than anyone else. His *Glimpses of the Ages; or, The 'Superior' and 'Inferior' Races, So Called, Discussed in the Light of Science and History* presented the Edwardian reader with an insight into Britain from the perspective of a Black resident. Four years later in 1909, A. B. C. Merriman-Labor, from Sierra Leone, continued this theme in his book *Britons through Negro Spectacles, or a Negro on Britons, with a description of London*. The author's fresh-eye view of London tells of smog-ridden streets, with shops open seven days a week, where 'guides with thick blazon lights known as devil fires'[13] would lead you over a busy cross-road for a penny. He commented, no doubt with his tongue pressing hard against the side of his mouth, on the what he saw as the africanisation of women's fashion, where more skin was being shown, heads were left uncovered and some daring amazons were even seen in bare feet. He felt the parents of undisciplined, disrespectful British children could do worse than adopt an African approach where sticks were unsparingly used in the cultivation of its rising generations.

Merriman-Labor highlighted the contradictions over race and pigmentation inherent in Britain and its cultures through his discussions on attitudes to 'Negroes' in the press, on streets and in the legal system. Creating a fictitious newspaper, *The Afternoon Newsmonger*, as a representative mouthpiece, he criticises journalists and editors for their constant use of 'Nigger' in newspapers 'to which decent Negroes object'.[14] 'They do not care for the Negro. [They] delight to report, and that often, anything wrong or exaggerated about the Blacks as would throw discredit on the race as whole.'[15]

He was aware of the negative influence on issues of 'race' from across the Atlantic, citing instances of British correspondents who had replied to racist letter writers from the United States who had attempted to popularise an image of the Negro as a lesser being. Merriman-Labor recounts an experience in a London hotel where White Americans refused to eat in the same restaurant as him, eventually changing their meal-time. In the courts, the West African observer felt there was equality between Black and White, arguing the law and judicial system in Edwardian Britain were colour blind. Yet in the parks – 'where kissing and spooning are not unusual' – and on the pavements, especially 'in a low class suburb a black man stands the chance of being laughed at to scorn until he takes to his heels . . . bad boys will not hesitate to shower stones or rotten eggs'.[16]

Merriman-Labor's precious insight into the reception a Black person received in Edwardian Britain suggests it was a mixed bag where the day could bring heartening displays of friendship and cutting stabs of harsh prejudice. He compared the political struggle of the 'Negro' for equality with the suffragette cause. What all Black writers make plain, however, especially those from the USA, is that, generally, cultural attitudes to brown skin in the UK were not as extreme and cruel as across the Atlantic.

While this Black intelligentsia and literary culture was enlarging and developing in both creativity and impact, at the opposite end of the cultural continuum, so to speak, the construction of the Black as freak was also attracting punters. A group of six pygmies, imported from Congo by their English manager James Harrison for the primary purpose of making money, toured the UK in 1905. Exciting interest as exotic curiosities from deepest Africa – that portion of the continent romantically revealed to British readers by Henry Stanley in his quest for Dr Livingstone – they featured on stage and in print, even attending a royal birthday party at Buckingham Palace.

These small people from the Ituri Forest of Central Africa were not the only 'freaks' on show from that continent. Edwardian entrepreneurs were keen to show that they came in all shapes and sizes. Gawping at Abomah the African giantess was another speculative crowd puller of the period.

Visible in Britain in the late 19th to early 20th century were people of colour inhabiting many walks of life. In some, such as sport, music hall and manual occupations, they were more prevalent than in others, such as politics, business and academia. By the first decade of the 20th century, there had evolved a vibrant sub-culture where those of African and Caribbean descent and heritage could look and find each other; places and spaces where their experience, over centuries, was articulated and presented to a wider audience.

4

The Children's Home and Orphanage

The Grace Hill Wesleyan Chapel, part of the Folkestone Methodist Circuit, had a financial and spiritual connection with the Children's Home and Orphanage (CHO) in Bethnal Green, whose motto 'to seek and to save that which is lost' was a literal explanation of its work. The Chapel raised money on behalf of Folkestone Methodist Circuit in support of the missionary activities of Reverend Dr Thomas Bowman Stephenson among London's young poor and homeless. CHO principal Stephenson, born at Newcastle-upon-Tyne in 1839, had been motivated to work among destitute children by his experience as a young Methodist minister in Manchester and Bolton during the Lancashire cotton famine of 1861–5. Inside the mills where children laboured in brutal, de-humanising conditions that disfigured their minds and bodies, and on the streets and in hovels pretending to be homes, he saw hunger, starvation and malnutrition. Appointed in 1868 as minister to Waterloo Chapel, Lambeth, in London, he witnessed further child deprivation, most notably abject poverty, parental absence and homelessness.

> Shoeless, filthy, their faces pinched with hunger and premature wretchedness, and I began to feel that now my time was come. Here were my poor little brothers and sisters, sold to hunger and the devil, and I could not be free of their blood if I did not do something to save some of them.[1]

With the help of £20 each from friends and colleagues Francis Horner and Francis Mager, in July 1869 he opened his original Children's Home at

8 Church Street, a small run-down cottage in Waterloo Road, Lambeth. Demand soon outgrew capacity. Looking around for larger premises, by chance Stephenson noticed that three houses and a yard were vacant in Bonner Road, Bethnal Green. They had been formerly used in the making of paving stones by the Victoria Stone Company. With rent of £190 per year, 37 boys and 6 girls of the CHO moved across the Thames with Stephenson and his staff in May 1871.

The trio of large terraced houses allowed the young minister to introduce his family system of care in which children would live in named Houses under the supervision of a Sister rather than in large, institutional dormitories. He wanted to create surrogate nuclear families within the extended family of the Home. This novel approach to childcare was inspired by German practice in looking after homeless children at Kaiserswerth and Hamburg that Stephenson had witnessed during his visit to the newly unified country in the aftermath of the Franco-Prussian war of 1870–1. Within two years the CHO had bought more houses nearby, enabling Stephenson to enlarge his 'family'. His pioneering work was not unnoticed.

> Dr Stephenson's Children's Home, at Victoria Park, is . . . engaged in giving a fresh start in life to many a destitute and friendless boy or girl . . . In these Homes everything that can be done is done to enable the children to overcome their bad habits, and to fit them for some useful occupation when they leave the Home. Industry and intelligence, order and cleanliness, cheerfulness and activity, are encouraged; religion is inculcated; and the whole discipline through which the children pass cultivates and improves them so much, that it is difficult to recognise in these sturdy, active intelligent boys and girls leaving the Home, the pale-faced, poor, neglected ones who entered it some years before. Many more lives would be brightened, if people, seeing how much we are all benefited by this work of rescue, would give of their charity.[2]

By the First World War the National Children's Home (NCH), as the Children's Home and Orphanage had become, had over 4,000 boarders in numerous institutions dotted around the country.

Correspondence between Folkestone and London suggests that, despite

Tulls' Methodism and the Folkestone Circuit's voluntary contribution to CHO funds, entry for the boys would not be a simple formality. The orphanage was consistently full.

> We receive children of all creeds and none. We deal with babies of a few days and with young men and women passing out of their teens. We are continually appealed to by Boards of Guardians, the Society for the Prevention of Cruelty to Children, the Reformatory and Refuge Union, the Ragged School Union, the Royal Patriotic Fund, and other Societies for dealing with soldiers' orphans; by ministers of all denominations, by police court [sic], city and town missionaries, deaconesses, parish visitors, rescue workers, and by all sorts of social and philanthropic organisations.[3]

The older Tull girls, Cecilia and Elsie, argued Adcock, could stay in Folkestone and help Clara with baby Miriam and other domestic responsibilities; while William was essential as the sole breadwinner. Initially, Elsie was due to go with Walter and Edward until a rethinking of options envisaged Cecilia going into service and Elsie becoming Clara's main help.

Adcock knew Stephenson personally, and was not shy of reminding him when advocating the boys' case, of the financial assistance the Folkestone Methodists had consistently provided for the CHO.[4] In an exchange of letters between the two in January 1898, Adcock emphasised the need of the seven-member Tull family for outside help is 'more urgent than I've already described'. He also pointed out the Grace Hill Chapel was helping with funds for 'rent for the present [and] a mangle' so Clara could take in washing to supplement the family's meagre income. In the application form, under 'Special circumstances', Adcock writes

> His [Daniel's] first wife's protracted illness (cancer) exhausted his little earnings. Stepparent mother was related to the first wife & married largely to mother the children. She has had a hard struggle to meet . . . disbursements occasioned by first wife's long illness. She is far from strong but if relieved of two children . . . she might with help keep a home for the remaining four children – three of which not being her own.[5]

He describes Walter as 'honest – truthful – somewhat quick tempered – afterward repentant and generally dutiful'. (These qualities of honesty and duty also came to be recognised by others, notably his fellow soldiers Major D. S. Poole and 2nd Lieutenant Pickard, who mentioned them in letters to Edward after Walter's death.)

In the application form for the CHO the North Board School provides a report on the academic progress of both boys, stating that in July 1897 Walter had been examined in standard three and had since been working in standard four, 'making steady progress'; while Edward had been examined in standard four and was subsequently taught to standard five.[6]

These statements are significant in helping to understand the emotional durability of the two boys. Despite the protracted illness and death of their mother; the remarriage of their father; a young stepmother replacing Alice; and the birth of Miriam, their education does not seem to have suffered. This suggests not only a cohesive, bonded family that emanated mutual support but one that was also bolstered by outside help from the wider family, notably the Palmers. No greater example of this is the arranged marriage to Daniel of his deceased wife's niece, Clara. Both Adcock and Stephenson were keen to see the boys enter the CHO.

Adcock could see first hand the Tulls' distress, especially the burden upon Clara as a single parent. No doubt he thought it his Christian duty, the family being members of his congregation, to prevent their decline into chronic poverty. If that meant sending away Walter and Edward so the rest of the family could stay together, so be it.

Stephenson, as principal, had a fiduciary duty to the CHO alongside his pastoral role as guardian of the children within its walls. These two roles were not always compatible, though without close watch upon finances, there would not be a CHO. He was anxious that the Elham Union should continue to contribute towards the boys' upkeep after they had been admitted. To this end there was negotiation of a financial contract through a round robin of letters between Lonergan, the clerk and superintendent registrar of the Elham Union of Poor Law Guardians, Stephenson and Adcock. In one of these, 22 January 1898, Lonergan asked if further funds, additional to the weekly contribution of the boys' maintenance, would be expected from the Elham Union for 'clothing, emigration or outfit when the children leave your home?'[7] In the same letter he pointed out 'the father of these children was a negro and they are consequently coloured children. I do not know if you are aware of this or whether it will in any way affect the application?'[8]

Stephenson replied that it made no difference. He is described by one biographer as a man 'singularly free . . . from any social pride or caste feeling of any description'.[9] In photographs of the Bonner Road Home there are children of varying ethnicities. Tolerance of difference courses through Stephenson's Methodism as bright as the tail of a meteorite except in his attitude to the Roman Church, in which he was 'fervently anti-Catholic'.[10] His enlightened feelings on race and colour were also apparent in his trips abroad to South Africa and the USA. An accomplished organist possessing a fine baritone voice, in both countries he preached, worshipped and sang at Black churches. He was overwhelmed by the singing in Cape Colony and Natal.

> A choir of Kaffir men and women, possessing voices which I have seldom heard equalled for compass and quality. They sang the full harmony, and specially remarkable were the rich, deep voices of the men, basses rolling thunderous at the bottom of the chord.[11]

In Washington he sung with, and to, Black congregations. He liked the relationship they had with their preachers, in which they would constantly reply with 'amen' and other comments throughout ministrations.

Stephenson was impressed with their cultural interpretation of worship and came back with the feeling that 'coloured people' should be able to 'work out their own relationship with God, under their own bishops'.[12] Stephenson, in his actions and thinking, was a fairly typical example of his nonconformist background and historical era. He believed the hope of achieving God's vision of a 'civilised' world lay through the global exploits of the greater Briton:

> It seems to me that to any thoughtful Englishman the British Empire is, next to the Christian religion, the greatest fact of these latter days. No man, who desires to measure at their true value the great social and moral forces which are making the world of the future, should neglect an opportunity to see that greater Britain which lies all around the globe, where men of our own blood, our own speech, and our own religion, are reproducing this dear

old England, with a freedom and elasticity which is not possible to us at home. I believe that in the accomplishment of His great purposes the Anglo-Saxon race is, and is to be, the most potent factor.[13]

The financial settlement agreed through the postal exchange resulted in the Elham Union subsidising the maintenance of the boys at the rate of 4 shillings per week each plus outfits on maturity at 18. This combined sum of 8 shillings per week was 2s 2d more than was paid to Clara by the same body for the upkeep of herself and five dependent children. Had they agreed to pay such a figure to the stepmother it may have been possible for the family to remain as one in Folkestone. With William's contribution of 7 shillings per week the total would have been 1 shilling more than the weekly wage of Clara's father William and Uncle Robert.

The Agreement between Clara and the Home stipulated there was to be 'no interference in any way' by her while the children were in the Home. Further, if the children (or child) were taken back 'without the agreement of the committee' the sum of 8 shillings per week per child times the length of duration in the Home, would have to be repaid. This was twice the sum the Poor Law Guardians allocated and was no doubt meant to be prohibitive, in the sense that de facto rights over the children would be determined by economic circumstances. Another clause gave the Home the right to send the children abroad. These conditions had to be agreed before the case for acceptance in the Home could be considered by the Committee.

Stephenson, principal of the CHO from 1869 until retirement in 1900 when he was replaced by Dr A. E. Gregory, had four aims for children in his care: to provide the love, care, discipline and stability of a surrogate family; to inculcate a moral code based upon Wesleyan Methodist principles (a more egalitarian version of orthodox Christian morality); to provide a basic education in core subjects such literacy, numeracy and religion in the orphanage's Elementary School; and to provide vocational skills, which in Walter's case meant an apprenticeship in the Home's print shop. In pursuing these aims the CHO would play its role in the mission of empire building, providing viable human resources usable at home or in the colonies.

After thorough medical examinations at which the boys' history of illness and vaccination was recorded, alongside descriptions of their intelligence and general health – Walter is observed as being in 'very good health'[14] having had measles but no other illness – they were due to be admitted on St Valentine's Day, 14 February 1898.

Leaving loved ones, the date could have been interpreted by the boys in their more melancholy moments of reflection as having an ironic significance. Yet Clara, Adcock, Stephenson and Lonergan had conspired in an arrangement motivated, in differing degrees, by love and concern. Their united hope was that the sacrifices made would be repaid by long-term gain in the shape of a family albeit atomised but saved from poverty and the necessity of vice. In fact, as we will see, the return was far greater than could have been imagined. Adcock had made arrangements with his Chapel for money to cover expenses for Clara to travel to Bethnal Green with her 'two dear sons, the little dark boys'.[15]

A few days prior to the 14th, Adcock received a telegram from Pendlebury, Stephenson's deputy and governor of the Bonner Road Home, saying there was 'no room'![16] Adcock was 'amazed'. Hadn't Stephenson told him the boys could come up 'at any time'? 'A misunderstanding,' replied the Rev. Dr, '"they may be sent for at any time" is what I believe I said'![17] The boys should come on the original date of the 14th:

> In all the circumstances of the case, however, I feel it much better that the children should come at once. There are no vacancies, but we can temporarily make arrangements by sending two other children to another branch where the numbers are not so strictly limited as here. We will, therefore, receive the children on Monday as you are aware.[18]

They didn't enter that Monday because Clara was ill. NCH records imply Walter and Edward, chaperoned by Adcock, were handed over to a member of the CHO staff at Cannon Street station on 24 February. However, a handwritten recollection by Edward states a 'kindly . . . heartbroken'[19] Clara took them to Bonner Road. Interestingly, Edward's notes for a 'talk' called 'The Film that Will Never Be Screened', subtitled 'The Boys from Dr Stephenson's Children's Home', were compiled in response to a 1937 film *The Boy from Barnardo's*. (For a discussion of why he may be proved wrong in his big screen assertion see the final chapter.)

Visitors to Bonner Road would arrive through large iron gates defending a large open space, The Big Yard, behind which a row of terrace cottages comprised a proportion of the living quarters. The other Houses formed Bonner Road itself. 'The families number in the aggregate 330 children'.[20] Today the site hosts a primary school. The opposite side of Bonner Road remains much as it was – a terrace of mid-Victorian step-ups speculatively built for an enlarging middle class. In Edward's 'Film' notes, which provide scenes and narrative but no dialogue, he describes, with a sprinkling of his characteristic dry humour, their induction into the orphanage, its geography, daily routine and the attempt at replicating an organisation of families within a Home.

At the entrance, which was situated in Bonner Road, London NE, you would be shown over the offices. Here the Governor's Room and Offices for the workings of the Home occupied a fairly large block of buildings. Carrying on past this building you would come to the Chapel which occupied the corner of a great big square or quadrangle . . . paved with wooden blocks and all around it are fairly big houses . . . There are names over each house, [each having been] gifted by the various people whose name they bear . . . [the] one in which . . . we . . . finished [our] stay in the Home is called Sunday School House. This house was gifted by the Methodist Sunday Schools of the country. Another is called Wakefield House . . . after Lord Wakefield . . . first treasurer of the Home.

In one corner [of the quadrangle] the noise of machinery and . . . printing presses. Through another door . . . cooking and baking. Another shows us a dining hall for the staff whilst another shows us a gymnasium. There is a little stairway at the side of the gymnasium . . . leading to a room that every boy and girl aspires to . . . the choir room. This Home had a famous choir of boys and girls conducted by a famous musician and it was the ambition of every boy and girl to become a member . . . a queer room, [it had] a series of desks which rose tier on tier at which one could only stand.

Let us go back to the quadrangle . . . set apart . . . in a lesser quadrangle of its own . . . the girls' Houses.

One corner I must mention – for cleanliness is next to Godliness. There is a big communal bath, something like the big football clubs have today and adjoining it is a swimming pool.

Highfield House was [our] very first house . . . as junior members . . . the Sister, as she was called, had fifteen boys in her charge and her accommodation consisted of three bedrooms, her sleeping room and her sitting room, a dining room, a play room and a washing room with lavatories . . . Each house was constructed on the same plan, but and it is a big but, each house was a home. Sister was the mother and the head of the house . . . All the work of the house had to be done by its occupants with the exception of the two oldest boys and girls. They were working girls or boys. Each boy or girl had his or her duties no matter what age and it was the Sister's duty to see that the house was perfectly run.

[We] had . . . been provided with clothing and unlike many Children's Homes . . . kept these clothes. Each child in the National Children's Home had their own distinctive clothing, which is important. Dr Barnardo's did not follow these lines. Our boys were given their separate lockers to put their own possessions in and shown where to place their separate clothing. They each had their separate beds in a room that slept six.

A bell rings . . . it is 6.20 am. All the boys in their room rise and dress, after which they make their beds. In the Reception House . . . boys have been shown what to do, so they fling off all the bed clothes, turn the mattress and make the bed leaving the top sheet with the correct six inches turned down and the night gown carefully folded. Following the other boys downstairs they go to their locker to get their own towel, brush and comb to proceed to the washing room to wash in cold water . . . They proceed to the play room and stand in line. Sister makes her appearance and sees that every boy is present and then the boys proceed to their various tasks before breakfast. Being newcomers [we] start at the bottom and naturally the bottom is cleaning of boots or rather shoes. Not one pair, but all the pairs of the household . . . the Sister's especially. No fancy pastes such Ki-wi in those days, it was the good old fashioned blacking that was lubricated with, I can find no better word, water. Having finished fifteen pairs of shoes, an inspection by the Sister was enacted and if favourable, put away in various lockers. Breakfast came as a happy relief, but what had the other boys been doing?

The two eldest boys, who were called Working Boys, had gone off to the printing shop and bakehouse, but as the house has to be cleaned, as your house has to be cleaned, the other boys had various tasks. The three older boys had the bedrooms to scrub and the bedrooms were bare boards. This was the procedure: each took a bucket, scrubbing brush, cloth and soap with pail and cold water, and each took a strip of those boards. At every fourth patch the water had to be changed until the room was finished. One boy was set to clean the brass taps of the washing room, not with Brasso but with Globe Polish, whilst another scrubbed the floor (concrete). Another had to scrub the playroom, which was tiled, whilst another set the breakfast table. Every boy had a task that kept him occupied until breakfast time and no task was finished until Sister had passed it satisfactorily. Breakfast consisted of bread and magarine with cocoa and as soon as that meal was finished and the dishes washed the whole house walked in order accompanied by the Sister to the Chapel for morning prayers.

Each house was fully represented in the Chapel and the prayers were conducted by the Governor. The choir was made up of about 40 boys and girls. A hymn, a prayer, a bible portion and the Benediction was the usual order of Service but on Monday morning instead of the Reading a boy or girl from each house had to stand and repeat a Text that had been chosen by the Sister. There was no Chapel on Sunday because the Home went to the Methodist Church in Bonner Road about 200 hundred yards away and the Home Choir led the Priest at morning and evening services.

After prayers came school for the majority of children. The school was beside the Chapel. Two boys aged 13 proceeded back to the house. They were house boys and only went to school in the afternoon. The senior house boy had the Sister's quarters to clean and look after whilst the junior had to dust, clean and prepare downstairs . . . the boys' quarters. Dinner was a one course meal – soup one day, meat pie another, fish another. Plain wholesome feeding one would call it but the boy with taste would call it many things. The boys whose duty it was to wash up after dinner had to stand by 'til the Sister inspected the dinner dishes. This duty rotated – two boys were [picked] each week to do the dinner dishes.

School again in the afternoon and tea at 5 pm, but before tea a thorough personal washing. The boys stripped to the waist and washed from there upwards. That didn't finish it. Sister required every boy to appear before her for inspection and that inspection was no careless thing. Hands and nails were first looked at, then under the armpits and finally the ears. I remember one small boy who had difficulty with his ears. Strive as he would he would never seem to get his ears clean. Tea consisted of the same course as breakfast, bread and margarine with cocoa.

For two hours after tea the boys could use their time as they liked in the play room except the choir boys who might have a choir practice, but no noise was allowed and at 8 pm the boys stood in line preparatory to going to bed in an orderly manner and with the common greeting of 'Goodnight Sister'. No talking was allowed in the bedrooms.

In the summer time the leisure hours were spent in the quadrangle just as you boys or girls spend your time out of doors, marbles, skipping ropes, spring tops, etc.

Edward's fascinatingly detailed account allows us a taste, feel and smell of life in his late Victorian/Edwardian orphanage. While the life-style of routine, order, hierarchy and discipline are typical of such out-of-the-ordinary, enclosed settlements be they prisons, boarding schools, monasteries or barracks, he is keen to emphasise the CHO's concession to individual identity in allowing boys to wear 'their own distinctive clothing' (in contrast to the rule at Dr Barnardo's).

From 1878 Sisters were formally trained, Stephenson pioneering the specialisation of institutional childcare in the UK. That the women mothering the Houses should see their role as a vocation, ideally God-given, he was passionate. In 1890 he published his thoughts on the subject in a book typeset at the Bonner Road printing department.

The experience of thirty years in connection with such work has convinced me of the necessity for specially trained women to do this work . . . The experience ordinarily obtained in public institutions is not only no advantage, but a positive disqualification. Generally it hardens those who acquire it. Their life tends to become more and more mechanical, their discipline more rigid, and they thus come to feel more and more that they are but parts of a system of police.[21]

Candidates for his Sisterhood should be 'of good education and address', approaching 23 years, members of an evangelical community and Christian, preferably Methodist. Overseeing the programme at the training centre, Willard House, in the year of Walter and Edward's entry, was Sister Ruth Northfield. She summarised the personal and professional skills developed and instilled in her students.

> You must be able to warn them that are unruly, comfort the feeble minded, support the weak and be patient to all . . . to answer the child's questions, to read aloud to them . . . to improve their manners and their morals, their grammar and their tempers, to enter into their play and foster their ideals.[22]

Training consisted of bible theory and practice, medical instruction and studying Christian biography and philanthropy, along with work practice. Those who had completed the three time periods of the course – a three-month trial followed, if successful, by a further nine-month trial, then a year's working probation – would be inaugurated into the Sisterhood through a ritual whereby Sisters would agree to devote their lives 'to seek and to save that which is lost', with a bible and badge given them as tokens of 'faith and fellowship'.

If a Sister married or left within two years of graduating they would be expected to pay back the cost of their training. During their schooling in the craft of childcare they would be provided with board and lodging but not expenses, unless there were exceptional circumstances. There were two working uniforms: indoors, a blouse fastened at the neck, a plain navy blue dress worn with stockings and black or navy blue shoes; outdoors, a cap, plain blue coat, blue or grey scarf and grey, navy or white gloves.

These carers were the nearest a child would get to close adult affection – or rejection – in the tight-knit, individual house system of boarding. While these uniforms almost invite physical and emotional rigidity, a glance at the numerous websites focussing upon the NCH provides evidence of how dedicated some of these women were; and of the respect, love even, that many ex-boarders held for them. Though there is no surviving evidence of Walter building a lasting, affectionate relationship with a particular Sister he did write to members of staff once he had left the Home. In a letter written from the Front in 1916 to Mr Hodson-Smith, principal of the Harpenden branch of the NCH, to which the Bonner Road branch moved in 1913, he thanks him for 'the feast' sent out to him. He is also concerned about the welfare of

> Mrs Jeffrey formerly cook at Bonner Road. I should feel very much relieved if you could visit her personally & see if you can do any-thing to help her as I believe she is having a hard struggle to make ends meet whilst the war is on. I know she has had to work very hard since the Home removed to Harpenden, & I rather fancy that the work is beyond her strength.[23]

Stephenson was superintendent of the Methodist Church that members of the Home attended each Sunday. It was nearby and, importantly, part of the wider Methodist community. While it was only a short walk once a week, the effect of meeting with people not connected to the Home was refreshing, vital and a large step in helping the children feel part of the world outside their walls. It would afford each child an entry point and reminder of a society from which they had been torn or which they had left behind but to which they would return at some point in the future.

Stephenson tried to foster a culture of care, responsibility and disciplined order within his Home. Yet, beyond its iron gates, lower-middle-class Bonner Road and picturesque, leafy Victoria Park, with its bandstand and boating lake, were in one of the poorest, most densely occupied boroughs of the largest city in the world.

Walking down Bethnal Green Road toward Shoreditch, Walter and Edward would have skirted the southern border of the Nichol, an impov-erished working-class ghetto of around 6,000 that had been fictionalised by Arthur Morrison in his much publicised and widely read novel, *A Child of the Jago*, published in 1896. After being criticised for sensationalising the criminal sub-culture of the Nichol, Morrison responded that he wrote as he found after 18 months of participant observation. A real-life 'child of the Jago' at this time was Arthur Harding, whose oral recollection of growing up in what was considered London's most feared slum is contained in Ralph Samuel's *East End Underworld* (1981). Harding tells of a close-knit community with intense tribal loyalty where gangs, guns and prison were as much a feature of life as overcrowding, vermin and incursions by middle-class missionaries. Interestingly, a rival firm from nearby Commercial Road was named after their leader, Darkey the Coon, a flamboyant 'man of colour',[24] also known as Ikey Bogard. He won a Military Medal in the First World War and is discussed further in the chapter on Black people in the armed forces.

Growing up fast was a necessary consequence of the rapid change which had occurred in Walter and Edward's short and eventful lives. Protected as they were from its roughest, harshest quarters, the borough of Bethnal Green in the late 1890s and early 1900s was no place for the naïve.

Edward felt Walter was hardier and better equipped to cope with the initial shock of entry and subsequent emotional acclimatisation. '[I was] homesick and a little frightened. [Walter] being of a sturdier mould seemed ready to sample new ways and new means.'[25] If applicable, it was usual practice to allow new boarders visits from their families. Letters arrived frequently from Clara, William and Cecilia – Cissie – requesting to see the boys. Two months after she had left them, Clara, in a postcard, writes of her desire to see her exiled stepchildren. By the end of the year her longing remained undiminished:

> I should like to come and see the to [*sic*] little boys tomorrow Thursday as I am in Tottenham my to dear little sons the dark boys. I hope it will not put you out and in any way as I have not been able to write before so shall arrive about 3 o'clock tomorrow afternoon.[26]

The Tull correspondence in the NCH archive reveals a stepmother and siblings who were ever-concerned for the boys' welfare and development, determined not to let the seismic emotional upheavals break their family bond. During the summer of 1899 William asks if he can spend time with his brothers; the following summer he requests that they stay with him for a two-week holiday; while in service at Mrs Broadbank's house, Cissie asks to visit.

After a few days in the Home, they were assigned to Highfield House and the care of Sister Ethel. Walter and Edward spent 33 months together with visits to, or from, their family. All three brothers were close, but Walter and Edward extremely so. When Walter enlisted in the army in 1914 and had to name next of kin, Edward was registered.

Stephenson's love of singing and playing music, his belief in its therapeutic and evangelical influence, had inspired him to form a CHO choir and band in the 1870s. Each year on Temperance Sunday, celebrating the joys of abstinence, they would be led through the streets of Bethnal Green by 'Black Bob, a converted drunkard' who would put on a show of dexterous gymnastics by tossing his iron bedleg high above his head and catch it, followed by a quick and neat exchange of hands.[27] (It isn't known if Bob's name was an accurate description of his ethnicity.) Stephenson's beloved solo was *Blind Bartimaeus*. His excellent baritone voice was a crowd puller to his services, initially at the Waterloo Road Chapel, Lambeth and later at the Approach Road Chapel, Bethnal Green. A working man standing outside the former, listening, commented 'it's worth half a crown any day to hear a parson sing like that'.[28]

The first choir and band tour of the country was in 1878, with 26 musicians aged between 10 and 14 and an unspecified number of singers. Performed favourites were *Onward, Christian Soldiers*; *Stand Up! Stand Up for Jesus*; *Mine Eyes Have Seen the Glory*; and *O Safe the Rock*. The dual purpose of these tours was to raise much needed money for the running of the expanding CHO network and showcase boys and girls available for adoption.

With their caps as much in their hands as on their heads, in 1900 the CHO choir of boys and girls once more toured the country fund-raising. As well as singers, the ensemble had an impressive array of musical instruments, including dulcimers, drums, mandolins and bells. Performing at Glasgow's main Methodist church, St John's, Edward was noticed by a Glasgow couple, James and Jean Warnock. Listening to his melodic voice, a quality much commented upon in obituaries of Edward, made an irrepressible impression. Through an intermediary, J. W. Butcher of Claremont Street Wesleyan Church, Glasgow, their place of worship, the Warnocks offered to adopt.

> I have what I consider to be an excellent offer for Eddie. His host is a dentist whose clientele is mainly among the poorer people. He is willing to take Eddie – treat him as a son, teach him a profession

& if the boy proves worthy eventually work the connection into his hands.[29]

The 'connection' was Mr Warnock's St Vincent Street dental practice. Butcher finishes his letter to the new principal of Bonner Road CHO, Dr Gregory – Stephenson having retired some months earlier – with a persuasive flourish.

> Your children on this trip have in power of behaviour surpassed all my former experiences & they were good. I think I shall when all cheques are to hand be able to send you between £65 and £66 nett [*sic*].[30]

As was the case in Adcock's communication with Stephenson over the boys' application to the Home, those who rely on charity are often reminded of their vulnerability, and Butcher was not slow in making Gregory aware who was doing who a favour in this exchange.

Both Butcher and Gregory accepted the role of money in the saving of souls: for the Home to take in more children it needed both funds *and* to be able to place those in its care in order to create space for new entrants. Devising ways and means of attracting income was an integral feature of the CHO culture. Public collecting boxes were distributed; public subscriptions advertised in newspapers; and, in 1899, the Young Leaguers Union (YLU), was established to encourage the rising generations in fundraising, especially ex-CHO boarders like Edward, who was a member.

Edward was fortunate in not crossing the sea in order to step across his new threshold. Sending CHO children abroad to anglicise Britain's expanding empire and ex-colonies was annual practice. By 1909 it had sent 2,000 children to Canada. For example, in 1894 33 boys and one girl were shipped to Hamilton, on the *Labrador*; three years later 34 boys also docked at the same port, bound for new homes.[31] While the reader may shudder at the thought of sending children thousands of miles to start anew, poverty-induced economic migration was a feature of working-class and rural communities. An estimated 10 million people from England and Wales left to try their luck elsewhere between 1861 and 1900.

Clara – now Mrs Beer – was delighted Edward had the opportunity to move to a domestic and social environment in which his life chances would be greatly improved, so much so that she sent a basket of food for a celebratory last supper at Bonner Road. Her gift, while accentuating the positive step for Edward, was not an insensitive ignoring of her other stepson's increased vulnerability.

The Warnocks formally adopted Edward, hyphenating Warnock to his surname and promising to regard him as their son. However, the Glasgow dentist and his wife, in completing the legal papers, refused the Home's contractual clause stipulating they find Edward a job.

> Some of the conditions we have not complied to as we do not intend putting the boy to work at present. We consider him smart and intelligent and would like to send him to school, in order to fit him better for the occupation we desire him to follow.[32]

A range of competing and conflicting emotions must have coursed through Walter as Edward walked out of the gates for his new home 400 miles away on 14 November 1900. No doubt he would have been pleased for his brother, going to a relatively affluent family home where he would have his own room and fire – a definite necessity in this second city of the empire – and the opportunity to study for a profession. Yet the person on whom he relied most was gone. Walter's isolation was now more acute than it had ever been.

However, both he and Edward were determined to remain close in spirit and, in pursuit of that goal, they certainly had the Warnocks' support. Within a day of his arrival Edward wrote to Walter saying he felt 'happy' and 'quite at home' and that he would be learning French and Latin and 'piano for pleasure'.[33] In fact the couple actively encouraged a continuance of their relationship. In July 1903, they sent 52 shillings – a sum roughly equivalent to two weeks' wages for a manual worker – for Walter's train fare to Scotland after Edward had written in May to the CHO:

> I again take the liberty of writing to you concerning my brother's holidays. We should be very pleased if you would permit Walter to visit us for a fortnight. We will send his return fare on receiving a letter from you, I may also add that although I cannot be with you on Founder's Day yet I think of you and hope you will have a happy time. I keep in touch with the Home affairs by collecting

and being a member of the YLU. I hope you will see it convenient to allow Walter to visit us and oblige with an early reply.[34]

Walter was also invited to stay with another boy who had been adopted, Fred Wrigglesworth, an alumnus of Newcastle House, Bonner Road. Taken in by the Lockley family of Longroyd Bridge, near Huddersfield, they too offered to pay Walter's fare. The Wrigglesworths had a printing business and, like the Warnocks, initially saw their adoptive son and Walter while listening to the CHO choir on a fund-raising tour.

The coincidence of the Wrigglesworths' printing business and Walter's apprenticeship in the trade may have been just that. The Bonner Road print shop had been in operation since the 1870s and, according to the NCH version of their history, had built an admirable reputation for the quality of work its compositors produced.

Walter spent seven years at Bonner Road in an institutional environment described by Edward as 'harsh and disciplined but not unbearable'.[35] Reg Ferm, one of the few orphans to write of his experiences, does not remember his days in a 1920s Home with much affection: 'True to the best traditions of orphanages of the period, all traces of comfort had been eliminated'.[36] Ferm hated his time in what he felt was a cold, dispassionate and austere institution where daily routine was punctuated by religion and once-weekly baths . . . in the same water! (The cleansing of souls more important than bodies?) Developing a working relationship with staff was fundamental to survival: 'To an orphan the most important people . . . [in] an orphanage are the matrons . . . and can determine whether life is happy, bearable or thoroughly miserable'.[37] Cold winter nights in bed alone exacerbated Ferm's feelings of loneliness. Once he ran away. Caught, and back at the orphanage, he was punished twice over, for absconding and for stealing the clothes in which he escaped! Visiting Edward's daughter, Jean, and her husband, the Reverend Duncan Finlayson, at their remote Rhugarbh Cottage in North Shian, a few miles from the small, picturesque coastal village of Port Appin, Argyll, I found she was keen to emphasise that her father did not think the CHO regime brutal.

Yet for Walter, while the daily routine and relationships with those responsible for his care were not as damaging as Reg Ferm's experiences, the physical loss of Edward was debilitating and unsettling. In 1903 Lonergan, clerk of the Elham (Poor Law) Union, Folkestone, enquired whether the

CHO still required 4 shillings per week from the Board for his upkeep now that he was 15. The Home replied that Walter is 'slow . . . not diligent in work . . . and is not ready to leave the Home'.[38]

Despite Folkestone Poor Law Guardians' desperation to erase Walter from their Relief list, it wasn't until he reached 18 in 1906 that they stopped making payments to the Home, a year after Walter started his apprenticeship in the CHO print shop at Bonner Road.

The years 1900 to 1905 were extremely difficult for Walter. The emotional impact of the loss of or isolation from the three most important people in his life at the ages of seven, nine and 12 was increasingly noticeable in his behaviour, as the observation of 1903 testifies. On one occasion even James Warnock wrote an apologetic letter in mitigation of Walter's misbehaviour.

At this crucial stage in his adolescence, despite trips to Scotland to see Edward, the visits to and from Clara, William and Cissie, Walter may have realised he had to cope with his losses and grief, in large part, alone. That was his day-to-day reality. Around him he did not have his natural family for support, they were available only at a distance. For an adolescent undergoing biological transformation, the struggle to deal with the drip, drip effect of vicious emotional ruptures was just short of overwhelming. It was hard to keep it all together, not to collapse under the weight.

Carers, staff and other children within the Home would have lent a listening ear, aware of his pain. Sister Ethel was his nearest comforter, his surrogate mother at Highfield House. But to seek special attention in an environment where all housemates, because of their circumstances, warranted these humane necessities was to assume a position of false privilege. This would bring only resentment and irritation. The smooth functioning of the House as a unit took precedence over consistent attention to individual wants and needs.

Yet Walter had dogged persistence, a quality of character that colours his life. He did not like to quit. However difficult, unmanageable, unbearable circumstances seemed, his reaction was to dig in. In this trait, perhaps, we can find the answer to his reliance upon, and superior ability in, football and cricket. These pleasurable instruments he used to sustain and reinforce the durability of his inner self. Both games allowed him space to enjoy his life, where he could forget, re-focus, concentrate, exclude, indulge and feel good about himself. The momentum, the dialectic, the synthesis between his tenacity, his sporting aptitude and the distance separating his emotional state and requirements, produced an aspirational sportsman. Sport was cathartic: the outside air cleansed; the competition focussed; the team ethos disciplined; success enjoyed; losses a test that galvanised. It was the ideal antidote.

Walter played for the orphanage football team, initially left-wing then left-back. In the only team photo existing, taken around 1902, he has an enigmatic, Mona Lisa smile. They played on Victoria Park in Hackney and Stamford Hill Playing Fields further north, toward Tottenham. Though we do not have further photographic evidence it is almost certain he played cricket while at the orphanage because, as a Clapton FC player in 1909,

> Standing 5ft 8in., and scaling 10st 10lb, Tull, who is a non-smoker and total abstainer, is considered by those who have seen him play both games to be a better cricketer than a footballer. Last season he took 76 wickets at 3 runs apiece, and in 1907 he had a batting average of 26.5. Playing against Garrison Artillery, Gosport, two years ago, he scored 61 and 31, both not out, and carried his bat through each innings.[39]

And, with his father a native of Barbados, it is not stretching the imagination to suggest an evening or Sunday game of cricket with Daniel and the rest of the family helped develop his skills with the bat and ball from an early age.

In 1905 Walter began his apprenticeship in the printing department of the CHO. Two years later, in September 1907, the Home eager for his bed, a young man his independence, a waged Tull packed his trunk and lodged with a number of other ex-CHO young men at Mr Maynard's Lincoln House hostel, 28 Darnley Road, South Hackney, a half-way house for those leaving the orphanage. To walk to the print shop in Bonner Road from his new address, as he would have six days a week, it would not have been out of his way to pass Dr James Jackson Brown's house at 63 Lauriston Road and maybe exchange greetings with the Jamaican doctor as he made his way to the London Hospital in Whitechapel. At Lauriston Road, a short walk across Victoria Park from Bonner Road, Dr Brown opened a practice that continued until the 1990s, long after he had died.

Living at Darnley Road, Walter could either take his midday meal with him to the print shop or return to eat. Walter preferred neither option and instead claimed the 6d allowance that was paid to another boy who had already chosen not to eat the hostel's lunch. Maynard refused and wrote to the Home arguing 'I have more than one reason for refusal which I am sure would meet with your approval'.[40] Did Maynard think Walter would spend his tanner on drink, drugs and women? After a succession of letters Walter was vindicated and received his allowance. A small affair, it says a great deal about Walter's willingness to stand his ground: he felt his landlord was being unfair and he wasn't having it. The incident has echoes of his father Daniel's vengeful visit to the house of Mr Massiah!

Walter lived at Darnley Road hostel for two years. By the end of the 1908–9 season his football career was evolving at a speed even the most enthusiastic of Tull's admirers could not have imagined possible. An extra benefit was the necessity of finding digs nearer the best-supported club in southern England. An address given on his Army Effects Form in 1915 was 77 Northumberland Park, Tottenham.

5

Football

The 1908–9 football season, beginning in September at the tail-end of a wet London summer, began in much the same way as many previous ones for Tull, turning out at left-back in the halved shirts of the orphanage team at Victoria Park and Stamford Hill Playing Fields. For the skilful, robust left-footer it must have been increasingly frustrating competing against keen but limited park footballers.

The 20-year-old would have read much in the plethora of daily, evening and sporting newspapers about the summer sporting festival across the city, in west London. At the 68,000 capacity White City Stadium, Shepherds Bush, the Great Britain soccer team captained by Spurs centre-forward Vivien Woodward had won gold in the football tournament of the fourth – and very controversial – Olympiad of the modern era. British football, at the elite level, stood unchallenged in the world. Woodward and his Olympians played the game in an arena and form light years from the park lump and bump style to which Tull was accustomed. Yet this season would climax with him standing shoulder to shoulder with the Olympic captain, both dangling medals on their chests. It was an ascendance that, for all his youthful fantasising, Tull could never have imagined, let alone expected.

By the season's close, as centre-forward with one of the best amateur sides in the country, Clapton, Tull had won three medals; agreed to sign for London's wealthiest professional club; and played against the Football League first division runners-up, Everton, in the Argentine capital, Buenos Aires (in June). It was a journey of unparalleled velocity for the Black Briton who harboured no ambition to become a professional footballer.

The transition from nobody to somebody was instigated by an anonymous friend – 'a chum of mine at Westminster College'[1] – who suggested he write for a trial to nearby amateurs, Clapton FC. An Isthmian League club, they had won the Football Association (FA) Amateur Challenge Cup in 1907 and had been beaten finalists two seasons earlier. After Tull dropping his handwritten plea into the mouth of a round, red, cast-iron postbox advertising collections throughout the day, the Forest Gate club secretary invited him for a trial with the 'A' team, against Woodford Albion in October 1908. Winning 6–1, Tull was soon promoted to the Reserves. On Boxing Day, against local rivals Leytonstone, he wore Clapton's red and white striped cotton shirt at centre-forward for his first-team debut.

Four months later, down the road at Ilford FC's ground, Clapton having already beaten Atherstone Town in the semi-final in front of 3,000, Tull played in the Amateur Cup final against Northern League Eston United, from a mining village near Middlesbrough in North Yorkshire. Clapton's winning score of 6–0 was a record margin. The run-around given by Tull and the other forwards, who 'were neat in their movements', was too much for Eston's J. Callaghan who was 'compulsorily retired'[2] – sent off – half an hour from the end.

The opening months of 1909 marked a triumphant introduction to senior competitive football for the young Black Briton. Though finishing a disappointing fifth in the Isthmian League, Clapton, who played at the wonderfully evocative Old Spotted Dog Ground in Upton Lane, won two other trophies, the London Senior Cup and the London County Amateur Cup, to add to the FA Amateur Challenge Cup. Charles Rance, who was to join Tull at Spurs in 1910, also played for Clapton in the Challenge Cup final.

Tull's excellent form had London's *Football Star*, 20 March 1909, describe 'our dusky friend [with] his clever footwork . . . as without doubt . . . Clapton's catch of the season'. Up to the date of this eulogy, Tull had not played in a losing Clapton side.

Tottenham Hotspur FC 1909–11

Haley's Comet whizzed into and out of the earth's atmosphere during the first half of 1910, 76 years after its previous visit. Tull's entry into the higher echelons of London football one year earlier, and his exit, also had that celestial quality of dramatic appearance and rapid fade.

It was inevitable that the glowing match reports written about Tull's performances for Clapton would have scouts from the capital's big hitters catching the match-day tram to E7. None were more affluent than the White Hart Lane club, Tottenham Hotspur, who were looking for a centre-forward to replace the legendary, free-scoring England international Vivien Woodward, who had chosen to transfer to Chelsea after his Olympic success. His was a hard act to follow.

Created in 1883, the north Londoners began charging admission fees to their ground in Northumberland Park in 1887–8. Officially turning professional in December 1895 and joining the Southern League, four years later Spurs moved to the site of their present ground in High Road, Tottenham, playing Notts County in a ceremonial opening match. Having won the Southern League in 1900, they became a recognised force in English football after their replayed FA Cup final win against Sheffield United in 1901.

Success on the field attracted ever increasing numbers which in turn provided impetus for expansion. In their first season as a professional club, income was £1,166 from crowds that never exceeded 15,000. Ten years later, with support doubling, total income had risen to £12,000. At the close of the season in which Tull joined, gate receipts had risen to over £20,000 with a net profit of £5,945 (multiply by 100 for current values). A new grandstand was also finished, which would further increase income. Spurs were the only Football League (FL) team in north London, one of only four southern teams in the first division.

However, large crowds and revenue brought similar-sized pressures and costs, such as policing: a pitch invasion by some of the 32,000 spectators in the second round FA Cup tie against Aston Villa in February 1904 led to the match being abandoned with Spurs 1–0 down.

While Walter was playing for Clapton, Spurs had trialled him in their A and Reserve teams. In his first game for the As against Shaftesbury Athletic 'W. D. Tull, the Clapton player whose complexion shows that he hails from sunnier climes than our own . . . often caught the eye'.[3] Instantly, misconceptions over origin occurred! During the first half of April 1909, Tull turned out for Spurs Reserves against West Ham and Brighton Reserves before the Amateur Cup final for Clapton. At the end of the month he scored twice for a Spurs first XI in a friendly at second division Clapton Orient. From what they saw in these games, the club felt confident in inviting the 20-year-old on their close-season tour to South America. The two-month excursion to the southern hemisphere was both a money-spinning venture and a thank you to the team for winning promotion to the first division after just one season in the second, itself a reflection of the high standard of the Southern League from which they had resigned in 1908.

On 14 May 1909, nine months after making his debut for Clapton's first team, he boarded the 11,537 ton Royal Mail Steam Packet *Araguaya* at Southampton, en route to Buenos Aires via Lisbon, Pernambuco and Montevideo. His club's touring companions were Everton, who had just finished runners-up to Newcastle in the Football League and were themselves FA Cup winners in 1906. (This London–Merseyside combination had also toured Austria together at the close of the 1904–5 season.)

In a letter written on board the *Araguaya*, to a Mr Morgan at the NCH – possibly his tutor in the print shop – Tull reveals mixed feelings toward the game. It was still in his mind, he asserted, if he didn't make the grade, to 'get a place on one of the newspapers [as a printer], if I can't do that I shall work as a comp [compositor]'.[4] Falling short of an outright apology for putting aside his printing skills, he explains to Morgan that he had rejected an offer from an amateur club in the Midlands to play for money. Had he accepted, his conscience would have troubled him far more.

Why did playing football for money bother Tull? For a hint of an explanation we need to examine the reason for his writing to Clapton, an amateur side in an area of east London that was an extremely fertile hunting ground for professional clubs in the production of both players and supporters. The choice of Clapton was not motivated merely by geographical convenience. There may well have been moral pressure from the Home, family and friends to remain an unpaid player and pursue his career in printing and compositing having completed his five-year apprenticeship. Walter's conciliatory tone to Morgan suggests as much.

At the orphanage Tull was moulded by the Methodist ethos of Muscular Christianity: playing games to develop a fit body and active mind. According to this doctrine, payment to play any sport missed the point of the exercise which was about character building. To play football for a wage would change the nature of the game and the status of the player. The sport would become a commodity, with profit the ultimate objective, transforming its players to wage labourers at the expense of the development of moral character. Tull had, from the age of 9 at least, grown up in a moral environment that attempted to design lives and to fix them on a track from which it would be very hard to stray. In this sense, it was a laboratory of social engineering as much as an institution of charitable welfare.

Despite these ethical difficulties over professionalism, the practical reality of making ends meet, in the wider context of the desire to be one's own man, led Tull to put his name to a contract with Spurs for a £10 signing-on fee and a £4 weekly wage, the maximum allowed. The envisaged transformation of his life-style no doubt added an extra incentive to put aside his aspiration for a career in printing and indulge in this temporary rush of joy, fame and modest fortune, even if the average first-team career of a footballer is between seven and ten seasons.

Tull, even with the tragic low points in his short life, had, by accident and design, managed to accumulate a range of skills that few from his social and ethnic background could better. Even so, for a young, working-class Black Briton the luxury of having two options of relatively well-paid employment on maturity was unusual. To be equipped with a relatively large amount of cultural capital – a sound elementary education; a viable, lucrative trade; and excellent skills for a game that had exploded, during his short lifetime, into a mass spectator sport and wage-paying industry – was akin to finding a pound, buying a lottery ticket and then winning the jackpot. It represented an uncommon amount of good fortune.

While Tull agonised over the morality of taking wages, others, such as Spurs' own Walter Bull, alongside Billy Meredith and Charlie Roberts of Manchester United, fought for the right to form a union and earn a wage determined by the marketplace – an arrangement, they argued, with which many chairmen acquiesced while wearing similar hats in other industries. The rapid commercialisation of football during the 1890s – an era which echoes circumstances today, where an abundance of wealth is enjoyed by the big clubs – and the industrial relations climate it produced, contributed to a sense of class consciousness among a number of players, leading to a wider debate about their overall rights and conditions. In his letter to Mr Morgan at the orphanage Tull wrote

you were very disappointed when you heard I had signed professional forms for the Tottenham FC. But I fully intended when I said goodbye to you, to remain an amateur. If I had gone to the

Midlands as I said, I should have been a 'paid' amateur which in my opinion is far worse than taking wages.[5]

The amateur club in the Midlands is not known.

The decision to turn professional was the act of a rational man. He did it in circumstances not of his own choosing, to paraphrase Marx. Quite simply, the adopted Eastender knew that he could earn more from professional football than from printing and playing as an amateur with payment for expenses only. And as a mixed-heritage man of colour in a predominantly White society, the respect of the community and the potential for fame that was almost guaranteed by signing for the capital's leading club was too good to refuse whatever the doubts raised by those White Britons of comfortable means. The labels 'amateur' and 'professional' were metaphors for class. Exaggerating the moral superiority of the amateur player and game was another tactic employed by middle- and upper-class minorities – who raced the same track, trotted the same turf and batted in the same team as the grimy occupants of cramped back-to-backs – to maintain social distance. The formation of the Amateur Football Association in 1907 – initially and revealingly called the Amateur Football Defence Federation – over the issue of admittance of professionals to county football associations, was essentially a southern-based, public school alumni reaction to the growing might of northern working-class professional clubs. For many southern gentlemen, allowing the muck and brass brigade into the privy council of football was akin to asking the moneylenders back into the temple. Such cleavages between the haves and the have-nots had occurred in other sports, most notably rugby, with the split between the southern bourgeois Union and northern working-class League in 1895. Indeed, at Spurs in 1893, controversy had raged over the 'Ernie Payne's boots affair', when the (then amateur) club's seemingly innocuous decision to purchase a pair of boots for a debutant player brought the anti-professional wrath of the southern, avowedly amateur, football establishment upon the region's most popular club.

Viewed with hindsight, the amateur/professional debate was characterised by snobbery, greed and hypocrisy. The elite amateur Corinthian Football Club, almost exclusively ex-Oxbridge, often charged more in 'expenses' to play than the weekly wage bill of their professional opponents. Amateur cricketers could receive unlimited income from benefit matches.

And, crucially, the majority of amateurs didn't depend on their sport for a living. They played to fill time, pursue and enjoy their pleasures, socialise or seek excellence. If they played badly, the disadvantages were a loss to ego and pride, not to the pocket. Sport, for the amateur, was not the only source of nourishment for the spirit. Those who excelled and who chose to remain unpaid did so, primarily, because they didn't need to be paid. Their lives had other dimensions providing for body and soul. For these fortunate few, loss of form wasn't the demon-with-material-consequences that shadowed the exploits of the working-class professional. For most sportsmen at the top of their game, though, life did not present such clear-cut choices.

Complicating the issue were 'shamateur' clubs like the anonymous Midlands outfit Tull mentions in his letter to Morgan, offering cash under the table, in the boot or wherever else they could secrete the envelope. They wanted to use the same instrument as professional clubs – money – to build a successful team, while remaining unsullied by the grubby practice of openly paying to beat opponents; to acquire kudos by dining at the top table, alongside the excitement of partying at the music hall. The economic and social conditions that produced the amateur produced the shamateur.

Most footballers would not have worried about the morality of signing professional. After all, before the ink was dry, the step would be lighter, the sun brighter, the girls prettier and life – well, life would be great from now on. The 'problem' irritating Tull's conscience was the Muscular Christian ethos of his Methodist orphanage background which believed sport was an instrument, a process, through which an individual develops physical and emotional wellbeing and a sturdy moral character. However, the attitude of powerful people and organisations to the colour of his skin added an extra practical dimension to the ethos that other White Muscular Christians didn't have to consider: limited life chances.

Tour to Argentina and Uruguay, May–June 1909

Publicity about the tour began appearing in local newspapers in April. *The Weekly Herald*, 30 April, notes that the Argentine promoters wanted Spurs and Everton to leave in early May and return in August. As neither club agreed to such an extended stay they eventually embarked from Southampton on 14 May with the first game scheduled for 6 June in Buenos Aires, with departure booked for 25 June.

Tull was not a well man while travelling to this seven-game excursion to Buenos Aires and Montevideo, suffering from 'sunstroke and [feeling] very queer for a few days'.[6] In a letter to *The Weekly Herald*, Spurs chairman Roberts reports that 'Tull had a headache all the way from Lisbon, but he is better – the sun, I think, had hold of him'.[7] It would be interesting to know how Tull would have reacted had he seen the newspaper article. Three months earlier, the football correspondent of the same newspaper had attributed his brown skin to growing up in a warm climate!

Tull and another forward, J. Curtiss from Gainsborough Trinity, were two signings out of a total of 14 to the club that season. Spurs had a young team that had been promoted to the first division in their inaugural season in the Football League. The transition in football culture that Walter would have undergone by going on tour with 'the first truly great professional side in southern England'[8] would have been profound. Yet, like 15 minutes of fame, it was to be a short orbit of the football stratosphere. The year 1909, or more precisely the six months between Clapton's cup wins in March, and October, after a run of seven first-team games for Spurs, represented the highest playing level and most numerous medal haul of Tull's football career.

The tour to Latin America was hosted by the Argentine FA Council, with the Committee of the Sociedad Sportiva, Argentina, liaising with the FA in London over practical arrangements such as travel, fixtures, training facilities, hotel bookings and the like. The first round of the Argentine FA Cup and League matches had been postponed to accommodate the visit. Along with Everton, Tottenham played the top club side in Buenos Aires and representative teams of the Argentine and Uruguayan Football Associations, 12 games in all. (Two other professional clubs, Nottingham Forest and Southampton, had already visited the continent.)

Though neither team lost to their South American hosts, some players – including Tull – still found issues about which to complain, like the quality of their living quarters at the Hotel Metropole. Like spoilt, arrogant prima donnas they complained that 'none of the waiters spoke English . . . [and] the aspect of the bedrooms was anything but cheerful'.[9] It was also cold and there were no fires or easy chairs! Proof that pampered footballers who whinge are not a uniquely contemporary phenomenon.

Yet climate, décor, balcony view and language barrier were secondary irritations. They were in this south-east portion of Latin America to do a job of work and it was in the earning of their daily bread that they encountered their greatest aggravation. Despite the predominantly British influence in establishing and developing the game in that part of the world – the committee of the first recorded soccer club in Argentina, Buenos Aires FC, founded in 1867, comprised of T. Jackson, T. B. Smith, T. and J. Hogg and W. Heald – the difference in playing styles and interpretation of rules, what was acceptable and what was not, was a source of friction that often ignited.

Spurs' 4–1 defeat of an Argentine League XI developed into more of a maul than a match. An off-the-ball foul on Tottenham forward D. Clarke was 'the filthiest charge in the back it is possible to imagine', argued the sports correspondent of the anglophile English language daily, *Buenos Aires Herald* (*BAH*).[10] Another Spurs forward, Minter, was sent off unfairly, continued the *BAH*. Following protests by the Spurs team and the intervention of chairman Roberts and other club officials, who came down to the pitch from the stands interrupting play for nearly three minutes, Minter was reinstated. It is unlikely the Tottenham officials would have tried this chauvinist stunt in England.

The *BAH* was not slow in asserting the moral superiority of Anglo-Saxons over their less-civilised gaucho hosts.

> It shows one what kind of a sporting spirit the native has, when I say that they laughed and clapped their hands with joy when they saw Clarke reel. [These] fine chaps from London [had been] treated very badly.[11]

The matches, argued the *BAH*, illustrated the gulf in tactical awareness the Latin Americans had to bridge, one major weakness being their positional play. The visitors were much better organised and more fluid in their co-ordination and movement, especially in running off the ball. (Whatever their deficiencies in 1909, their neighbours across the River Plate were quick learners. In the 1924 and 1928 Olympics, Uruguay stood on the winners' podium of the football competition before hosting and winning the inaugural World Cup in 1930.)

That gulf in tactical awareness has not only been closed in the ensuing

100 years but reversed, if World Cup wins by Argentina and England are compared. What hasn't changed is the clash of cultural styles and values that matches between teams from the two countries represent.

In contrast to the game against the Argentine League, the first match of the tour, on 6 June, pitted shipmates Everton and Tottenham, and was a relatively untroubled, though exclusive, affair. Tickets were $3 and $1 and the match was attended by president of the Republic, Figueron Alcarta, to whom the teams were presented at half time. Spurs struggled to a 2–2 draw with Tull netting. His performance was one of the highlights, the *BAH* noting Tull 'early in the tour installed himself as favourite with the crowd'.[12] In a physical game he gave as good as he got and 'took his punishment well not afraid to have a fair tussle with the opposition'. Sometimes, though, 'his enthusiasm . . . makes one think he is a bit too rigorous at times'. Yet the journalist saw a promising future ahead: 'He is the latest convert to the team and will improve in such good company. Besides being able to go through on his own, he knows how to draw his man and then send out to the wings'.[13]

Interestingly, the report ends by suggesting players wear numbers to make identification easier, an innovation eventually adopted simultaneously by Arsenal and Chelsea in 1928. Spurs lost the return two weeks later, a triple body blow for the Londoners as the players of both clubs opted for money rather than prizes in this two-match 'rubber'. And, no doubt, the journey back to England, with the Evertonians asserting bragging rights, helped Spurs to develop thick skins! Their matches were the first between two Football League clubs in Argentina. Playing in front of a 'poor crowd of 4,000', in this second meeting Tull did not have a good game: 'Besides being dreadfully slow, Tull showed a tendency to dilly-dally when a crashing shot might have scored. He was too much of the individualist and individualism against a half-back line as Everton possesses, doesn't come off'.[14]

Not only did the visit of the English clubs hold national importance for the development of football in that part of the continent, it also provided an opportunity for the Argentine leader to indulge in a bit of grandstanding.[15] Given both the suppression of the previous month's strike of 200,000 workers in Buenos Aires and the price of the tickets, Alcarta may well have been looking for a collective thank you from his well-to-do backers and supporters.

The tourists were surrounded by people and institutions who wanted to make political capital out of their presence: the Argentine president, the football establishment of Argentina and Uruguay and, most shamefully, the mouthpiece of the British colonial settlers, the *BAH*. The *Herald* did not hold back in proclaiming the superiority of Spurs and Everton: better because Britain was better, and Britain was better because it had an empire, and one of the reasons it had an empire was because Britons were better at sports, and therefore war, than other nations. The editorial message broadcast by the *BAH* was simple and explicit: game playing, nation building and war are complementary activities. They are an inseparable trio. This vision was explained in its *Mission of the Athlete* address welcoming the tourists.

We look upon [the footballers] as men with a mission . . . Every unit in a football team, is a missionary who teaches the gospel of sport by strenuous example. Sport is essential, exercise is vital, to the well-being of nations and individuals alike. The people who do not love field sports will not take kindly to field campaigns. War is best waged by those nations who have learned the absolute truth of the saying unity is strength. Disciplined unity, which involves instant and cheerful obedience to even unwelcome orders, is the secret of success not merely on the football field but on the field of Mars.

Our 'missionaries' then, are here today to preach the gospel of individual fitness, and demonstrate the value of their teachings. They are here, too, because in Argentina there is a growing willingness to learn the game in order that the Argentines of the rising generations may, in their turn, play the game. The youth of Argentina are finding out that the sensuous life, the life of the sybarite, is not conducive to glory, or even commercial pre-eminence. Politics and cigarettes may round off a feast, but they will not extend a territory, or keep the flag flying proudly.

England was fated to bear a great part in the building up of the nation . . . On the battlefield of old the foundations of British enterprise in Argentina was laid, and on Wednesday next we may go down and see yet another of the long series of great efforts made by Britain to develop Argentina's resources.[16]

It did not, of course, mention the inconvenient truth that 'crowd favourite' Walter Tull had African heritage.

There were no tears and waving hankies at the dockside when the teams left. The tempestuous matches had resulted in a rush of correspondence on the letters page of the *BAH*, with editorials questioning the 'adaptability of the Latin races to strenuous games such as football'. The newspaper thought it would be 'some time' before other British clubs visited. However, it did note that trouble at a Celtic–Rangers match a month earlier limited its authority to 'moralise . . . when the canny Scots set such an example it seems hardly just to think too harshly of the warm blooded "criolle" players and spectators who are unable to keep their excitement and enthusiasm within rational limits'.[17]

Tull had mixed fortunes in his football rite of passage to Argentina, Uruguay and the Big Time. It was a stern, harsh, exotic and unique introduction. Though suffering on the journey over – added to by the discomforts of the hotel! – his enthusiasm to play seems not to have been affected. Unfortunately, the Spurs management were not as impressed as the *BAH* and the Argentine crowd. The match following the opener against Everton in which Tull had scored – an easy 8–0 canter against the Uruguayan League in Montevideo – saw him sitting in the shade of the stand. When selected for his second tour game, the turbulent battle against the Argentine League, he played at centre-forward, Spurs experimenting with combinations of front lines after the departure of V. J. Woodward to Chelsea. Any replacement was expected to follow Woodward's example of leading the line with class and finding the net with regularity. Spurs were an attacking side, scoring 67 in 38 games on winning promotion the previous season and 29 goals in 7 games on their Latin American sojourn.

In the comments and opinions section of the *BAH* summing up the tour both Spurs and Everton thought Alumni the best of the home teams they played, even though the north Londoners won 5–0. Tottenham chairman Mr Roberts, relaying tour tales for readers of *The Weekly Herald* back home in his part of north London, thought the tour a success. They had been well treated by their hosts, who had conferred honorary membership of the Buenos Aires Jockey Club – 'one of the greatest clubs in the world'[18] – upon all. On the downside, he didn't like the press articles 'belittling the professional footballers'.

The fans, continued Roberts, were difficult to handle, the majority 'having no idea of the game'.[19] And the less said about the refereeing the better! His descriptions provide an outsider's take on local conditions. The Argentine militia, it seems, were masters at crowd control. In one tour match the cavalry rode into the fans and attacked with the flats of their swords, forcing the supporters out of the ground. Play was delayed for a number of minutes. Apparently some supporters had charged a gate and entered without paying.

The players would have liked more entertainment arranged, especially as they didn't speak Spanish. (Readers can make up their own minds as to the sub-text of that appraisal!) They were looking forward to returning to the comforts of home. The reference to home comforts may have been a coded allusion to a seaborne scare while docking at Pernambuco in Brazil on the way out when 'a monster shark' sprang out of the sea and attacked the basket in which they were transferred from ship to boat! Lives and limbs have been lost in the past, remarked chairman Roberts.

Unscripted entertainment, like the shark attack, seems to have been a feature of the visit. On another occasion, a Spurs group, including Roberts, went to

a tin shanty which they found to be a kind of music hall. The company had been seated barely five minutes when they heard the reports of several pistols outside. Immediately there was a stampede. But order was soon restored and the entertainment was resumed. The nerves of the Englishmen were too much upset, however, for them to enjoy the programme and they left. Next morning they learned that in the affair outside three policemen and two civilians had been shot dead.[20]

And, if chairman Roberts' entry into Argentina and visit to the shanty was dramatic, his departure was no less so. Late at the dockside, with the ship hooting for the last time, Roberts and his party were forced to accept an extortionate demand by boatmen for rowing them to the steamer. Close by, Roberts signalled the situation to those on board, who aimed automatic pistols at the oarsmen. The chairman then paid over the correct fee for the water taxi.

On the trip home the players of both teams took part in the ship's organised and much less scary fancy dress party, Tull turning out as Man Friday.

He and Robinson Crusoe won first prize, the edge over their competitors perhaps achieved by using the ship's pet parrot as an authentic symbol of their desert island re-creation. On disembarkation the parrot was presented to the Spurs party. It remained happily mimicking the various accents within the club offices until that fateful day in March 1919 when Arsenal were given Spurs' place in the first division, whereupon it dropped off its perch, dead with shock and indignation! According to Adam Powley and Martin Cloak in their amusing collection of Tottenham trivia, this incident marks the origin of the phrase 'sick as a parrot'.[21]

Tottenham 1909–11

Tull played four tour games, the sum total of his performances earning selection for Tottenham's first ever game in the first division in September. His displays in the hothouse atmosphere of Argentina and Uruguay had also confirmed his ability to withstand hostile pressure.

It was a wonderful summer for the 21-year-old. Arriving home to Bethnal Green from a fascinating adventure in South America, greeted by his three gold medals shining brightly, a glowing career in senior football beckoned. After a few days finding his feet on terra firma – which must have been wonderfully difficult given his rapidly changing world – Tull officially signed professional forms with Tottenham on 20 July 1909 for a £10 signing fee and wages of £4 a week. Relaxing on a bench by the duck pond in Victoria Park on those warm late July evenings, the handsome, athletic, affluent Londoner envisaged a world very different to the dark, tortured vista nine years earlier when Edward had left the orphanage.

If he wasn't whistling with a light step around the pond or listening to the musicians in the bandstand, he may well have been playing cricket, a game at which he displayed all-round talent. In a match between Spurs and Chelsea footballers on 19 August, batting at number two, Tull scored four and took four wickets. Was one of those V. J. Woodward's, the centre-forward he had replaced at White Hart Lane? The following week against Wadham Lodge he hit 60 and took two wickets. With the new football season due to kick off in the first week of September, cricket was a pleasant, enjoyable way of keeping fit during the close season, according to ex-Spurs manager and player and secretary of the Players' Union, John Cameron.

In his book *Association Football and How to Play it*, published in 1909, he covers, among other topics, tactics, training and football as a profession. A progressive thinker, Cameron recognised the destructive effects of drink and cigarettes, the necessity of a disciplined life-style and the benefit of getting a trade to fall back on. He cites V. J. Woodward as the complete player: a great captain, 'clean, clever and cultured'.[22]

Yet the profile he constructs of the ideal-type footballer – non-smoking, teetotal, a minimum of vices, skilled in a trade – also applied to Tull. And, like Tull, Cameron had doubts about football as a profession, the contemporary player little more than a 'slave'. This term was used in the summer of 2008, by Sepp Blatter, the head of FIFA, the governing body of world football, when describing multi-millionaire player Cristiano Ronaldo's contractual relationship with his club Manchester United. The Portuguese footballer wanted a move to Real Madrid – which he achieved the following year – while his manager Sir Alex Ferguson was refusing to let him go. Not only does Blatter's description castrate the potency of the term, it is an absurd categorisation. 'Rich spoilt brat' might have been a more accurate portrayal of Ronaldo and less of an insult to the memory of people who really were slaves.

Cameron's book is a mixture of ideas, forward thinking for the time, that are now accepted wisdom. Yet in some areas, such as food intake before games and maintaining fitness during the season, his suggestions would today raise eyebrows and widen the mouth. While the following observation on the pre-match meal may have partially satisfied the nutritional requirements of pre-Woodward Chelsea's first captain and goalkeeper, 28-stone Fatty Foulke, if religiously followed by trainers seeking to keep up to speed with the latest thinking, it would soon have had opposition crowds singing 'Who ate all the pies?':

> The game is so strenuous that a substantial meal should be taken at least 2 hours before a match . . . beef steak well cooked, with stale bread and vegetables that are well done, always excluding potatoes.[23]

On fitness, Cameron once more exposes the limitations of Edwardian sports science:

During the season walking and some practice at kicking, with an occasional sprint, are quite enough to keep the player well . . . Special training is not really necessary, even from a professional point of view. Instead a good esprit de corps should be encouraged with a disciplined life-style.[24]

Cameron's opinions are better understood in historical context. For the vast majority, work in the early 20th century was labour intensive. Most day-to-day activities needed muscle and sweat. Factory workers, where machines usually supplied the raw power, still needed inordinate amounts of elbow grease to keep them working; tradesmen did not have power tools; coal was dug with pick and shovel (by millions).

It is not surprising that in such a demanding era, in which debilitating and life-threatening disease and illness were common, the emphasis in Cameron's training manual was on revitalising the body and saving it from unnecessary exertion. Those from whom the football industry recruited would have had a decent level of day-to-day fitness as a consequence of class and life-style. Industrial, urban Britain took its toll upon the body, as differences in height and mortality rates between classes testify, exhibited to the nation by the Boer War. To punish the body with unnecessary exercise would weaken the constitution, making the player susceptible to illness and injury. So, a good walk and the occasional sprint would suffice!

In the week prior to the start of the season it wasn't clear who was going to follow Woodward into the famed centre-forward position. *The Weekly Herald* felt another new signing from Forthill Athletic, David Brown, was favourite. Whether by the spin of a coin or a cool, detached analysis of aptitude and talent, the new signing from Clapton got the nod from Spurs' trainers and directors.

The historic double of Tull's Football League debut and Spurs' initiation into first division football was deflated by the result, a 3–1 defeat away to Sunderland in front of 10,000. If any game can so brutally illustrate the maxim 'pride before a fall', it's football. (The result was an eerie repeat of history: the first Black professional Wharton also made his FL debut at Sunderland and his team, Sheffield United, similarly lost by two goals.) *The Wednesday Herald* reporter felt 'Tull dallied too much, and did not open out the game sufficiently'.[25] Took his time on the ball? *The Daily Chronicle* hack was even more scathing.

Tull, the coloured centre forward, was as far removed from Woodward as it is possible to imagine. The most one can say of Tull is
that his selection is ill-advised and unprofitable. He was incapable
of getting beyond Thompson, and the Hotspur attack were very
weak until Minter went to the centre forward berth early in the
second half.[26]

A reading of the match reports in the north-east newspapers gives a slightly
different impression of Tull's league debut, noting that the 'coloured man
... placed the ball beautifully for Middlemiss';[27] and 'Tottenham's coloured
centre forward Tull was conspicuous with a drive that Roose had difficulty
in saving.' In these commentaries Tull seems to have been more involved
than he is given credit for by the Tottenham papers. 'Tull then sent a beautiful pass across the goalmouth.'[28]

The result was not a collective embarrassment. Sunderland was a respected
club and very successful team. Since the FL's inauguration in 1888–9 they had
won the first division four times and finished runners-up three times. The
previous season, 1908–9, they had finished third, beaten to runners-up
spot by Spurs' next opponents, Everton.

For their next game the following Saturday Spurs kept faith with Tull.
Before an estimated 20,000 at the purpose-built Goodison Park came
another defeat, 4–2. Yet it seems the Londoners' forwards were starting to
knit together as a unit, giving a 'fine display'.[29] Tull's display improved,
suggested the *Daily Chronicle*, now warming to his potential, com-
menting he 'showed much promise', quite a change from their previous
assessment. This revised evaluation could be explained by the practice of
papers relying for reports on away games from local correspondents often
seeing opposition players for the first time and judging their performances
without preconceived opinion.

No doubt the post-match socialising gave players the chance to compare
and share their busmen's holiday snaps! At least this match against their
tour companions was only a couple of hundred miles north-west of
London, in the northern hemisphere and the ride home a matter of hours
rather than weeks.

Despite these scores against two of the country's top three teams, an
initiation that could only have been tougher had they played champions
Newcastle, over 32,000 paid to watch their first home match against FA

Cup holders and Players' Union strikers, the self-proclaimed 'Outcasts', Manchester United. The massed White Hart Lane faithful, 10,000 larger than any other crowd in the country on that day, went home with half a smile, their heroes winning their first point with a 2–2 draw, 'Darkie' Tull having been brought down at the Paxton Road end for a penalty. ('Darkie' was a common nickname for players of colour at the time.) *The Wednesday Herald* wrote

> Tull can be satisfied with his debut at Tottenham as a professional . . . The West Indian was not quick enough at times in parting with the ball, but he showed enterprise and no small degree of skill.[30]

The *Daily Chronicle* reporter was more enthusiastic.

> Tull's . . . display on Saturday must have astounded everyone who saw it. Such perfect coolness, such judicious waiting for a fraction of a second in order to get a pass in not before a defender has worked to a false position, and such accuracy of strength in passing I have not seen for a long time. During the first half Tull just compelled Curtis to play a good game, for the outside right was plied with a series of passes that made it almost impossible for him to do anything than well. Tull has been charged with being slow, but there never was a footballer yet who was really great and always appeared to be in a hurry. Tull did not get the ball and rush on into trouble. He let his opponents do the rushing, and defeated them by side touches and side-steps worthy of a professional boxer. Tull is very good indeed.[31]

The most widely read and trusted national sports newspaper, *Athletic News*, was similarly warm with praise, though damping down its enthusiasm with a suggestion for improvement that entailed Tull supplying more of the heat.

> Tull, the West Indian . . . has the unique distinction of being the only coloured player in operating in first class football . . . [He] revealed an excellent knowledge of the game. His control of the ball and his passes were alike excellent but he should put a little more fire into his work.[32]

The profile that emerges from these reports is of an intelligent, skilful, robust young footballer who had the ability to produce a high level of performance but who also exhibited the common failing of youthful players, inconsistency of form.

Tull scored his first League goal in a 5–1 away defeat against an improving Bradford City the following Saturday. (The West Yorkshire club eventually finished seventh after being third from bottom the previous season.) 'Tull was left with only the goalkeeper to beat. Spendiff rushed out to tackle the West Indian but was too late. Tull equalised the scores with a clever shot'.[33]

He wore the same scoring boots in a midweek evening friendly against Reading, arranged as part of a transfer deal, netting twice in a 3–2 win. Surprisingly, despite three goals in two games, Tull did not play in the next match against Sheffield Wednesday. 'There has been some surprise expressed in certain quarters . . . Lyle being selected instead of Tull'[34] – a strange decision, because injury is not mentioned. The first priority of a centre-forward is to score goals. To drop a forward when he is finding the target is not only irrational but damages confidence, the core ingredient needed for success.

Whatever the reasons for choosing Lyle, Tull was reinstated for the following match against Bristol City, the defeated FA Cup final opponents of Manchester United, where 'as energetic as ever [Tull] was responsible for some pretty work',[35] being 'a class superior to that shown by most of his colleagues'.[36] (We'll return to this important and defining game in the development of Tull's career.)

If there was a fixture where the pain of disappointment at having to sit it out in the stands was alleviated by the comforting realisation that playing would entail being kicked around the park for 90 minutes, the following home game against roughhouse Bury would have been the one to miss: 'Bury had gone in for smashing up tactics, and many hard knocks were given, the referee often having to admonish the visitors owing to their rough play . . . Tull also played very well'.[37]

The Lancashire club had come down to the capital to teach the upstart southern nancies a thing or two about playing in the first division. Fortunately for football, Spurs won 1–0, sending home their 29,000 faithful confirmed in the belief that artistic flair backed by muscled resilience was superior to brawn and brute force. In a tradition that has continued to this day, the Bury match emphasised the club's (controversial) policy of prioritising style over graft.

This approach did not work against Middlesbrough, resulting in a 3–1 home defeat, Tull giving 'a poorer display than he has done before'.[38] The following week Spurs had two matches in three days: a League game against Preston North End and a London Professional Football Charity Fund match with Woolwich Arsenal. Tull played in the latter, scoring twice in a 3–2 win. He was then relegated to the reserves – the 'Stiffs' – where he remained for the rest of the season, having played just seven first-team games in the League.

Quite why Tull was never given another chance in the first team that season remains open to speculation. Here's my theory: the match reports, as we have seen, suggest he was good enough, when on form, to have merited selection. And there is little in these commentaries indicating a sustained loss of confidence. Although he was not in top form against Sunderland and Middlesbrough – defeats in which the team did not play well – these below-par performances were surely more than compensated by the above-ordinary and outstanding displays he gave in the five other matches. Additionally, there is his unexplained non-selection against Sheffield Wednesday during a short burst of goalscoring, a knock to the confidence from which he recovered with a competent performance against Bristol City.

In this match on 2 October 1909 Tull was the target of sustained, vociferous and ferocious racial abuse. So incensed was *DD*, the correspondent of the *Football Star*, that, uniquely, his match report had the sub-heading 'Football and the Colour Prejudice':

> he is the Hotspurs' most brainy forward. Candidly, Tull has much to contend with on account of his colour. His tactics were absolutely beyond reproach, but he became the butt of the ignorant partisan. Once, because he 'floored' Annan with a perfectly fair shoulder charge, a section of the spectators made a cowardly attack upon him in language lower than Billingsgate. Let me tell these Bristol hooligans (there were but few of them in a crowd of nearly twenty thousand) that Tull is so clean in mind and method as to be a model for all white men who play football whether they be amateur or professional. In point of ability, if not in actual achievement, Tull was the best forward on the field.[39]

The local journalist *Centre forward* of the *Bristol Evening News* did not see it in quite the same way as Londoner *DD*.

> Spurs did not know what a football battle was until they came to Bristol today. When West meets South there is usually a tug of war, but Chelsea and Woolwich are but passive resisters compared with the rivalry engendered by the meeting of the City and Spurs.[40]

What is certainly clear, as was noted by *DD*, is Spurs did not lie down in the face of the West Country team's aggression. And, of the Spurs players, Tull was at the forefront in returning like for like. In front of a crowd of 15,000, Bristol's biggest gate of the season – 'with a big London contingent'[41] – the first half of the boisterous match left players 'sprawling all over the ground'.[42] Continuous inflammatory outbursts scorched the game's canvas, with the referee adding to its fairground boxing booth/music hall flavour.

> An extraordinary incident . . . R. Steele raced away on his own, and was tackled just as he shot. To the amazement of everybody an ordinary free kick was given inside the penalty area. The ball rattled against several players' legs, and appeared to go through, and while the Spurs were congratulating themselves, the referee was pointing for a goal kick. This incident was followed by another.

There you have it in black and white, eccentric refereeing decisions are not a strictly modern phenomenon. In this over-physical encounter, incomprehensible pronouncements by the official were not what was needed to calm things down.

Early on in the second half Bristol forward Burton was injured. No substitutes were allowed, so unless the player couldn't walk he usually stayed on, if only to be a body in the way of the opposition. Soon after came the incident between Tull and Annan, the reaction to which incensed *DD*. Yet, in contrast to the latter, the Bristol reporter makes no mention of the racist nature of the abuse.

> An unpleasant incident occurred when the West Indian Tull upset Annan with a heavy charge. Annan protested vigorously; and

the spectators took up the story, but the referee ignored the incident, although he penalised Hanlin [of Bristol] for charging over Curtiss.

(Shoulder) charging was very much part of the game. And Tull, at 5 feet 6 inches and 10 stone 11 pounds, used his full weight in tackles. But both the referee and *DD* felt Tull's tackle was legitimate. In all the match reports I have read of Tull, none mention any proclivity for foul play. In fact, quite the opposite, as *DD* indignantly points out. However, what is noticeable in many summaries where Black players have featured is the violent response to them: Arthur Wharton was often nose to nose with irate forwards who didn't like his goalkeeping technique; Leith Athletic winger John Walker was clumped by Airdrie full-back MacFarlane for making a monkey of him on one occasion too many.

In his appraisal of the bruising Bristol–Spurs encounter, *Centre forward* argued

> Spurs asserted their weight at every opportunity; the [Bristol] players sprawled and protested, while the referee occasionally tootled his warning . . . Cowell was tackled until he scarcely had a shot left . . . Spurs . . . hammered their way through in their own particular way. There were fouls galore.[43]

Perhaps Spurs had learned a few survival lessons from their match with Bury a few weeks earlier. The Bristol match is especially significant because the racism of the crowd was reported. This was very unusual, if not unprecedented. It is the first report of a football match I have seen in which racism made the headline. A friend of the West Indies cricketer Learie Constantine, the Marxist writer C. L. R. James, noted in his seminal book on the social influence of colonialism on cricket and Black identity, *Beyond a Boundary*, that the reporting of racism at sporting events in the British press was almost non-existent, as if scribes were either ignoring incidents or downplaying their significance. 'Writers on sport . . . automatically put what was unpleasant out of sight even if they had to sweep it under the carpet. The impression they created was one of almost perpetual sweetness and light.'[44]

To have racial abuse reported *and* headlined was a quantum leap. During the career of Arthur Wharton, 1882–1902, racist shouts and comments were commonplace. Yet never, to this writer's eye, did a report introduce its commentary with reference to the insults, let alone headline the abuse. Old journalistic habits die hard: having suffered, during the last quarter of the 20th century, watching and hearing BBC *Match of the Day*'s John Motson studiously avoid mentioning incidents of racist chanting at matches, James' criticism, written in the 1960s, is entirely believable.

If it is the case that this report in 1909 was the first of its kind, we owe a great debt to the anonymous *Football Star* hack with the nom de plume *DD*. He began a tradition that took another 80 years, at least, to consolidate.

It is in the response to this uncomfortable afternoon in the West Country, by a nervous Chairman C. D. Roberts and his ambitious directors, that an answer to Tull's demotion may be found. The history and political geography of Bristol as a port whose wealth, growth and importance was a consequence of the slave trade may explain, in part, the vociferous prejudice of City's supporters. To this potent cocktail of local, cultural factors we should add an event that occasioned a free-for-all against people of colour. The assassination in London on 1 July 1909 of Sir William Hutt Curzon Wylie, a former agent to the governor-general of central India, by Indian nationalist Madan Lal Dhingra, at a function hosted by the National Indian Association, inflamed passions nationwide. Among a sizeable minority a public show of grief by the political establishment engendered a primitive mood of racist hostility to non-Whites. A Black doctor whom we have already met, James Jackson Brown, living in the same east London borough as Tull, commented 'every coloured person had a hell of a time'.[45] Dhingra's life expired at Pentonville Prison on 17 August with a punitive drop and retributive tug of the hangman's rope.

Football is dominated by opinion. Player, fan, manager, coach, director, chairman, granny and mother-in-law all have views on the abilities of players and teams. Universal agreement is rare. It is difficult, then, to say conclusively why Spurs did not give Tull much of a chance. Quite probably there were those with power and influence who felt he was not good enough. Maybe there was an internal problem, within the dressing room, which remained hidden. Yet, in his defence, he was popular with some influential people at Spurs, director G. Wagstaffe Simmons writing fondly of Tull and his abilities:

W. D. Tull, an inside forward of parts, who joined the Tottenham ranks before the Great War, was one of the best amateurs in Metropolitan football when he decided to enter the professional ranks. He soon became a great favourite, but at the time the Spurs were rich in inside forwards, and he was not given many chances to appear in the League side. In the Reserve games he was an outstanding success.[46]

If, in our evaluation, we allow for the factors mentioned above – 'common-sense' prejudice against people of colour as a result of the pervasiveness of the ideas of 'scientific' racism; Bristol's involvement in the slave trade; and the general mood of hostility after the murder of Wylie – it could be argued that the Spurs board, after the Bristol match, felt they should exile the target of the abuse for the sake of team spirit, form and, most importantly, the gate. A loss of form would mean lower crowds would mean less money.

If this speculation – built, admittedly, on circumstantial evidence – is accurate it was a weak and dishonourable response that did not do justice to the inner strength of Tull, at 21, still young in a game where most do not reach their peak until the mid- to late 20s; or to his many team-mates who, surely, would have weathered the storm had the club not consigned one of its brightest prospects to the lower decks; or to those club officials who had the moral courage to sign Walter. (Arguably, the transfer of Ardiles in 1982 as a consequence of the Falklands/Malvinas war suggests the cup-tie culture of the Spurs boardroom had changed little in the intervening 73 years – up for the infrequent big games but lacking the dogged tenacity to plough through the hard times that brings League success.)

If this speculation isn't accurate it is it hard to find a football reason for Tull's virtually permanent demotion from the first team. He was, on the basis of a trawl of contemporary opinion, a very competent player, even a very good one. While Spurs had good forwards and a competent team it did not have outstanding forwards, or an outstanding team. It was a decision that defied logic.

During the 1910–11 season, Tull studded the sunlit turf and breathed the rarefied air of the first team only three times: two games over the hectic Christmas period, scoring once, against Manchester City; and his third and last game, in April 1911, against south Londoners Woolwich Arsenal at Plumstead, a 2–0 defeat.

In consolation, Spurs Reserves won the South Eastern League (SEL), Tull making 27 appearances and scoring ten goals, finishing as third highest scorer. He netted three of these in the first half of a match one cold February Saturday afternoon against Northampton Town Reserves. Another scorer in this game was ex-Clapton team-mate and Amateur Cup finalist, Charles Rance, who had joined Spurs at the start of the season. Tull also played for the SEL representative team against Chelsea in the season's finalé. Despite this success it was a frustrating time. It was plain that he was going to find it difficult establishing himself as a first-team regular.

Though his employers were confining his talents to the localised competition of the SEL, serendipitously Tull may have bequeathed them a curious international legacy. Spurs toured Germany in May 1911, playing six games in Hamburg, Berlin, Leipzig, Frankfurt and Brunswick, winning all, scoring 33 and conceding three. In the last named city they were hosted by Eintracht Brunswick who included a tall, blond, handsome 18-year-old centre-forward, Otto Harder. He joined Hamburger FC (later HSV) in 1913 but it wasn't until the inter-war years that his career blossomed as a robust, English-style centre-forward, scoring 14 goals for the national team in 15 appearances. By then he had adopted the nickname 'Tull', having 'allegedly got his nickname from an English player he was said to resemble'.[47]

It appears that, as a young Eintracht Brunswick player, Harder was captivated by a Spurs forward who played with a rugged, precise and thoughtful determination he admired and came to emulate. Or, did Harder's team-mates see qualities in the dual-heritage Londoner mirrored in their raw, young centre-forward, conferring the nickname with both irony and respect?

Whatever the circumstances, the incongruity of this particular player using Tull's surname grew in tandem with the all-enveloping Nazification of 1930s Germany. Harder, the international star of 1920s Hamburg SV, joined the NSDAP – Nazi party – in 1932. By the decade's close he was working as a guard at Sachsenhausen concentration camp, Berlin. For a brief period near the war's end, he was head of the guards at Neuengamme concentration camp, Hamburg.

According to Nazi ideology, racial struggle was the motive force of history. Competition at its most naked was not over the control of material wealth and the means by which a society creates that wealth, but between 'races' for purity, survival and dominance. Only the unadulterated and non-miscegenised would endure. The salvation of the human race – in effect, for Hitler, the biological struggle for Aryan pre-eminence – was only possible through the elimination of all other (sub-) species. Thus the apparatus of racial oppression and destruction, genocidal in scale, so characteristic of Nazism: official denigration of minorities; ethnic ghettoisation; forced and slave labour; concentration camps and the application of eugenic and ethnic cleansing. Had Tull survived the First World War, as a Black 'auxiliary' of the United Kingdom he would have been accorded the same racial status as Jews, Gypsies, Slavs and the same social status as communists: an 'Untermensch'. (One mixed-heritage Black German who did survive growing up in his Nazi fatherland was Hans-Jürgen Massaquoi.)

The absurdity – surrealism – of Otto 'Tull' Harder modelling himself on a Black British footballer then joining, working for and defending the practices of a party whose ideology dismissed such people as inferior beings is maddeningly difficult to understand. Yet in Harder's mind there must have been some attempt to deal with the contradiction. It is tempting to assume it was a nickname that had been given in 1911, stuck, and that after the First World War, when he resumed his football career, its Teflon quality stubbornly remained. But, he shows no attempt at dropping it.

Perhaps this is approaching an explanation from the inside out – looking for reasons within Harder – rather than searching for social causes that affect individual behaviour. The Treaty of Versailles, the contract of agreement and settlement that formally ended the war between Germany and its enemies, was a purposeful humiliation of this advanced industrial power. While it didn't have the same linguistic decoration of pre-2003 American promises made to Saddam's Iraq of 'bombing it back to the stone age', it nevertheless implemented a punishing regime designed to rein in and limit the pre-war momentum of German industrial, financial and geographical expansion. Germany in the 1920s was certainly not an equivalent of the horror that is post-2003 Iraq but there are remarkable similarities: a meltdown in the economy, a rapid rise in unemployment and inflation, expensive basic necessities and an undeclared civil war – between left and right, proletariat and bourgeoisie – creating the conditions for an authoritarian populist such as Hitler to force ideas of race purity, eugenics, ethnic cleansing and German unity on a weary nation desperate for solutions that would restore a pre-1914 order.

The case of Harder does illustrate the seminal contradiction that plagued Tull: the dissonance between his subjective identity – his character – and his objective identity, defined by the attitudes of the powerful to people of colour. Harder could willingly accept Tull as a role model as a footballer and forward, but would energetically collaborate in the destruction of his race and all Untermenschen. In his few months supervising the guards at Neuengamme, at least 200 captives were murdered. In his trial for war crimes, Harder argued it wasn't murder but self-neglect. 'The "inmates'" inner organs were weakened through malnutrition in the Jewish ghetto, so that they couldn't take the good and plentiful food in the concentration camps.'[48]

If any inner-workings were at play in the death of these poor victims it was the self-delusion of Harder and his Nazi accomplices, a self-delusion on a par with that displayed by the tabloid press each time England qualify for a World Cup – but with, of course, a radically different outcome.

Tull's arrival at Spurs, at first garlanded with praise and promise, ended unsatisfactorily. His turbulent three seasons on the Tottenham High Road – including a loan spell at Midlands League Heanor Town during 1910–11 – resembled weather patterns affected by global warming: wave upon wave of extreme highs and lows.

In October 1911, Tull signed for Southern League Northampton Town – winners of the competition in 1909 – 'for a heavy transfer fee', according to the *Northampton Chronicle*.[49] The deal included the exchange of R. C. Brittain to the north Londoners. As for Tull, the report noted, 'He is regarded as quite a good centre, and has several times assisted the Spurs in that position, although not one of the regular first team'.[50]

There is some confusion over the details of the deal. Two seasons later, when Brittain was transferred by Spurs to Cardiff, the Northampton *Football Echo* reported that the Cobblers had received Tull plus £1,000 for Brittain and suggested that Leicester Fosse had offered Spurs £500 for Tull and been refused. Such opacity is not surprising because, from inception, the financial detail of transfers in professional football has been hidden within a culture of secrecy.

The move to the Cobblers – so nicknamed because Northampton is a town dominated by the shoe and boot-making industry – was a step down the football ladder. Not a chirpy cockney, the changing room banter as he said his goodbyes would have been worth hearing.

Player 1: Never be down at heel there, son!

Player 2: A spiritual move, Walter? Looking for your inner sole?

Throughout his time at Tottenham Tull had struggled to secure a first-team place in a club that was battling to maintain and further its noviciate status among football's elite. We do not know how things would have worked out had he stayed. What cannot be denied is that his choice of Northampton, under the guidance of a young Herbert Chapman, was providential. What appeared a backward step was to prove the making of Tull as a player. The Spurs programme notes of 21 October 1911 commented 'Walter Tull, who has been with us just over 2 seasons, has been transferred to Northampton Town. He should render the Cobblers good service, and we wish him the best of luck with his new club'.

The Cobblers were desperate for a class forward who could create and score. *Tapper*, the football correspondent of the Northampton *Football Echo*, in February lamented that in 13 of their matches Northampton Town had failed to score.

> That is to say the team have been kicking a ball about 19½ hours – the best part of a day and night – and has never smelt of the net. The weakness has been in the centre and the left wing.[51]

Tull, having played centre-forward, and favouring his left foot, fitted requirements perfectly.

Northampton Town, 1911–15

Herbert Chapman, from the pit village of Kiveton Park near Rotherham, was a manager sympathetic to the additional pressures faced by the few players of colour in the professional game. He was ahead of his time, revolutionising tactics, formation and strategy, introducing the stopper centre-half, developing counter-attack into a precise art and one of the first to number shirts, use floodlights and provide supporters' facilities fit for humans. A former Spurs player, the Cobblers' manager later became uniquely successful with Huddersfield Town and Arsenal (after the latter had moved to north London and dropped Woolwich from their name). So revered was he in N5 that his bust used to greet visitors to Highbury stadium as if permanently keeping protective watch over the club he transformed: a cockerel astride a cannon? Yet it was at Southern League Northampton Town that he made his name as a successful manager, winning the championship after taking over when the team had finished bottom in successive seasons.

Rugby Union had established itself before enthusiasts of the 'dribbling game' decided to establish an Association club in the town. At the time of writing, Northampton Rugby Club still attract more supporters than the Cobblers. If Chapman did not manage to overcome Rugby Union's pre-eminence permanently, he certainly challenged it. Chapman's legacy in football is so impressive that he was inducted into England's National Football Museum Hall of Fame at Preston in 2003. Less than two years later, in March 2005, at 6 Haslemere Avenue, Hendon, a blue plaque was unveiled announcing the avant-garde football boss lived within between 1926 and his death in 1934.

During a managerial career spanning 27 years, from combining the role with playing at Northampton in 1907 through to Arsenal, the club he brought to greatness as the roaring 20s metamorphosed into the depressive 30s, Chapman re-defined the role of manager and transformed tactics, team culture and team–manager relations. He developed counter-attacking football into an art, constructed new, intelligent formations by playing half-backs deeper in an effort to provide more room for forwards to improvise goalscoring opportunities. He disliked lump and bump, preferring his defenders to find a player in the same coloured shirt, instead of sending the ball long for territorial gain.

Within 12 months of taking over at the County Ground, in 1907, Chapman improved a team of no-hopers to eighth place. The following season they won the Southern League, at which juncture he retired as a player. It was customary for the champions to play for the Charity Shield with the winners of the Football League. Opponents Newcastle United, champions for the third time in five seasons, narrowly defeated the Cobblers 2–0. The standard of the Southern League was considered equivalent to second division Football League.

Chapman's ultimate goal while manager of Northampton Town was to secure Football League status. This was problematic as new entrants had to be voted in. He suggested adding a second tier, the Football Alliance, from which there would be promotion into the FL. As with many of his ideas, proposals and suggestions, though rejected this four-division structure later provided the template for the enlargement of the FL in 1921.

Tull may have caught the visionary Yorkshireman's eye scoring that first-half hat-trick against his Reserves the previous season in a 7–1 win. Newspaper talk had it that competing to sign the Black Briton were Aston Villa, Leicester Fosse and Clapton Orient. Villa were one of the outstanding teams of the pre-war period. Of the first 12 Football League championships, to 1900, they captured six. They were not used to being turned down. Maybe Chapman was a great talker, selling the 1909 Southern League champions as a club for the future? Maybe Walter thought his chances of getting a regular first-team place would be better at a smaller club? *Councillor* on the Northampton *Daily Echo* commented that he had to

> Congratulate Mr Chapman upon having captured Tull, the clever West Indian forward of the Tottenham club. This step I really believe, is a great stroke of business, as Tull is a great player, and I have no hesitation in saying he will prove a decided acquisition to Northampton's front rank.[52]

What is not open to conjecture is Chapman's experience of playing with, and under, a Black professional, a positive outcome of his time as a young-ster with Stalybridge Rovers in 1896 where Arthur Wharton was player/coach of the mill town club.

Having numerous football contacts in South Yorkshire, Wharton often went back to sign promising talent while playing in the Manchester region. Apart from a six-year spell over the Pennines, 1896–1902, employed by Stalybridge Rovers, Ashton North End and Stockport County, the goalkeeper had lived in South Yorkshire from 1888 to his death in 1930, playing for Rotherham Town and Sheffield United. (He lived in Darlington while playing for *the* Lancashire club, Preston North End, between 1886 and 1887.) When Chapman joined Stalybridge Rovers in 1896 the team, dubbed by local journalists 'Wharton's Brigade', was firmly under the control of the West African who, quite possibly, enticed the raw 18-year-old with an inviting roll of greenbacks waved under his nose, a friendly arm across his shoulder and few 'thee', 'thou', and 'brother me lad's uttered reassuringly in his ear.

Another factor linking Tull, Chapman and Wharton was their Methodist belief. Before the safety net of the Welfare State provided a thin veil of protection for the working class against the bitter winds of laissez-faire capitalism, these congregations acted as networks of aid and assistance as much as religious communities. It was the Methodist Wesleyan Missionary Society that had employed Arthur's father Henry Wharton; Arthur had been sent from Accra, Gold Coast (Ghana) to a Methodist college in Cannock for his education; the Methodist community in Folkestone ensured the Tull family was not left destitute once the children were orphaned, and indirectly set Edward and Walter on career paths by enabling them to live in institutions – the Warnock household and Bonner Road – that acted as springboards for their future careers.

Walter didn't explode onto the scene at Northampton, but rather took the stage quietly, almost shyly. His debut in front of 5,000 to 6,000 against Watford didn't inspire a great deal of talk or writing. In the 2–2 draw, though, he made the pass to Freeman for the latter to score the equaliser, 'Tull, the new centre, did not show to great advantage, but it would be unfair to judge him on just one exhibition'.[53]

In the following game against New Brompton, now Gillingham, Tull was paid the compliment of special attention, namely elbows and kicks, leaving him bruised, hobbling with an ankle injury, and slow. Not the quickest of players on the best of days, this wasn't the beginning he hoped for. After his third game, Tull was dropped to the Reserves, the 'Stiffs'. It would not be until the end of December, two months later, that supporters saw him again in the first team, scoring against Coventry.

Over three months later, in the warm spring breeze, a substantial regeneration of Tull's form occurred. In three games during April 1912, he scored six goals. Poignantly, he scored four of those against Bristol – Rovers, not City! The quartet of strikes may not have been bettered in terms of the satisfaction they returned. Wrong club, maybe, but Tull would not have needed reminding that supporters of both clubs read the same sporting press. It was an emotional and supremely satisfying conclusion to another difficult season. While he had scored nine goals in 12 first-team games, with the team finishing third in the League, he had not secured a regular place.

The following season Chapman took over at Leeds City. Tull's change came in his position, converting to wing-half from centre/inside-forward, a position better suiting his talents. Equating to the modern-day midfield playmaker, it inspired a revival in form: 'Tull has now settled in the half line in a manner which now places him in the front rank of "class" players in this position'.[54]

Once more the Spurs–Northampton connection was instrumental in providing the replacement manager, Walter Bull. In 1907 he had originally been recommended by Chapman for the job that the latter took. Like his ex-Spurs team-mate, Bull also registered as a player for the Cobblers.

In 1910 Bull had been transferred from Spurs to Heanor Town, the club that Tull joined on loan in 1910–11. During October, playing comfortably well at wing-half, Tull established himself in the team and as a 'favourite with the crowd'.[55] While he had found a position which suited his style and approach, his ability as an all-round player was utilised after right-winger Fanny Walden's transfer to Tottenham. 'Tull played at outside right for Tottenham in ten league games and one could tell by the way he shaped, after the first quarter of an hour, that he was no stranger to that position.'[56] While the reporter's confusion as to the extent of Tull's previous experience wide on the right may have heightened expectations, playing there against Coventry he featured highly in one of his team's most memorable games. Heavy rain meant the pitch cut up immediately, the central sections and goalmouths resembling a ploughed field. So, as a winger out in the green zone, he received a lot of ball. Catastrophically, despite 'centres excellently placed by Tull',[57] Northampton were 4–0 down at the break.

Returning from their half-time fags, cups of teas and odd nip of whisky, was a transformed claret and white team. Within less than 10 minutes a centre by Tull was redirected into the net by King, who went on to score two more for his hat-trick. A minute from the final whistle, after the ball was played out to our temporary outside right

> Over to Freeman came the ball from Tull . . . [who] transferred to King a dozen yards out [who] crashed the ball forward. It struck the post – and such a yell. Two players slipped and fell in the mud . . . there was a surging wave of struggling forms, and the ball was at the feet of Robert Hughes. Two feet of goal left vacant, half a lake and a sodden ball. There would have been every excuse for a slip. But Hughes made no slip.[58]

One of Northampton's great second-half comebacks! However, it was at left-half that Tull found his niche, playing over 110 first-team games.

Soon after signing for Northampton, he moved house to the small market town of Rushden, lodging with team-mate Eric 'Wassie' Tomkins, a local man who had joined the Cobblers around the same time. Tomkins was an accomplished cricketer. It is likely that he introduced Tull to the Rushden Town and Thursday Cricket Clubs for which both played. It is within this small, close-knit Northants community that another enduring but far more personal secret of Tull's life is hidden. A little while after sharing with 'Wassie' Tomkins, Tull moved into the lodgings of Miss Annie Williams, at 26/39 Queen Street, Rushden, depending upon which newspaper we rely. In the 1901 Census Annie Williams is detailed as 4 years old and living in North Street, Rushden. Was 16-year-old Annie Walter's lover? (At enlistment in the British Expeditionary Force in December 1914 Tull's address is 33 Albany Road, Northampton.)

Tull's love life is a continuing mystery. There is no evidence that he had one. Although it would be naïve in the extreme to assume that a man in his physical and intellectual prime, with a relatively glamorous (if short-lived) career, was celibate, there is no supporting data to deny or confirm this supposition. It is more likely that there are a number of reasons we cannot find, or there no longer exist, letters, photographs and other such confidences passed between lovers. It may have been a reflection of Tull's desire to keep this aspect of his being hidden from view. From the age of 10 he had been reinvented as a public person, an orphan, the property of an institution in which every moment is either supervised, regulated, standardised or observed. Formal contact with the world outside the Bonner Road yard was recorded in the children's personal files. They were watched bodies.

On leaving the orphanage as a boarder, Tull lodged at Mr Maynard's hostel while serving his printing apprenticeship, a home environment with rules, hierarchy and limitations on personal freedom. Walking from the Darnley Road hostel to the NCH print shop, Tull would enter a workplace regulated by contract, his actions monitored for signs of commitment and progress.

As a professional footballer his work would be scrutinised by the trainer, manager, directors and, on match day, by the paying public and journalists. His every touch and move, his thoughts almost, played out and exposed to thousands of critical eyes. He had moved from an enclosed, hierarchical, rule-bound institution – the orphanage – to an equally regulated but far more public institution, the professional football club.

That there was no hiding place would have been a fact of existence from his days in Folkestone as a boy of colour, from a family of colour in a town and country overwhelmingly White. Attracting public gaze and scrutiny would not have been unusual; nor would the rule-bound existence he experienced on leaving the Kent town.

It has been argued by many historians that Victorian society and family life was deferential, with order enforced if necessary with the sanction of violence. It has also been suggested that parental culture within Caribbean families has a far more relaxed attitude to the use of physical punishment. It would not be unimaginable to assume that Daniel Tull conformed to the cultural practices of his time and enforced rules with violence if he felt such a sanction necessary to maintain his power and authority over the children.

In those dimensions of Tull's being over which control was compromised – work and his identity as a public figure – there was little room for individual manoeuvre and volition. He may have felt that it was only in that very personal domain – his love life – that control could be exerted to a degree that gave him shelter from the ever vigilant and prying public eye. He would not offer this portion of himself for the appraisal of others. And that evaluation, uncalled for and unsolicited, would surely occur if he was emotionally involved with a White woman, whether married or single. He would have seen and heard negative public comment with his mother and father. He would not have wanted to replicate this situation in his adulthood.

Residents of the small market town of Rushden were unused to mixed relationships. While some would have accepted the love of two people as a blessing for the community, there would have been those opposed, both to the fact of the relationship and the prospect of the physical expression of such 'unnatural' love between 'races' in later years running about the streets and sitting in the classroom with their children.

If 24-year-old Tull was living with his 16-year-old landlady, their relationship, for reasons other than mere differences of colour, would have been a topic of gossip over the garden fence, in the public bar and on the terraces. For a man who was talked about a lot, further food for mouths to chew upon would not have been on the top of his shopping list. He didn't need the additional emotional expenditure, which is why he may have done all in his power to protect this precious oasis from external pollution with an unusual level of secrecy.

Alternatively, as was suggested confidently by two 30-something women at a talk I gave at the National Army Museum in October 2007, he may have been gay. Again there is no evidence to deny or confirm (though cultural myths linking institutionalised boarding at school age and homosexuality would strengthen the case!)

6

Other pioneer Black footballers in the UK, 1872–1918

If Walter had managed to survive the war and fulfil his pledge to Rangers he still would not have been Scotland's first Black footballer. Ged O'Brien has claimed this distinction for Andrew Watson but, after much diligent searching among dusty backcopies of Victorian newspapers and club records, Richard McBrearty of the Scottish Football Museum has unearthed Robert Walker, given the nickname 'Darkie' – a common soubriquet, right up to the 1960s, for players who have darker skin. His discoverer writes:

> The first time that we come across Robert in the Queen's Park records is on 11 August 1876 when he renews his membership of the club. This suggests that he was a member of the club for at least one year previous to the date of the record.
>
> An article by J. Shaw Carmichael in the *Weekly Record*, 23 July 1916, mentions that in 1875/76 season Walker was one of three Queen's Park players who moved to Third Lanark to help out in Scottish Cup ties when the (Cathkin) side were hit with injuries.
>
> 'Thus in the first round of the Scottish ties some of the Thirds players were injured, and the late Major Cassels, the life and soul of the Third then, applied to his old comrade-in-arms, Captain Joseph Taylor, for the loan of three players to assist the Third in the ties. This request the Queen's captain graciously and gallantly conceded, the trio who marched from Old Hampden to Old Cathkin Park being John G. Crichton, Robert Walker (i.e. "The Darkie"), and William Drinnan. They doffed the pleasanter-looking black

and white stripes for the then flaming fiery soldier solid red jerseys of the Third. So well did they and the team of which John Hunter was the captain play that they reached the Scottish final, and who do you think they met in that classic event, why none other than the Queen's, from whom they had been loaned.'

The Scottish Cup final took place on 11 March 1876 at Hamilton Crescent. A crowd of 10,000 watched a 1–1 draw. The replay took place one week later with 6,000 spectators returning to Hamilton Crescent to see Queen's Park win 2–0. Walker played in both matches.[1]

Walker's ethnicity was not always highlighted in match reports. However, McBrearty has found another, confirmatory reference in *The Scottish Referee*, 8 February 1904.

Third Lanark are the only team to have a half caste playing for them; this was Darkey Walker, a familiar and conspicuous figure from 1874 to 1878.

It seems Walker was playing for the second team of Queen's Park, the Strollers, when he was loaned out to Third Lanark in 1875 to play in the Scottish Cup. Queen's Park in the 1870s was Scotland's most formidable club. There was no League programme – this didn't begin until 1890. The Scottish and FA Cups were the only national trophies for which clubs in Scotland could compete.

Queen's Park were FA Cup semi-finalists in 1872 and 1873, the first two years of the competition. Perhaps they are the only team to go out at this stage without losing. They didn't play either semi because they could not afford the expense of travelling down to the London venue, the Kennington Oval. Had they done I might have been able to claim a family connection: during the 1860s and 1870s my great great-grandparents, Alice and John Borgars, lived at addresses in the Kennington/Vauxhall area. John worked in the gasworks, alongside the Oval.

Ten years after their second non-appearance, Queen's Park had saved enough money to go all the way, losing in the final to Blackburn Rovers, 2–1. The following season, 1884–5, the two teams met again in the final at Kennington Oval, with the Lancashire side once more scoring two. At the other end the Glaswegians couldn't find the net. I don't know if walrus-moustached John and the feisty, matriarchal Alice Borgars watched either final!

While the Queen's Park teams would have been more than disappointed at losing the finals, in compensation the club had won the Scottish Cup in its first three seasons, 1873–4, 1874–5 and, of course, 1875–6, when Robert Walker played against them while signed to them! Attendances for the first six FA Cup finals did not exceed 3,000. It wasn't until the 1884 final, featuring Queen's Park, that the crowd topped 10,000. The difference in attendance figures between the Scottish and FA Cup finals reflects the faster development of the game in Scotland which evolved a more cohesive, team-oriented, *scientific* passing style, as opposed to the individualist approach of the English teams. This Scottish superiority is further confirmed by the results of 11 international matches between England and Scotland between 1872 and 1882, where the blue shirts conquered the whites on seven occasions, the latter winning just twice, in 1873 and 1879.

This Scots dominance continued until 1888 when England, bolstered with professional players preparing for the inaugural season of the Football League, won 5–0. Given the relative excellence of both the Scottish game and Queen's Park, Robert Walker's standard as a footballer was above ordinary.

Of undoubted ability was the next Black Scottish footballer to play in both Scottish and FA Cups, Andrew Watson. I first came across the Queen's Park and Scotland footballer in 1998. Checking some details as I was putting the finishing touches to the manuscript of *Colouring over the White Line: The History of Black Footballers in Britain*, he jumped out at me while looking casually at an 1880–1 team photo of the Hampden Park amateurs in a club history by Richard Robinson. My heart jumped; my mouth opened. I may have even dribbled! In short, as soon as I saw this brown-skinned player with curly hair among his White team-mates I realised I had a problem. The biography of Arthur Wharton, *The First Black Footballer*, was at the publishers being readied for its launch in September. Usually, any find of a long-lost Black footballer would be welcomed. However, the ramifications of this find worried me: the possibility of having to rewrite not one but two books, and having the first edition of the former pulped before it reached bookshops.

After a little preliminary investigation which delivered even less, I wrote to Queen's Park asking for further information. Not untypically, I didn't get a reply. Football clubs are hit and miss in this respect. The eye of the first reader is often crucial in determining what happens next. Of clubs in Scotland, Celtic, Rangers and St Johnstone have responded to queries and more, the Parkhead club sending a photograph of Gil Heron and the Perth club a Saints first-team shirt. Others, whom I won't mention, have been, well . . . very forgetful!

After a lot of deliberation I decided I didn't have the necessary energy and time to rewrite the *Colouring* manuscript. It was contracted to come out in hardback and, on the basis of its sales, I thought a decision would then be made as to a paperback version. This is what I'd been led to believe was the usual procedure. My reckoning, as a virgin author, was I'd have time to research Watson before *Colouring* came out in softcover. It never did! However, I was able to amend the backcover of *The First Black Foot-baller* to read that Wharton was the first Black *professional* footballer. And, in a telephone interview with Sukhdev Sandhu for his review of the biography, *A League of His Own*, in the *Guardian* on 3 April 1999, I ensured he noted my re-evaluation that Wharton was probably not the first Black footballer. Unfortunately, in the article Sandhu claimed he 'wasn't the first black professional footballer'.

Football records from this early period of the Association game are randomly scattered, incomplete and inconclusive but McBrearty's research does revise the now-accepted wisdom that Andrew Watson was the first Black player – of Scottish and Guianan heritage – to play in the Scottish Cup.

Watson was actually born in Guyana but the evidence now tells us that Walker was a contemporary of Watson's if he was also playing from 1874. Walker is also the world's first black footballer to have played in a national final (Watson didn't reach the Scottish Cup final until 1881). Unfortunately we have not yet come across any images of Robert Walker. We have images of course of Andrew Watson as well as Major Cassels (the man who asked for him to go to Thirds) and Joseph Taylor (the man who allowed him to go). Third Lanark were formed in 1872 not long after the first international had been played in Glasgow. In their day a leading Scottish club (Scottish Cup winners twice and League Champions in 1904) Thirds sadly went out of business in 1967 under suspicious circumstances.[2]

In 2002 Ged O'Brien, then of the Scottish Football Museum, publicly announced the findings of his research on Andrew Watson, appealing for further help and information: 'We believe the findings, dated between the 1870s and 1880s, could prove that the first black British footballer was Andrew Watson who played for Queen's Park (Glasgow) and Scotland'.[3]

Douglas Lamming, in his 1987 *Who's Who* of Scottish internationals, profiles Watson, characterising him as a 'fast moving defender possessed of a huge kick and a doughty tackle',[4] but makes no mention of his ethnicity. Watson is the first Black international, captaining Scotland in their 6–1 thrashing of England at Kennington Oval in 1881. While he won just three caps, one of the most respected and knowledgeable football journalists of the Victorian and Edwardian eras, J. A. H. Catton, editor of the popular and influential *Athletic News*, writing as *Tityrus*, selected Watson in his team of Scotland's greatest players.

Watson's entry in the *Scottish Football Association Annual 1880–81* emphasised his rapid progress on joining the Hampden Park club – also headquarters of the Scottish FA – after playing for Glasgow junior sides Maxwell and Parkgrove.

> One of the very best backs we have; since joining Queen's Park has made rapid strides to the front as a player; has great speed and tackles splendidly; powerful and sure kick; well worthy of a place in any representative team.

Playing, and for a short while between 1881 and 1882 acting as secretary, for Scotland's elite club, Watson was from a similar class background to Arthur Wharton. The son of Peter Miller, a plantation owner in British Guiana, and Rose Watson, from Georgetown – his place of birth in 1857 – he attended public school. In 1875, continuing into higher education, he enrolled in the Arts Faculty at the University of Glasgow to study natural philosophy, mathematics and civil engineering and mechanics. He didn't graduate but, according to Lamming, utilised his engineering knowledge, working in that profession in Liverpool in 1887.

Wharton also came from a wealthy, mixed-heritage background and he, too, did not graduate from his college with a formal qualification. Additionally, like Watson, he played for a top club, Preston North End – the Invincibles – who in the latter half of the 1880s were reputedly the best in the world. (This status was hotly disputed by Glasgow's Renton FC!) This is where the similarity ends. While Watson's clubs are a name check on the socially elite, big-city amateur sides of the 1880s – Queen's Park, Corinthians and London Swifts – Wharton's working-class teams from northern England were about money, joining those from whom he could earn a living. He was a professional in every sense of the word, excelling in those sports in which he took a wage or received remuneration: football, athletics and cricket. Watson was a gentleman amateur at a time when money did pass hands but only in the shadows, for 'expenses' and 'testimonials'.

An application by Wharton, while he was a professional footballer, for a post in the Gold Coast Colonial Service was turned down because of the 'ill-repute' of his sister, Clara and the alcoholism of his brother Charles.[5] Whether in resigned acceptance of a pre-determined fate or by choice, Wharton stayed in England, working as a miner at New Edlington colliery once his ability to secure a wage from sport had ended. He had a sad end, dying in a workhouse sanatorium from cancer and venereal disease. Buried in a pauper's grave without a headstone – until 1997 – he paid a price beyond death for fathering two children by his sister-in-law. His wife Emma refused to be buried in his grave, preferring instead to lie in another cemetery. In 1902, notes Lamming, Watson was reported to be living in Bombay. O'Brien suggests he died in Sydney.

There was, remarkably, another Black Walker to emerge from Scottish football in the Victorian era, left-winger John, from the port of Leith, now part of Edinburgh. His manor is *Trainspotting* territory and, indeed, when he was playing for his first adult team, Leith Primrose, the steam locomotives were still pulling in and out of Leith station. In the year, 1898, that Sudan was colonised by the British and the Scottish TUC was formed, 'Walker, the darkey' signed for neighbours and betters, Leith Athletic, of the Scottish League second division. Making his debut against the Edinburgh-Irish club from across the Links in Easter Road, first division Hibernian, he scored, 'making an excellent impression'.[6]

The local youngster continued his good form at the beginning of the following season, so much so that he was now being clumped for his skills and referred to as the

> 'Black Jewel' [whose] consistent and brilliant play won for him fresh laurels and new friends. It also gave him one enemy . . .

R. MacFarlane, the Airdrie right back. So often did he outwit the latter that the back . . . deliberately struck Walker. [7]

Edinburgh's other first division club, Heart of Midlothian, fancied parading the jewel on their turf, signing him at the end of October for an £80 transfer fee. However, the sparkler didn't mesmerise. His individualist (English!) style did not endear him to the Tynecastle committee who preferred a player more suited to the club's tried and tested passing game, often selecting David Baird or John Blair in his position. Despite his lack of success, Walker did win a medal while at Tynecastle, playing in the East of Scotland Shield final in March 1899, when Hearts defeated rivals Hibs 1–0. A few months later, after Hearts had finished the season as runners-up to Rangers, Walker was on his way to the fens of eastern England and Lincoln City of division 2 of the Football League. He didn't settle in the cathedral city either, making only six appearances for the Imps. One of the reasons, according to Lincoln FC historian Alex White, may have been the racist comments made about him in the local press.

Journalists' frequent reference to colour and physical appearance would not have been considered racist in the modern sense and context of the term. Most Victorians, but certainly not all, accepted the 'common-sense' assumption of Black inferiority. A flavour of the debates about 'race' occurring in regional newspapers can be found in an article, responding to a previous article, in the Edinburgh *Evening Dispatch*, 9 September 1899. The original, by a female writer from a southern state in the USA, sought to explain why Blacks ended up with broken necks: she said that Negroes are inferior; they are in a majority in some states; White women will not give evidence in court against Black men because their husbands won't allow it, therefore lynchings! The follow-up article outlined how the UK was different. 'Americans are astonished at the readiness of the English people to associate with members of the coloured race on terms of equality.'[8] But, it continued, this is probably because there aren't great numbers of people of African origin in the Kingdom.

The 'race' discourse had changed during the 19th century. Pre-abolition it had been characterised by debates that asserted or refuted the common humanity of all peoples. Those who argued for abolition often did so citing Christian and enlightenment principles that espoused the equal worth of individuals. Post-abolition, the battle won, arguments about race from those who believed separation was preferable switched to concerns about culture and miscegenation; about maintaining a distinct way of life and racial purity. 'Races' were graded and ascribed particular, ingrained characteristics. The inference was that you couldn't escape the genetic/ biological inheritance denoted by your (skin colour and) physiognomy. While all were of equal worth as humans and/or God's children, the 'races' have evolved at different speeds and it would be best if they continued to develop separately. As these columns were being written and read, Walker was being watched and evaluated. He returned to Scotland in January 1900, dying prematurely eight months later.

John William 'Jack' Cother and younger brother Edwin 'Eddie', born in Uxbridge, Middlesex, in 1873 and 1878 respectively, were the first professional footballers with South Asian antecedence. In fact they were Eurasian, or what was later termed Anglo-Indian, having a British mother, Clara, and an Indian-born father, William, who may well have been Anglo-Indian himself. This would not have been unusual. Many British men working or serving in the military in India married local women. Indeed so common was the practice in the late 18th and early 19th centuries that the colonial authorities in India did everything in their power to end it. The descendants of both still live in the Watford area. In discussing the brothers they were unsure about the precise genealogical details of their South Asian lineage.

Jack was the more successful footballer. His first recorded club was Colne Valley in Lancashire, during 1891 and 1892. It is rumoured he played for them professionally but this was never substantiated. If he moved to the north-west to play football rather than for other work, it would surely have been for money. After this excursion, he played the rest of his career in and around Watford, officially turning professional in 1897 with Watford St Mary's. Taken over by Southern League division 2 West Herts the following season, the combined team became Watford FC (WFC). With a reputation as a hard, robust full-back, he made over 140 appearances at Cassio Road, scoring three goals. It was a bumpy and emotionally turbulent career, Watford winning promotion in 1900 and being relegated three years later. They then appointed as manager ex-Preston North End and England legend and team-mate of Arthur Wharton, John Goodall. It took the former 'Invincible' just one season to recover his club's place in the top division.

After Jack Cother's career ended in 1905 he continued his association with the club, selling programmes and helping out on match days. He died in 1946, aged 73, and is buried, fittingly, at Vicarage Road Cemetery, close by the present Watford ground.

While Jack was the model of consistency, dedication and, given his continued attachment to Watford FC after his career ended, commitment, it is brother Eddie who captured my imagination for reasons beyond football. Five years younger, his professional career was short, lasting only one season officially (but maybe longer given the practices of the time, in which payment was sometimes made outside of a formal contract). His clubs, for whom he played in the mid- to late 1890s, included Watford Athletic, Watford St Mary's, West Herts and Watford. At his best he was a formidable half-back (midfield). The *Watford Observer*, 14 January 1899, noted 'With any amount of dash and go, he combines ability to find the net, and is a worker for the whole 90 minutes'. Yet, by 1900, the 22-year-old's professional career was over. This is where his story turns more interesting and touches upon issues that many 21st-century Black and working-class youth would recognise, such as intensive, disproportionate scrutiny and criminalisation for relatively trivial violations of the law.

On 8 October 1907, Eddie stood in the dock at Watford Police Court (WPC). He was charged with assaulting Albert Russell while trespassing and cutting watercress from a stream. Eddie counter-charged Russell with assault. The ex-footballer had one witness, Russell six, including a policeman who said Eddie was 'under [the] influence [of alcohol] and excited'.[9] Unsurprisingly, Cother was fined 10 shillings (50 pence) or seven days' hard labour. He was also ordered to pay £1 4s (£1.20) costs for having his counter-assault charge dismissed.

Many other court appearances followed. He may have turned out at WPC more times than he did for WFC. While he may not have been man-marked as a player, it seems one law officer, Police Sergeant Morley, followed Eddie around like a virus looking for a home. Morley was the arresting officer on a number of occasions, including those that led to court summonses for gambling in 1909 and assault on the Police Sergeant himself in 1911. Most of Eddie's run-ins with the law were for gambling (often while drinking), with the odd assault charge (justifiable in the PS Morley case?). His troubled life included spells in St Alban's Workhouse, an institution that held visions of terror for the working-class poor, in which he eventually died in 1951. His destitution resulted in him being buried in a pauper's grave at St Alban's Borough Cemetery.

While all the men so far discussed were indisputably footballers of colour, a similar assertion cannot be made for Fred Corbett of Thames Ironworks/ West Ham United (WHUFC). However, he has been included because of his appearance in WHUFC team photographs of 1900–1 and 1901–2, the final judgement resting with interested readers who have the time and energy to corroborate or deny my assertion with their own examination of Corbett's physical appearance.

Thames Ironworks, started by workers at the Canning Town shipbuilders, was Corbett's first professional club. Formed after a strike at the yard, the unspoken aim of the newly created 'Hammers' was to foster better relations between management and workers after a period of great militancy in the docks of East London.

Thames Ironworks turned professional in 1898 and joined division 2 of the Southern League for the start of the 1898–9 season. Thirty new players were signed, and only three retained from the previous campaign. Corbett, an 18-year-old goalscoring right-winger, was employed the following season, at the end of which the club changed its name to West Ham United. He played a total of 39 games scoring 12 goals – including a hat-trick against Wellingborough – before moving to Bristol Rovers in January 1902. He also signed for Bristol City, Rovers again (twice), Brentford, New Brighton and in 1912–13 Merthyr Town, his last club. In 14 seasons of senior competitive football in the Southern and Football Leagues, Fred played over 280 games, scoring 101 goals – a good rate for a winger. It is quite possible he played against Jack Cother of Watford who was also in the first division of the Southern League in 1900–1 and 1901–2.

West Ham and Tottenham were the local professional clubs that attracted the support of those living in north-east London, such as Tull. It isn't known if Walter did support either as a boy, or if he watched them. But, if he did manage to get himself along to White Hart Lane, the Memorial Ground, West Ham's home until 1904, or the Boleyn Castle ground, he might have seen Corbett, Jack Cother even, in action.

Black amateur footballers also played at senior competitive level during this period. Edward Tull, while training to be a dentist, between 1904 and 1912 appeared for Ayr Parkhouse of the Scottish League division 2, Girvan Athletic and junior club Ballantrae and was characterised as 'a tricky inside forward and a menace in the goal area'.[10]

The eldest of the Tulls, William Stephen Palmer, a sapper in the Royal

Engineers during the First World War, according to the feature article on Walter in the *Football Star*, 20 March 1909, played for two Kent clubs, Folkestone and Dover St Mary's.

The most prominent amateur footballer of colour of this period is forward Hassan Hegazi, the first Egyptian to play in the Football League when he appeared for division 2 Fulham in November 1911. Despite scoring on his debut, a 3–1 win over Stockport County, he did not play for the Cottagers again. He had come to the west London club's notice turning out for amateurs Dulwich Hamlet, for whom he had signed earlier in that 1911–12 season. The 20-year-old Cairo-born student attended the University of London (or Dulwich College, depending on which local newspaper is used as source), having graduated from Saidiq Secondary School in Egypt. The *Fulham Observer*, 17 November 1911, commented that while 'it was apparent the Egyptian was playing out of his class . . . with persistence something might be made of him . . . Hegazi has the makings of a League player'. (In the report he is a University of London student.) Hegazi signed for Southern League Millwall in 1912, playing one game, but soon returned to Dulwich Hamlet. Never one to allow himself the luxury of a relaxing moment, he enrolled at St Catharine's College, Cambridge, in 1913 to study Arabic and history, staying just long enough – two terms – to play in the annual match with Oxford, earning his Blue in a 2–1 win.

A player Tull would not have seen but who appears fleetingly and momentarily in the year of his death is

> Costa, who figures intermittently on the Southport left-wing, has the characteristic pace and lack of robustness of the black. But he is more of the Red Indian than the African Negro type, with long black hair and copper coloured skin.[11]

Not much more is known about this Southport Vulcan player who featured in just a few games in the Lancashire Regional Tournament at the beginning of the 1918–19 season. (The Football League resumed the following season.) The *Southport Guardian*, 7 September, reporting Vulcan's 3–0 victory over Blackburn Rovers, thought him 'the most dangerous man on the home side . . . cleverly he dribbles, and then centres accurately'. Yet a month later Southport signed former Preston North End winger George

Barlow and no more was seen or heard of Costa, possibly the third Asian footballer to play at senior level in Britain.

Brown-skinned players of African, Caribbean and Asian heritage whom Tull could have seen or heard of from the 1890s to his death in 1918 number at least six, not including Robert Walker, Andrew Watson and his brothers. Of all the Black footballers in Britain up to 1918, who number at least 12, four – Robert Walker, Andrew Watson, Arthur Wharton and Tull himself – played at the highest level, the first divisions of the English and Scottish Leagues, with Watson captaining his country while winning three international caps. If the success of Watson, coming before Tull's birth in 1888, did not filter into the consciousness of the young Black Briton as he was growing up in Folkestone and Bethnal Green, it would have been difficult not to have heard Wharton's name being mentioned. Walter's father Daniel Tull was a literate man and the exploits of this West Africa-born Black Briton would surely have not gone unnoticed. There was little overtly positive comment in the press about people of colour, and the achievements of Wharton as Amateur Athletics Association (AAA) sprint champion in 1886 and 1887, world professional sprint champion in 1888 and professional footballer for two first division clubs would have provided a rare opportunity to share the warm reflection from the public discussion of his deeds. Sporting achievement is, sins of cheats aside, unqualified: victory or defeat; triumph or failure. Only with great difficulty could it be diluted with caveats and excuses by those with an ideological agenda. A public victory on the sports field by a person of colour would not go unnoticed or unfelt by others of a similar pigmentation.

The 'Kaffirs'

A team that certainly did not go unnoticed by the newspaper-reading public was the first Black Association football team to visit Britain, the 'Kaffirs', of the Basuto people from what is now Lesotho, South Africa. They docked at Southampton in September 1899. Never before had a Black African squad played outside that continent. Indeed, they may well have been the first African football tourists – even if we include White South Africans. The Basutos' trip to Britain was organised by the Orange Free State Football Association (OFSFA) which was controlled by administrators of British origin. (The president was a Mr Hudgson, chairman of Bloemfontein's Rangers FC.) Afrikaners favoured rugby. G. A. L. Thabe's 1983 history of Black football in South Africa, *It's a Goal: 50 Years of Sweat, Tears and Drama in Black Soccer*, makes reference to an Orange Free State Bantu soccer club active in 1898. This was almost certainly Oriental FC, club of the tourists' captain Joseph Twaji.

There were a number of reasons for the tour: to raise funds for OFSFA, who, it seems, were determined that the team's visit to England would pay its way and more; to encourage and improve the playing of football in the Orange Free State by raising its profile with a visit to the home of Association football; to pay for a working visit home by officials of British antecedence; the players' novelty, freak show value; and expressly political reasons which will be discussed below.

Thirty-six games had been arranged against the best teams in England and Scotland. The punishing schedule, with more fixtures than a division 1 season, was to have begun on 1 September against Aston Villa, the current Football League champions, but the liner *Gaika* on which the footballers had sailed berthed nine days late, eventually arriving on the second day of the month. The re-arranged programme had the Basutos kicking off on 5 September in the north-east rather than the Midlands, pitching them against first-division Newcastle United at St James' Park. There was much pre- and post-match publicity, the language describing the physical characteristics of the visitors hinting at, and subtly exploiting, the European obsession with the (relatively unrepressed) sexuality of the African.

> The visitors [are] a fine lot of men . . . reputed to possess remarkable staying powers. [They are] clever at the game . . . Some of them remarkably good looking, and of an intelligent cast of features.[12]

A large crowd of 6,000 assembled, with 'a sprinkling of the fair sex'.[13] Some inquisitive folk had even gone to the Central railway station to welcome them. Compared to their opponents Twaji's team, wearing orange shirts with dark blue collars and shorts, were not very good. In fact, they were awful. The Geordies coasted to victory 6–3, as did all but one of the teams the Africans faced. (The final statistics read: played 36, won 0, drawn 1, lost 35, with 235 goals conceded.) Other north-east opponents were Sunderland – big boys of the region, having won the first division three times in the

1890s – to whom the 'Kaffirs' lost 5–3, and Middlesbrough, who won 7–3. In all three games the Black footballers were treated patronisingly, as over-grown children

> they are a very heavy lot and caused a great deal of amusement (v. Newcastle United); the delightful darkey returned to the centre line as proud as the proverbial dog (v. Sunderland); From a corner just on the interval, the Kaffirs amidst loud laughter were permit-ted to score (v. Middlesbrough).

Without irony, this reporter also noted that 'the darkeys played a very gen-tlemanly game, and it says much for their good temper – which must have been sorely tried – that they did not utilise their obvious strength of body and cranium'.[14]

The various quotes illustrate confused attitudes toward the 'Kaffirs'. They were big and strong, handsome yet excruciatingly naïve and honest. However, while it would have been simple, literally, to portray the 'Kaffirs' as freak-show footballers for the amusement and entertainment of the 'master race', matters became complicated by the unfolding tragedy of the political and military crisis in Southern Africa, which descended, in October 1899, into the South African War. A feature of the political debate surrounding the crisis was the allegiance of the Black – or 'Kaffir' and 'Bantu' as they were often (disparagingly) labelled – populations. Basutoland, the homeland of the 'Kaffir' footballers, was sandwiched between the Orange Free State, which was a Boer republic, and Natal, an English-speaking colony. With whom the Basutos would side was a live question in British newspapers.

Not unexpectedly, but certainly unenviably, the Africans found them-selves on a tour organised by administrators of British descent in a country at war with the Afrikaans-speaking government and population of the Orange Free State. This political dimension created a dilemma for report-ers and editors, some of whom continued to work the tourists as malleable raw material with which to stir up public prejudice. The (Southampton) *Football Echo and Sports Gazette* informed its readers of the 'Kaffirs'' arrival – 'up come Eleven Little Nigger Boys from Savage South Africa'[15] – via a cartoon situated centrally on its front page, featuring a sturdy but shaken John Bull reminding readers of Kipling's description of Britain's Black col-onies as the 'White man's burden'. The *Athletic News* followed in similar vein. Like the cartoon in the *Football Echo and Sports Gazette* it was placed so readers could not miss it. Instead of a group of Africans it had an individual, in football kit but wearing only one boot, holding a spear and tomahawk with a ring through his nose and feathers in his hair, kicking a ball. Underneath is the caption: 'Jeeohsmiffikato the crack Kaffir centre-forward thirsting for gore and goals'.[16]

Others were more sensitive – to the political needs of imperial Britain! During war-scare September there were fears expressed in the press that 'Boer spies' were inciting the Basutos to rise up against Natal. In light of this should not the tourists be utilised in the anti-Boer propaganda offensive? If so, disrespecting them as 'savages' was unwise as they and their peoples may well be needed as allies should the emergency escalate into a South Africa-wide war. Much of the ambivalent language used in the reporting of the 'Kaffirs' reflected the environment of naked, competing propaganda that war scares generate. To provide a flavour of this politicised hysteria, we need only cast our minds back a few years to the conspiracy of lies deployed by the US and UK governments in their ideological window dressing for their invasion of Iraq. In their build-up they obsessively linked the attacks on the World Trade Center and other targets in the USA in 2001 with the Iraqi government, rather than Saudi Arabia from which most of the 9/11 attackers came. Prime Minister Tony Blair, smiles and frowns theatrically employed in equal proportion, warned Parliament on 24 September 2002 of Saddam Hussein's ability to launch his weapons of mass destruction in 45 unstoppable minutes. (Interestingly, when I tried online to retrieve this speech to Parliament which had been available at www.number-10.gov.uk/output/Page1727.asp I found it had been *archived*.) US Secretary of State Colin Powell's speech at the UN on 5 February 2003 detailed with charts, diagrams, slides and statistics Saddam's Weapons of Mass Destruction (WMD) arsenal. One particular accusation, supported by graphics, alleged Iraq had bio-weapons labs, mounted on trucks, that would be virtually impossible to find! The WMD have been as elusive as verification and corroboration of the evidence supporting their existence. A war which has cost hundreds of thousands of lives, created millions of refugees and destroyed the fragile normality of a country was built upon words that had no depth, origin or substance other than the prejudice in the minds of their utterers. Not since the 1991 Gulf War scare had the maxim 'the first casualty of war is truth' been so obvious!

In the UK of autumn 1899, a pressing political objective was the concoction of a public mood of patriotic fervour in support of kith and kin in South Africa. The zeal with which various Victorian journalists tailored the ideological content of their output to suit this foreign and colonial policy agenda demanded overriding and contradicting 'common-sense' notions previously held. Thus, during the War Scare period, the Dutch-origin Afrikaners became light-skinned savages, a redefinition that contributed to the later justification of imprisonment in concentration camps. As with many top-down propaganda campaigns, not all recipients accepted the devilish reconstruction of the Boer unquestioningly. There was sizeable opposition to the war in Britain, led by Emily Hobhouse and David Lloyd George.

Many events have unintended consequences, the South African War, or Second Boer War as it was popularly known, being one such. Because such a high proportion of the men volunteering as recruits to the British Army were so puny and underdeveloped, the government created the Committee on Physical Deterioration in an effort to socially engineer a more muscular British man. One of the solutions offered was more exercise. Drill and physical education was introduced into state schools. This was the first time the government took an official interest in sport and it probably marks the beginnings of the use of sport for unashamedly political ends. And, to compound this irony of the world's most affluent and powerful country defectively reproducing itself, 'several of the [Basutos were] over 6ft high and proportionately built'.[17]

As the war escalated over the winter of 1899–1900, Boer became Black and Black became something else. An example of this contradictory and confused state of affairs is the description of the human exhibits of the Savage South Africa exhibition at Earls Court as the 'magnificent men from the Zulu country'. Yet so 'magnificent' were these men that, soon after opening, London County Council officials instructed the exhibition manager Edwin Cleary to section off the 'native kraals' in order to prevent the public – particularly nubile young women – from fraternising with the 'heathen warriors'.

The Boys from Basuto, bombarded by goals, also succumbed to the propaganda barrage. In their rescheduled fixture with Aston Villa, gate receipts went to a Boer War fund. And it would have been more than a blanket full of farthings and ha'pennies because, despite their inability to match the organised teamwork of their opponents, the Southern Africans attracted large crowds. Against Tottenham, gate receipts totalled a hefty £89. Christmas Day was 'celebrated' with a 3–2 defeat by Brentford at Griffin Park.

At Bramall Lane v. Sheffield United the legendary Billy Foulke, perhaps the only footballer who could match the Basutos for size, being over 6 feet and 28 stone at his most complete, played at centre-forward and scored two goals. Arthur Wharton may even have taken a trip back across the Pennines to his old club to watch his fellow Africans play his ex-team-mates, in particular 'Fatty' Foulke, the goalkeeper he could not dislodge from the first team.

Hopefully the Basutos would have gone back to South Africa better footballers, though with war raging there was little immediate opportunity for them to apply the knowledge they had gained from their experience of playing the best teams in Britain.

The 'Kaffirs' were not the first Black footballers to visit Britain. That pioneering status goes to the Maori tourists of 1888, the year of Tull's birth. The 26 New Zealanders – including five Whites – played 74 games under the Rugby code, with a few practice matches under Association rules as relatively insignificant extras.

The existence of other Black footballers, though sparse, would have provided the young Tull with a notion of what was possible. While he played at school, in the street and park, there were other brown-skinned professionals doing it for money. And football was not the only sport in which darker-skinned characters were having their exploits broadcast far and wide as will be discussed in the next chapter, on other Black sports people.

7

Bloods, sweat and fears: other Black sports people

A giant of Victorian cricket was K. S. Ranjitsinhji, a thin-built Indian prince who used his willow bat and body to produce fleeting moments of wonder and lasting memories of beauty. During the summer of 1899 he beat the scoring record of the legendary W. G. Grace by accumulating 3,000 runs over the season. In his seminal book on cricket, ethnicity and class, *Beyond a Boundary*, C. L. R. James leaves the reader in no doubt as to the elevated status 'Ranji' held within the sport. An England international, revered by followers of cricket, he is irremovable from the pantheon of great names.

The Illustrated Sporting and Dramatic News, November 1899, recognised the political and social role of sport in Britain and its Empire, cricket in particular, at the onset of its war with the Boers in South Africa. On the use of volunteer native Indians in the conflict, and the possibility of forced enlistment of poor working-class men in the UK, it commented:

> It is sometimes said on the continent that the cricket playing Briton is the finest man in the world. But this includes the cricket playing Greater Britain, and it is their love of sport which has lately made a success of our colonial troops, hastily raised and ill-trained. As a sportsman the colonial is more English than the Englishman. And it is not simply physical training which has made him a soldier . . . War is a sport, and, like every other sport except croquet, has its moral side . . . skill and daring are requisite and it is, we English believe, through these qualities that, like the meek, we inherit the earth. Conscription may 'level up' the sub-merged tenth, much to the discomfort of the other nine-tenths,

but the commandeered self-starved ruffian will still be a tenth of the value of the volunteer sportsman.[1]

For loyalists who believed that sport was cultural cement binding disparate peoples of the Empire, Ranjitsinhji was physical evidence. In him was embodied the evidence that class and cultural affiliation was indeed more important than difference of colour. At a dinner held at the British Sportsmen's Club in London some thirty years later the Maharaja of Patiala, a nephew of 'Ranji' – now Jam Sahib of Nawanagar and 'Maharajah of Connemara'[2] – reaffirmed sport's crucial role as a uniting force.

> Sport, it seems to me, is among the greatest ties that bind together the far-flung Empire of the King. I always find myself happy in the company of fellow sportsmen. Despite differences of race and creed, we feel ourselves to be really one together.[3]

The English-speaking Caribbean's most popular game also thrived among its expatriates in Britain. Dr John Alcindor played for an amateur club in London, as did Dr James Jackson Brown, for the London Hospital. The pioneer professional cricketer was St Vincent-born Charles Augustus Ollivierre, who arrived in England with the West Indies team in 1900. Amassing over 800 runs on the tour, he was quickly recognised as the Caribbean representatives' premier batsman and quickly signed by Derbyshire, for whom he played until 1907. According to Jeffrey Green in *Black Edwardians* he holds the distinction of being the first African-Caribbean West Indies international to play county cricket. After being forced to retire from the first-class game, Ollivierre played for club sides in Yorkshire, where he might have come across a middle-aged Wharton playing for Rotherham Town Cricket Club in the latter half of the 1900s.

The existence of Black cricketers and footballers confirms the existence of a rainbow, polychrome sporting world in late-Victorian/pre-First World War Britain. As early as the 1860s a renowned athlete was the first American long-distance runner Deerfoot Hagasadoni, known also as Louis Bennett. In Sheffield, a contemporary of Arthur Wharton on the sprint track was Black Yorkshireman Billy Isaac, a formidable professional who also trained athletes. The runner credited with popularising the crouching start was Scotland-based Maori, Bobby Macdonald.

I Single father Daniel Tull with Elsie on his knee and, *right to left anti-clockwise*, Edward, William, Cecilia and Walter, probably taken in Folkestone around the time of Alice's death in 1895

2 *(left)* 51 Walton Road, Folkestone, home of the Tull family from at least 1891

3 *(below)* North Board School, Folkestone, one minute from the Tull home in Walton Road. Walter and Edward were pupils in the 1890s before they were sent to the Children's Home and Orphanage in London

4 *(above right)* Dr Stephenson's Children's Home and Orphanage, Bonner Road, Bethnal Green, London, *c.* 1900

5 *(below right)* Walter and Edward with housemates and sister at the orphanage, between February 1898 and November 1900

6 Walter in Dr Stephenson's Children's Home and Orphanage football team, *c.* 1902

7 Clapton FC, 1908–9, with the FA Amateur Cup and London Senior Cup. They also won the London County Cup that season

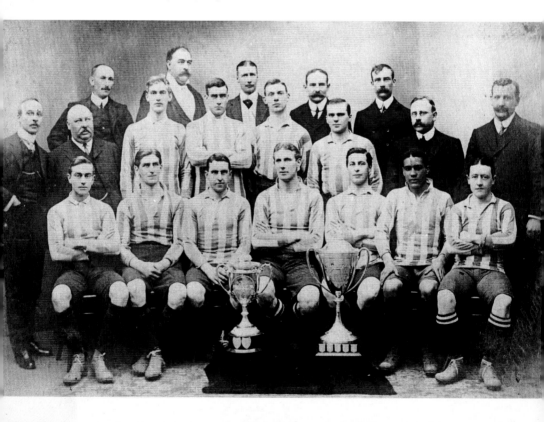

8 Tull in action for Clapton, Amateur Cup final against Eston at Ilford, April 1909

9 Letter written by Tull from the RMSP *Araguaya*, en route to Argentina, May 1909, to Mr Morgan at the NCH explaining his decision to sign as a professional with Spurs

I hope to get a place on one of
the newspapers, if I can't do
that I shall work as a comp.
The heat for the last week or
so has been awful. I think I
had just a touch of sunstroke
& felt very queer for a few days
It is getting cooler now, although
we only "crossed the line" yester-
day. Last night we had a Fancy
Dress Ball & the deck looked
like Fairy-land. The Captain
said it was the best that had
ever been held on his boat
I shall be very glad to get
home again, in spite of the
interesting voyage we are having
Please give my kind regards to
Mrs M & Nellie. From yours very sincerely
Walter D.

R.M.S.P. "ARAGUAYA"

Dear Mr Morgan,
    I expect you were
very disappointed when you
heard that I had signed
professional forms for the
Tottenham F.C. But I fully
intended when I said goodbye to you, to remain an
Amateur. If I had gone to the
Midlands as I said, I should
have been a "paid" Amateur
which in my opinion is
far worse than taking wages

10 *(above)* Walter in action in his and Spurs' first home game in the first division, 11 September 1909, against Manchester United

11 *(below)* Walter's third season at Tottenham (1911–12)

12 *(right)* Walter, Spurs *c.* 1910, in his 'to do is to dare' pose

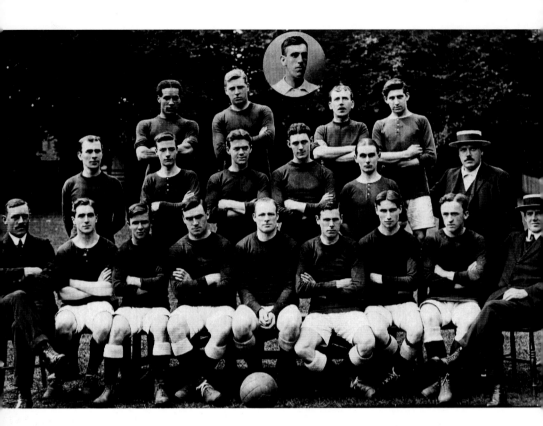

13 *(left)* Northampton Town FC (1913) – Walter at his most contented as a footballer?

14 *(left below)* A call to arms not intended for men such as Walter

15 *(right)* Portrait of the newly commissioned officer, spring 1917

16 *(below)* Walter, Edward, Cecilia and Mrs Jean Warnock, Girvan, Scotland, spring 1917 – the last period of time Walter would spend with his family

17 *(left)* 2nd Lieutenant Tull with regulation moustache and pipe

18 *(right)* Officer training, Gailes, Scotland, spring 1917

19 *(left)* 2nd Lieutenant Walter Tull, Scotland, spring 1917

20 *(above)* 2nd Lieutenant Walter Tull, drawn by the UK's best artist of footballers, Colin Yates

21 *(above)* Andrea, Fionnulla and Alex Vasili find Tull's name on the memorial wall at Faubourg d'Amiens war cemetery in Arras, France

22 *(left)* Tull memorial, Walter Tull Way, Northampton Town FC

23 *(above right)* Rita Humphrey, William Tull's granddaughter

24 *(right)* Edward Tull's daughter Jean and her husband, the Reverend Duncan Finlayson, Appin, Argyll, Scotland 1995

23rd Middlesex Regt
17 April 1918.

Dear Sir,

Of course you have already heard of the death of 2nd Lieut. W.D. Tull on March 25th last.

Being at present in command of "C" Co:— (the Captain was wounded)— allow me to say how popular he was throughout the Battalion. He was brave & conscientious; he had been recommended for the Military Cross, & had certainly earned it; the Commanding Officer had every confidence in him. & he was liked by the men.

...... Now he has paid the supreme sacrifice pro patria; the Battn & Company have lost a faithful Officer; personally I have lost a friend. Can I say more! except that I hope that those who remain may be as true & faithful as he.

Yours sincerely

R.H.Pickard 2/o

25 Letter written by 2nd Lieutenant Pickard to Edward after Walter's death saying he had been recommended for a Military Cross. (The words partially cut off in the photo say 'Now he has paid the supreme sacrifice pro patria'.)

James Peters, a Black dockworker born in Manchester, represented England at rugby in 1907 and 1908. Playing for Plymouth RFC and Devon, he had been mooted as an England candidate for many seasons prior to his initial selection. Jeffrey Green quotes the *Western Morning News*, 17 March 1907, reminding its readers that 'claims for international honours have been repeatedly put forward, but he had been overlooked'.[4] The first man of colour to play the Union game for England, Peters was innovative in other ways, attempting to popularise the professional League version in Devon. His experiment didn't catch on and he eventually moved back north, signing for League club Barrow-in-Furness.

The reality of sports participation in Britain was that people of colour were kitted up all over the place. They were also at the velodrome and in the ring: African-American racing cyclist Marshall Taylor beat British and continental opponents in 1902; South African boxer Andrew Jeptha won a world title in London in 1907; and ex-slave Bobby Dobbs fought in Britain in 1898, returned in 1902 and stayed for another eight years. He had a spell as waged pugilist in fairground boxing booths. This was the most punishing way of boxing for a living and often featured Black fighters. Contests were fast and frequent, the opposition untried and untested. Vanessa Toumlin's *Fair Fight: An Illustrated Review of Boxing on British Fairgrounds* reveals numerous Black pugilists challenging all-comers on a daily basis. Men such as Bob Scanlon, who made a name for himself in both pre-First World War Britain and France, and the fascinating Johnsons, William – 'Billy' – and sons Len and Albert. Like Daniel Tull, Billy migrated to England after working on ships, in 1897. Marrying Margaret Maher, who bore him four children, he boxed in fairground booths. Len followed his father's boxing boots and eventually, after beating some of the best middleweights of inter-war Britain, ran his own booth. He later became a grass roots activist in Manchester, acting as spokesman for, and representative of, the city's Black communities. He also wrote a boxing column for the *Daily Worker*, the newspaper of the Communist Party of which he was a member.

The prevalence of Black booth boxers was not an accident of history. Some years after the Jack Johnson–Bombardier Billy Wells débâcle, which will be discussed below, a colour bar was officially implemented by Britain's boxing administrators. Black pugilists were not allowed to fight for British titles during much of the inter-war period. It was not until 1948 that a Black British boxer, middleweight Randolph Turpin, was allowed to contest a domestic title with a White Briton. This funnelled many good young Black boxers into the more welcoming environment of booth boxing. Indeed, some booth-holders, including Billy Wood and John Stewart, advertised for *coloured* boxers in newspapers such as the *Showman* and *World's Fair* and featured them on their hand-illustrated frontages enclosing the booths.

Boxing was the sport in which Black participation had been longest and most numerous. Because of its core elements – controlled aggression and muscled agility – and the personal qualities required to be successful – strength, character and durability – contests between Black and White, of which there was a long history, had significance beyond the ring.

Black prowess caused enormous problems for White supremacists. Peter Jackson, born at Fredericksted, Virgin Island in the Caribbean in 1861, won the Australian heavyweight championship in 1886. Arthur Ashe in his book on African-American sports people cites Jackson as the first Black man to win an official national title. Shunned by White heavyweights in the USA he sailed to England for a match. On 11 November 1889, the Virgin Islander won the British heavyweight title from Jim Smith. On returning to the USA he challenged James Corbett. After 61 rounds the fight was declared a draw. Corbett, who was to win the world championship from John L. Sullivan a year later, described Jackson as the best boxer he had met. The latter wanted a return against Corbett for the undisputed championship of the world in 1893. Corbett refused. There was a 'race' to lose in defeat. The overthrow of White supremacist ideology by the triumphs of Black athletes, in particular boxers, vexed racists. Public appeals were made for the best sons of the White race to come forward, defeat and thereby subdue the animalist threat. Sports editor Charles Dana of the New York *Sun* was apoplectic.

> We are in the midst of a growing menace. The black man is rapidly forging to the front ranks in athletics, especially in the field of fisticuffs. We are in the midst of a black rise against white supremacy . . . Less than a year ago Peter Jackson could have whipped the world – Corbett, [Robert] Fitzsimmons, . . . but the white race is saved from having at the head of pugilism a Negro . . . There are two Negroes in the ring today who can thrash any white man in

their respective classes . . . Wake up you pugilists of the white race! Are you going to permit yourself to be passed by the black race?[5]

The newspaper was widely read and influential. The open letter addressed to its (White) readers – expressing the sentiment that Black–White bouts were first and foremost racial, therefore political, contests – was not received as the obscure ranting of an extreme and isolated crank. Ashe argues it 'was the most provocative piece of racist sports journalism yet seen in America and caused a sensation that lasted for years afterward'.[6] The success of African-American Jack Johnson in becoming the first Black world heavyweight champion in 1908 – the boxing authorities were forced to wrap the belt around him in Sydney, Australia, because they had been unable to find a venue in the United States – would no doubt have caused editor Dana another paroxysm of racial fury. In fact, his public tirade merely lifted the lid on the latent prejudice that bubbled to the surface in the USA when notable Whites athletes were defeated by Blacks. The bruising caused by each jab, hook and upper-cut in Johnson's taunting, smiling demolition of White contenders was felt many times over by White supremacists, whose suffering was further intensified by the boxer's pride in himself and delight in his blood-spilling achievements.

White hostility to Black prowess created an atmosphere of heightened racism in other sports, and boxing in particular. Johnson's win led to numerous lynchings and attacks upon Blacks throughout the United States. If the future of the White 'race' could not be assured in the ring, outside it the futures of some Black men would be terminated. The defeat of Johnson by a 'Great White Hope' became a burning passion. For others, such as the Reverend F. B. Meyer in the UK, the mere matching of Black and White was unfair. He campaigned to stop Johnson fighting 'Bombardier Billy' Wells in London in 1911.

> The present contest is not wholly one of skill, because on the one side there is added the instinctive passion of the Negro race, which is so differently constituted to our own, and in the present instance will be aroused to do the utmost that animal development can do to retain the championship, together with all the financial gain that would follow.[7]

Reverend Frederick Meyer was no one-dimensional racist. An evangelical Baptist, he was known inside and outside his nonconformist movement as a crusader against sexual freedom and alcoholic indulgence. His Wikipedia entry claims he was instrumental in shutting down many brothels. Yet his public fight to have the Johnson–Wells fight banned sees him stepping into an arena he had previously entered only in a spirit of fraternal solidarity. He had supported the Pan-African Conference in London in 1900; been an activist in the Christian Brotherhood Movement which supported Black emancipation; in the League of Universal Brotherhood, an organisation whose members pledged never to enlist for war and dedicated themselves to work for a world without boundaries and barriers, in which God was recognised in every human, Meyer was vice-president; he also assisted in nurturing and facilitating good relations between the Metropolis and colonial subjects in West Africa. He was a Christian moralist who perceived his God-given duty as steering humanity away from its self-destructive path of corrupt excess, usually pleasures of the flesh. His words and actions in the burning, record-breaking summer of 1911 are in contrast to his words and actions on race before and after.

As Meyer was lobbying politicians such as Winston Churchill, and newspaper editors, in support of his campaign that held innate racial difference to be a fact of God-created life, approximately 1,000 people of varying ethnicities from over 50 nations were meeting in London as part of the Universal Races Congress. Their aims were simple and straightforward: respect of all, by all. One of the organisers, Gustav Spiller, concluded that 'an impartial investigator would be inclined to look upon the various important peoples of the world as, to all intents and purposes, essentially equal in intellect, enterprise, morality and physique'.[8]

Such a geographical juxtaposition of opposing causes provides an example of the competition raging for people's hearts and minds in the world's most influential city at the heart of the most powerful empire on the planet.

In Meyer's lay anthropology are three core concerns – biological, economic and political – of White supremacists, a group whose ideology was seemingly at odds with the preacher's own beliefs: Black athletic success as symbolic expression of the degeneracy of the White race; the consequent rewards of this success as a threat to White superiority; that the collective confidence and spiritual sustenance given to Black communities by

Johnson as a heroic role model may inspire emulation. The champion was not only an Uppity Nigger who kicked White arses but he was also a rich UN who sexually aroused, slept with and loved White women. Inevitably, the giant Texan was stopped, a Bow Street magistrate prohibiting the match over a concern for public order. Johnson eventually lost his world title in Havana, Cuba, in 1915 to the 'Great White Hope' Jess Willard. Many then and today feel the fight was fixed.

The central tenet in Meyer's explanation for Black success on the sports field – the animal in the Black – was to become the common feature in the apologies offered by supremacists for defeats of Whites on track and field. The agility, physical dexterity, instinctive endurance and insentient durability of Black athletes, derived from their animalism, made contests between Black and White unfair. The former would always be at an advantage when human competition included only the physical dimension. Thus it was because Whites were more evolved and civilised, at a more advanced stage of human development, that they were incapable of inflicting those kinds of comprehensive defeats in sport on Blacks that had been achieved – for the 'race' – in the economic, political and social spheres. The animalist thesis represents an attempt to discount Black athletic success by devaluing the victory and, therefore, the social significance of defeat. They were unequal bodies in unequal contests.

This racialisation of a sporting contest, enthusiastically taken up by the press during the coronation summer of 1911, cannot have made easier Tull's desire to be judged on his sporting abilities alone. Moving out of London, a political and politicised city, to the less intense if more parochial environment of a town in middle England in the autumn of that year was beneficial to his football, which suggests he was more relaxed and at ease in other areas of his life. Reading the boxing press of that year he would have been informed of the bouts of a number of Black boxers apart from Johnson: 'At least six Black boxers had some fame in England in 1911. Sam Langford . . . defeated Australia's Bill Lang on 16 February . . . Langford's camp included Bob Armstrong . . . "Liver" Davis and Andrew Jeptha'.[9] The idea that humanity was made up of different 'races' invested Black sporting achievement with nonsensical symbolic value. In such a politicised, racialised sports environment the erasure from collective memory of Black triumph was profound and essential. For the public mouthpieces of the ruling elites, newspapers such as *The Times* and *Daily Telegraph*, to accept Black success at face value would undermine the crucial notion of biologically determined White superiority. If this ideological keystone was shifted, would not other ideas underpinning the hierarchical structure of society, such as those justifying class and gender inequality, also come crashing down? In reality, sporting contests between Black and White were anything but equally arrived at. The opportunity for most White athletes to develop their skill and talent was greater than for Blacks. The operation of the colour bar, official and unofficial, whether in Britain, its empire or indeed any part of the globe dominated by Europeans, sustained inequalities across the board.

Martin Offiah, a Black former Rugby Union international for England, was nicknamed 'Chariots' by his team-mates, referring to the film *Chariots of Fire*. It is the closest association any Black athlete has with this box-office success of 1981 which dealt with elitism, race and sport, among other issues, in the decade after the First World War. Yet one of the greatest sprinters in Britain during that period was Harry Edward, born in British Guiana in 1895. Wearing the vest of the Polytechnic Harriers club, he first forced attention upon himself in central Europe in 1914, when he ran 200 metres in 21.7 seconds in Berlin in June, following this up with a time of 22 seconds in Budapest in July. Though the outbreak of war shortened the duration of his career, it did not dull his astonishing speed. In 1920 he won the AAA 100 yards title in 10 seconds, also running the 220 yards in 21.6 seconds. At the Olympics of that year he won the bronze in the 100 and 200 metres. It was said that his faltering start at the shorter distance deprived him of the gold. In 1921 he beat British Jew Harold Abrahams – he and fellow runner Eric Liddle were the two main characters in the film – in both the 100 and 220 yards. At the 1922 AAA championship Edward won the 100, 220 and 440 yards titles *within an hour*. His outstanding performances won him the Harvey Memorial trophy, presented to the best athlete of the championship. Abrahams thought the young British Guianan 'one of the most impressive sprinters I have ever seen'.[10]

That the two runners, Abrahams and the Scot Eric Liddle, both came from ethnic minority backgrounds compounds the irony in the exclusion of Edward from *Chariots of Fire*. Furthermore, it was Sam Mussabini's excellence in nurturing Edward that propelled Abrahams to invite the part Arab-African, part Italian trainer to take him up. (Mussabini coached another Guiana-born Black British sprinter, John Edward 'Jack' London, to an Olympic silver medal in Amsterdam in 1928 and an AAA 100 yards title in 1929.)

The dramatisation, a romanticised and racialised portrayal of real sporting endeavour, was enormously popular and profitable. Both characters, Abrahams and Liddle, are brought together by their achievements on the track, each finding obstacles in his pursuit of excellence. For Abrahams it was anti-Semitic prejudice; for Liddle, God, in particular the spiritual turmoil caused by his attempt to combine time spent running on the track with time spent talking with God. The most significant manifestation of this running battle was Liddle's refusal to compete on the Sabbath. Paralleling the lives of these two athletes carried with it another sub-text proclaiming the egalitarian principles and practice at the heart of sport. Liddle and Abrahams evolve as personifications of the meritocratic ideal.

The opening dialogue of *Chariots of Fire*, 'let us praise famous men and our fathers that begat us', echoes two themes that were seminal concerns of Tull: memory and identity. Unfortunately, the film commits to celluloid posterity a selective, arbitrary and orthodox interpretation of the social history of British athletics in the 1920s. The Nation is White, overwhelmingly Anglo-Saxon and ruled by the fathers of God's Children. The only perceived threat to this structured-by-nature supremacy comes from the Jew Abrahams. (Liddle, though a Scot, is doing the work of God's chosen Englishmen as a missionary in China.) It won an Academy Award as 'best film of 1981'. On receiving the Oscar, actor Colin Welland, involved in the making from the beginning, warned the Hollywood audience to beware, with words that had an unmistakable symmetry with the narrative of the film: more British winners were sure to follow. However, it was the film's unspoken and missing dialogue, its silence, that was most eloquent, proclaiming British athletics monochrome and egalitarian where, upon the track, anti-Semitic racism could be pounded to dust underfoot. An early scene recalling Abrahams' induction to Gonville and Caius, his Cambridge college, reveals the contemporary texture of anti-Semitic prejudice through a sneering porter. Later, at a dinner welcoming freshmen, the master of the college pauses to solemnise the memory of those alumni who died in the First World War. 'They died for England, and all that England stood for.' His Little Englander character and sentiment, drawn from the same bank of ideas as the prejudice of the porter, embodied the values of a disintegrating pre-war hierarchy.

Liddle, as a Christian sportsman, acts as a bridge between the old world and the new. Inhabitants of the former, such as the master and porter, have a highly racialised view of the Nation. They suffer its decline and degeneracy caused by the introduction of universal suffrage, the harbinger of bourgeois subordination to the inferior majority race within, yearning for a return to *noblesse oblige*: rule by the elite in the interest of all. Sport in this order had a specific social role as a muscular activity exemplified by manliness, selflessness and hierarchy; a path of enlightenment to godliness, sobriety and patriotic duty. Sporting endeavour of this muscular Christian variety was a tool by which character was instilled and developed.

This acquired character that builds empire, forged through study of the bible and exertions of the body, was further customised by class. Elite participants at the public schools and Oxbridge would be equipped with the guiding principles necessary to rule. For working-class people such as Tull, it taught passive acceptance of higher authority from the referee, the governing body of the sport, employers, and political masters. However, sometimes a grand design does not achieve its objective.

C. L. R. James argued that cricket in the Caribbean – the social and ethnic composition of its clubs and their style of play – was a looking-glass which 'at any particular period . . . reflects tendencies in national life'.[11] In *Chariots of Fire* these 'tendencies' are represented as pressures in both sport and society for progressive change away from the stifling know-your-place regime of old. Abrahams, as a Jewish student at the University of Cambridge, which had historically barred Semites and Dissenters from enrolling, was confidently making his place in the new order of things: you were what you did and you did what you wanted to do, unhindered by class or creed. This was, and should be, the measure of you, how you should be judged. The practised egalitarianism of Liddle and Abrahams, as sportsmen, stood as metaphor for the fresh easterlies – cleansing political winds blowing through from revolutionary Russia – that flavoured this inter-war period. The film's narrative spoke against a return to an ethos, in sport or society, that advocated passive acceptance of inequality, hierarchy and elitism. Yet while addressing contemporary social and political tensions it did so in a timid, limited and monochrome style. Where were Harry Edward and Jack London? Indeed, Liddle's record time of 9.7 seconds for the 100 yards at the 1923 AAA championships broke for the first time Arthur Wharton's 'evens' set 37 years earlier.

Incidentally, Liddle too, like Wharton, was buried far away from his birthplace, in China, without a gravestone until his resuscitation in *Chariots of Fire*.[12]

Around Tull, as an amateur schoolboy and as a professional, were other Black sports people, all men. While he was playing for his orphanage team, Joseph Barbour James was a member of the Springfield College school team from Ealing in West London. (I haven't yet come across a Black sports woman, though it would not be surprising or illogical to find Black women participating in sport prior to the First World War, for the simple reason that they were present in British society.) In this sense he was not alone. He would have read, seen, heard, played against other people with brown skin, but not very often nor alongside. He would have recognised their existence and their similar place in the culture of sport in the UK because, injected into evaluation of their achievement, were ideological criteria that had nothing to do with scientific measurement of their success. And, as is often the way with such unfair practices, it made winning sweeter and losing harder.

8

War

'In the global ocean all states were sharks, and all statesmen knew it.'[1] This metaphorical description of political and economic relations between the major imperialist powers of the late 19th to early 20th century gives us a clue as to why the First World War occurred. To provide a straightforward explanation of the origins of the conflict is virtually impossible. The incident which led to Britain declaring war on Germany in August 1914 was the latter's invasion of Belgium and France. It was an incident in a drama that had many stages, sets and acts. And like all dramas, opinions varied on the reality contained within. What can be written without too much fear of contradiction is that the reach and depth of the war was unprecedented. Never before had so many major powers, so many people, so many guns, so much ammunition, so much technology, so much death been witnessed. For those involved there was nothing that could have prepared them. It was an episode for which the phrase 'hell on earth' could have been coined.

To argue that certain powerful people – industrial and finance capitalists, political leaders, militarists – wanted war and were blasé about its consequences would be a shameful over-simplification. Yet what can be argued is that while, in the early to mid-19th century, Britain was the supreme economic power, by the end of the century its pre-eminence was being challenged and threatened by rival economies. This rapid enlargement of national economic competition had a geopolitical dimension: imperialism. Britain, France, Germany, Russia, Japan, the USA and Italy were competing with each other in a global arena. While alliances were formed, rules were not kept. Capitalism in this imperial phase of its expansion was getting out of control. The world was its hunting ground: it

sought to devour peoples, their lands and resources. These were the political and economic conditions in which a political dispute between
European countries widened out, inevitably, into a global carnage.

Walter Tull travelled down from Northampton to London to enlist in
the British Expeditionary Force (BEF) at West Africa House, 64 Kingsway,
Holborn WC2 on 21 December 1914. He may well have been persuaded by a
letter from FA secretary Fred Wall, sent to all professional clubs south of the
River Trent a few days earlier announcing the formation of the 17th (Service)
Battalion Middlesex Regiment (1st Football) – commonly known as the
Footballers' Battalion – encouraging unmarried players to join. Tull signed
for a short service engagement in the battalion, the first Northampton Town
player so to do, with the service number F55 (suggesting he was the 55th
recruit). What drove a man of mixed heritage to join an army that operated
a colour bar; that did not want men of non-European descent in its ranks?

Social debt and personal duty seem to have weighed heavily in his consideration. Signing his Attestation form B 2505, his pledge of military allegiance to king and country, was not the act of a politically naïve man. Tull
felt he owed something to a society that had helped him and his family
when that assistance was most needed; and, as a Folkestone-born adopted
Londoner, he was conscious of his patriotic obligation.

While social debt and personal duty were motivating forces, peer pressure was another hidden hand that pointed Walter toward the recruiting
office. He joined a battalion of footballers and supporters – from the park
player to the international, from club secretary to the young terrace afi-
cionado – in which he would be known, in which he would not need
to continually prove himself to those strangers unable to see beyond the
colour of his skin.

Joining a 'pals' battalion' of fellow footballers, he also bypassed and
short-circuited the numerous obstacles faced by men of darker pigmentation when trying to enlist in the British Army, such as 'failing' the medical,
a ploy used by medical, recruitment and registration officers up until the
1970s:

Medical officer: Read the sight board please.
Man of colour: O, e, r, s . . .
Medical officer: Take three steps back please and start at the line below.
Man of colour: Erm, n, no, m, er . . . p, no q.

Medical officer: Thank you. Do you normally wear glasses?
Man of colour: No sir.
Medical officer: I'm sure you'll be able to do some useful work for the war effort here in England. Next!

In Tull's case, it would have been difficult to justify the rejection of a British-born man in the best of health. The recruiting sergeant, the Army's public face, its mouthpiece and persuader, was paid a fee for every successful addition he encouraged into the ranks. It was not in his economic interest to turn people away he thought might not be up to the task or potential rejects. Indeed, given the poor response of eligible males in the early months of the BEF's enlistment campaign, anyone showing the slightest interest in his spiel would be channelled toward the recruiting office.

Once inside the recruiting office the process of signing-up was a bureaucratic obstacle course of questions and answers, form filling and tedious personal examination, involving the recruiting and medical officers and forms B 2505, B 178 and D 418A. It presented these officers, acting as the Army's gatekeepers, with numerous opportunities to reject, overlook or suddenly find a candidate's deficiencies, from age, height, sight and chest to intellectual shortcomings. They were not working on commission.

The Army, prior to 1914, was an aristocratic institution, officered by upper-class men operating according to the feudal notion of *noblesse oblige*, the men in their charge trained into unquestioning obedience and acceptance of the status quo. Normal army recruiting strategies during the voluntary enlistment period, from 1914 to 1916, were adapted to appeal to working-class men who would not normally be interested in such a hierarchical life in khaki. The BEF was essentially a civilian force, and, to reach the ordinary man, wrote recruiting officer Coulson Kernahan, meetings should be held in the open air. The factory worker, mill hand and miner don't like to stand in a room and listen passively. They feel trapped and are likely to react negatively. A recruiting sergeant on an orange box in the market square is more likely to get his message across. Poems should be recited; patriotic songs sung. He cites T. W. H. Crosland's *Reveille* as *a* suitable example of the former. One verse runs 'And the words ain't "lovey dovey" nor "snookery, cowboy coon" but death and bloody slaughter, and the devil's wrote the tune'.[2] While the reference to 'cowboy coon' was acknowledgement that many cowboys were indeed men of colour, it was yet another demeaning characterisation used to whip up Anglo-Saxon national and racial pride.

Those who had signed in December were asked to present themselves at the Kingsway recruiting office on Monday 4 January 1915 in order to march to their HQ at the Richmond Athletic Ground. However, as Riddoch and Kemp point out in *When the Whistle Blows*, it was a false start for Tull, a member of the eager 120 who turned up in Holborn in their heavy overcoats on this cold winter day.

> Various photographs were taken to . . . cries of 'Goal!','Offside!' and 'Well tried'. The men were disappointed to discover that Richmond Athletic Ground had been deemed unsuitable by the authorities and that another headquarters had yet to be procured. Everyone was disheartened to be sent back home.[3]

The men were asked to reassemble the following Monday. For Tull, it was back to St Pancras for the return train ride to Northampton – after, possibly, a visit to Bonner Road to look up some old faces and friends? A week later over 250 congregated outside West Africa House

> including William Jonas, the Clapton Orient centre-forward, and the Millwall goalkeeper Joe Orme, both of whom had been sent off for fighting in Saturday's FA Cup match at New Cross. Having received their first pay, the men paraded in Keeley Street under the watchful eye of Col. Grantham.[4]

They marched – or, according to some bystanders, swaggered their way – to White City where they billeted in the expansive, draughty, uncomfortable Machinery Hall. Making room the next day for another 350, the battalion was still less than half strength.

It was a collection of talents from clubs, amateur and professional, around the country even though, officially, the battalion did not actively recruit north of the River Trent. Notable professionals included Chelsea's Vivian Woodward, Aston Villa's Walter Gerrish and Tom Barber, Fred Keenor of Cardiff City, Manchester United's Sandy Turnbull, Archie Needham of Brighton and Hove Albion and ex-regular soldier Frank Buckley of Bradford City who would later temporarily command the 17th Middlesex. After the war he went into club management, developing a style of management that was media savvy, authoritarian and financially successful. He reached his apex at Wolverhampton Wanderers in the 1930s where, at playing level and on the balance sheet, he propelled the club from the second to the first division, laying the foundations for it to become, after the Second World War, a powerful rival to Matt Busby's youthful Manchester United.

Most enlisters in the 17th Middlesex, however, were supporters, officials and those involved in the non-playing side of the game. Getting workmates, friends, relatives, neighbours to join up together into 'pals' battalions' had two purposes: generating peer group pressure to conform; and delivering a ready-made bond between recruits. In turn this created a collective discipline better able to withstand and hold firm against the extraordinary physical, emotional and psychological bombardment faced in the field. It was not king and country that held the BEF Tommy's primary loyalty, rather Ken and Curly, his mates with whom he served. And, surprisingly, this was a shift in identity that the Army Council and War Office were instrumental in forging. They recognised that in a mass civilian army with new regiments and battalions, pre-war methods of engendering a regimental esprit de corps – team spirit – through proud propagation of the regiment's martial history would be difficult, if not impossible. Instead, they fostered an affiliation that drew on working-class values of communal and local solidarity. The principal belief of unity in adversity was the magnet around which men pulled together; the totem that carried them further than they would like, want or thought they could go.

The Army Council's toleration and use of proletarian values and customs to maintain morale and sustain a fight-to-the-death culture included the facilitation of working-class leisure pursuits, such as concert parties, fairs and day trips to the seaside. However, it was football, playing and watching, that would quicken the heartbeat of most rank-and-file soldiers; bring them together; develop their fitness and recreate something of a feeling of home in the hell of the trenches. The Army's elite, in the light of the changing nature of warfare where small units, such as platoons and companies, were the primary fighting units, was not slow in recognising how passion for the platoon football team could be, and was, transferred to the battlefield. Hence, kicking the football over the top of the trench parapet was a signal for attack. (What the military authorities didn't want, of course, was the Germans kicking it back and 'war by other means' – a football match – taking place. After the spontaneous Christmas Day matches of 1914, orders prohibiting a reoccurrence were quickly issued and rigidly implemented. The magic of the game in bringing people together was useful only if it was carefully controlled, nourished with discretion and strategically deployed to destroy others.)

This cultural compromise didn't go down well with some of the old guard. Sir Douglas Haig was dismissive of football as a useful instrument, moaning that his troops 'run about and play football [instead of] resting'.[5] Lieutenant General Baden-Powell, founder of the Boy Scouts, viewed football supporters as effeminate, self-indulgent defectives:

> Thousands of boys and young men, pale, narrow-chested, hunch-backed, miserable specimens, smoking endless cigarettes, numbers of them betting, all of them learning to be hysterical as they groan or cheer in panic unison with their neighbours – the worst sound of all being the hysterical scream of laughter that greets any little trip or fall of a player.[6]

While there was a great deal of cultural pressure from wider society and within football, as Wall's letter suggests, on unmarried men to enlist. As a practising Methodist, Tull may have also been influenced by an article by renowned anti-militarist Frederic Harrison. In the *Wesleyan Methodist Magazine*, March 1914, Harrison did an ideological about-turn, warning of the increasing danger of war through rapid rearmament being undertaken by Britain's major economic rivals. To end war once and for all we have to fight war, he now argued. It was an alarming, prophetic and widely publicised essay, explaining Harrison's rethinking of his attitude to conflict, drawing a large response from readers outside the Methodist community, traditionally believers in talk and compromise rather than bayonet and bullet in the settling of international disputes.

The personalities behind the formation of the battalion were three Conservative and Unionist politicians: party grandee and MP for Brentford, William Joynson-Hicks, Privy Council member William Hayes-Fisher and Henry Norris, Mayor of Fulham and property developer who, for a while, was on the boards of both Fulham and Arsenal. (Norris was eventually banned from the game in 1927 for 'financial irregularities' at the north London club.) All wanted the professional game to continue but were conscious of the need to counter the bad publicity the sport was receiving, accused of a shameful record of supplying manpower for the war effort compared to other sports.

As football bosses and right-wing politicians Joynson-Hicks, Hayes-Fisher and Norris, in the formation of the Footballers' Battalion, were responding to pressure from powerful people and institutions, including the Archbishop of Canterbury, *The Times* and the Amateur Football Association, who had used the issue to further denigrate their professional opponents. They crowed how the call to arms was being enthusiastically heeded by amateur footballers: 16 players from Dulwich Wood FC enlisted in August 1914; amateur clubs and leagues cancelled their fixtures, assisting and encouraging their players to don khaki.

This finger pointing at professional footballers for their white feather tendencies continued throughout the 1914–15 season. Col. Grantham, commanding officer of the 17th Middlesex, complained to the FL Management Committee in March that the relatively small number of professionals in the battalion was shameful. The most vociferous of these moral crusaders disapproving of the professional game's continuance and lack of patriotic spirit among its players and supporters were Harold Tennant, Under-Secretary of State for War and Prime Minister Asquith's brother-in-law, and, more so, Christian soldier Frederick N. Charrington of the brewing family. They were supported by, among others, 'several editors of important London newspapers . . . [who] met and decided not to print any descriptions of the contests until the war is over'.[7]

Charrington was obsessive in his determination to mothball the professional game, writing letters to and visiting personally everyone and anyone of note in his address book. Lord Kinnaird, head of the FA, actually left London on 'holiday' to escape. At Fulham on 5 September Charrington tried to take on the crowd in a half-time public speech from the directors' box in which he castigated them for their attendance. Despite efforts to shut him up, he repeated his admonition, eventually being both physically prevented from continuing and escorted from the ground. Yet it was he who first raised the idea of a footballers' battalion.

The Football Controversy, as it became known, continued throughout autumn 1914. The political temperature was not cooled by the War Office's requisitioning of grounds, such as Everton's Goodison Park and Manchester City's Maine Road, for training, stabling and other military requirements. This pressure from above led to increasing tension between football's governing and administrative bodies, the FA Council and the Football League Management Committee. The former gradually relaxed their outright and firm opposition to calls for the postponement of professional football by setting up a war sub-committee; encouraging players without family commitments to enlist; and suggesting clubs donate receipts from friendlies to the Prince of Wales' National Relief Fund. In contrast, the latter remained unmoved, arguing players were under contract and had a legal obligation to their clubs until the end of the season.

There was also a class element delineating the responses of the two bodies to critics of football's continuance: while the FA's elite were largely aristocratic, public school and Oxbridge – president, Lord Kinnaird – and their involvement usually unpaid and voluntary, the FL's power brokers were entrepreneurial, monied club chairmen of business backgrounds who had invested in the game seeking a profit. Income from gate receipts had fallen in the opening months of the season and most were none too happy about seeing more of their wealth diminish through closure of the industry. However, conscious of the need to offset criticism by being seen to contribute to the war effort, in October the Management Committee ruled FL clubs divert 2.5 per cent of gross gate monies to the War Relief Fund.

In Scotland the relationship between the Establishment, their pro-war lobby and professional football was different. The Scottish FA had co-operated with the government recruitment drive. Heart of Midlothian players enlisted en masse in the 16th Royal Scots, an initiative of Lieutenant-Colonel Sir George McCrae, once MP for Edinburgh East. He had managed to get an agreement from Scottish clubs that they would pay enlisted footballers half their wage while they were in the Army and would re-sign them when peace resumed. From the War Office, McCrae won the concession that players would be allowed to turn out for their clubs until the season's end. Joynson-Hicks, Hayes-Fisher and Norris used McCrae's success north of the border as a template for their campaign in England.

In the first few months of the war the BEF was involved in heavy fighting, particularly around Mons in Belgium, suffering serious losses. At the end of October, Secretary of State for War Lord Kitchener issued another call for volunteers both to replace those killed and to enlarge further the BEF. This ratcheted up the pressure to suspend professional football.

Football is an excellent thing, even in time of war. Armies and navies can only be maintained so long as the community fulfils its function of producing means for their support; and healthy recreation is essential for efficient production. A man may be doing his duty in other fields than the front. But there is no excuse in diverting from the front thousands of athletes in order to feast the eyes of crowds of inactive spectators, who are either unfit to fight or else unfit to be fought for . . . Every club who employs a professional player is bribing a needed recruit to refrain from enlistment, and every spectator who pays his gate money is contributing so much towards a German victory.[8]

As a flag-waving patriot with a vested interest in the football industry, the aim of Norris in particular, supported by Hayes-Fisher and Joynson-Hicks, was to somehow absorb this criticism with the least political damage in order to maintain the difficult balancing act of keeping the turnstiles swinging and money flowing until the end of the season. It was important, therefore, to keep up pressure on single players like Tull in their enlistment drive, with the promise they could continue to play for, and be paid by, their clubs until the season's fixtures were completed.

Recruiting sergeants and their bands banged the drum and offered the king's shilling at half-time. Yet the initial push to get players signed up failed. Of the estimated 500 who attended the inaugural meeting of the Footballers' Battalion at Fulham Town Hall on 15 December 1914, a mere 35 enlisted. Of these, ten were from Clapton Orient. Forty-one of their members eventually enlisted, the largest number from any club, including chairman Captain Henry Wells-Holland, a former Mayor of Hackney. In a packed send-off, a gate of 20,000 watched Orient in their final game of the 1914–15 season, a 2–0 win against Leicester Fosse, after which a farewell parade led by the Footballers' Battalion was filmed for posterity.

The organisers of the Footballers' Battalion were hoping to raise a full strength outfit of 1,350. Even with their concerted recruitment effort, the numbers enlisting were not what were expected.

Lieutenant Arthur Tickler travelled around the country visiting professional football clubs and public venues. He was one of several officers given this important job . . . Despite all the hard work undertaken . . . by March [1915] only 122 professional players had joined up.[9]

A powerful, significant opponent to the postponement of football was the Manchester-based *Athletic News*, outraged by crude attempts to portray the game, and those civilian workers that had anything to do with it, as pro-German conspirators.

> The whole agitation is nothing less than an attempt by the classes to stop the recreation on one day in the week of the masses . . . What do they care for the poor man's sport? The poor are giving their lives for this country in thousands. In many cases they have nothing else . . . There are those who could bear arms, but who have to stay at home and work for the Army's requirements, and the country's needs. These should, according to a small clique of virulent snobs, be deprived of the one distraction that they have had for over thirty years.[10]

The *Athletic News*, with left-wing newspapers and journals like the *Socialist Pioneer*, argued that stopping professional football amounted to effective compulsion to enlist, which for all other groups in society was voluntary. By taking away the footballers' living the authorities would be acting unfairly and unlawfully.

In fact, it wasn't until April 1915, eight months into the war, that professional football's administrators succumbed, announcing that normal competition would close until the war was over. Their decision reflected the enveloping mood and momentum of war pervading society, a feeling seemingly confirmed by the first Zeppelin raid over London on 31 May 1915.

Military training of service battalions at this time took months rather than weeks. As agreed, the 17th Middlesex footballers continued to play for their clubs at weekends while undergoing induction and initial training at the huge, ostentatious White City complex in west London, site of the 1908 Olympics. As a battalion team they also played other clubs, including Hampstead Town, winning 3–1. (I mention this for selfish personal reasons only! I coach a youth team for an incarnation of the latter, Hampstead FC.)

Stephen Jenkins in *They Took the Lead* lists the typical daily training routine of the 17th Middlesex as:

06.30: Reveille – Get up, tidy beds, blankets and kit bags for morning inspection. Get tea and biscuits.

07.15: First Parade – Drill (marching about field, both at normal pace and at the double).

08.00: After breakfast personal hygiene is attended to (including shaving).

0900–12.30: Second Parade – Inspection and Company Drill.

1300: Dinner.

1400–16.45: Third Parade – Inspection and Drill.

16.45: Tea.

17.30–18.30: Lecture/Theory.

18.30–20.30: Free Period.

20.30: Everyone must be in camp.

21.15: Lights Out.[11]

It is uncanny how this structure matched that of the orphanage. In Edward Tull's summary of his day, the boys were woken 10 minutes earlier at 6.20 am. After making their beds and washing they were inspected before going about their allotted tasks. On completion they had breakfast. The bulk of the day would then be taken up with the primary daytime preoccupation of childhood and early youth, schooling. At training camp, the most important aspect of basic military education, drilling and marching, took up the best part of the day. Tea at the orphanage was at 5 pm, 15 minutes later than at camp. At both there was two hours' free time in the evening, after which bed. Having been conditioned from the age of 9 to live according to a precise rhythm, the enforced discipline of a camp/barracks regime would not have presented Tull with too many problems of adaptation.

During the autumn of 1914, when optimism that the war would be over by Christmas was still helping people cope with the reality of Britain's first major war against an alliance of European powers since the Napoleonic Wars some 100 years earlier, Stanley Lane of the 13th London Regiment was training at White City. He tells of meagre lunch rations – bread, butter and cheese – badly cooked food – franchised out to a private catering firm – and training in Richmond Park.

Marching through Putney to the immense royal deer park, they would practise extended order drill.

This consisted of running forward a short distance and flopping flat on the ground, then up and on again [a skill second nature to some of today's Premiership forwards] until we obtained our objective – an imaginary on the hilltop ahead.[12]

Lane's account of using Boer War Lee-Enfield rifles, wearing their civilian clothes and long journies to the rifle range in Purfleet, Essex, gives the impression of an ad hoc training programme for the massed ranks of the BEF, hastily put together.

The (shambolic) state of affairs reached tipping point one day after a long, late afternoon march in the rain back to White City. Dripping, hungry and impatient, the trainees were served with boiled eggs, shoulder of mutton and boiled potatoes, all 'uneatable'. 'Mutton and potatoes sailed through the air . . . Windows were smashed and tables overturned. Officers and Military Police appeared, heavily outnumbered'.[13]

In the second half of April, the season over, the 17th Middlesex were sent to another training camp at Holmbury St Mary, near Dorking in rural Surrey, the country house of Joynson-Hicks. With its elevated situation on Holmbury Hill, looking over the Surrey Weald, swimming pool, proximity to leafy lanes, woods, fields of wild flowers and green meadows, it was an aesthetically pleasing and inspiring alternative to urban west London. John 'Cosmo' Clark was commissioned 2nd Lieutenant into the battalion from the Inns of Court Officer Training Corps while it was at Holmbury. The lax disciplinary culture and easy-going ambience shocked the art student.

I am sharing a tent with Wade and we're both very comfortable – the poor men sleep ten to a tent the same size . . . My platoon of sixty men are a mixed mob who haven't (through bad teaching) realised what is expected of them as soldiers. In fact, the whole battalion are the same – the majority of junior officers let unforgivable little crimes slip by without saying anything.[14]

The 17th vacated Holmbury early in July, passing it on to their sister battalion, the 23rd Middlesex (2nd Football), raised in London at the end of June. They relocated in the East Midlands at Clipstone Camp, near Mansfield, a vast, purpose-built site that housed 30,000 soldiers. It was D. H. Lawrence country, a part of Nottinghamshire reliant on mining that would also, in 1915, have controversy thrust upon it with the publication of Lawrence's *The Rainbow*, soon banned and burnt for its sexual content. Copies that survived may well have fetched a high price within the Clipstone nissen huts!

During that unusually stormy month the battalion took part in a football tournament with the Sportsmen's and Public Schools Battalions. In one game on 24 July, between a sergeant's team and a battalion team, Tull played for the latter in a 2–1 win, Captain Frank Buckley refereeing. A couple of months later, in autumn, while the 17th Middlesex were training at their fourth and final location, Perham Down, on the edge of Salisbury Plain, Tull guested for Henry Norris' Fulham in their opening three games in the (wartime) London Combination League.

To raise funds and attract recruits the Footballers' Battalion also played against professional clubs. A match against Archie Needham's Brighton and Hove Albion drew an enthusiastic crowd of over 2,000 who cheered this cocktail of khaki footballers ceremoniously into the Goldstone Ground, led by a drum-and-fife band and 700 soldiers. At half-time Joynson-Hicks and the commanding officer of the battalion, Colonel Grantham, in the hope of enticing more recruits, addressed the crowd with the usual emotive rhetoric coloured by patriotism for the receptive, but drenched in guilt for the hard of hearing.

In terms of games and appearances, both in Britain and France, Tull doesn't feature much in the battalion fixtures. On the Western Front, where the 'Greater Game' was being played with mounting and mountainous fatalities, ever increasing and consistently replenished British forces had attacked German positions around Neuve Chapelle, Aubers Ridge, Festubert and Loos, yet they could not dislodge their stubborn enemy, firmly entrenched in Belgium and France.

On the day that British children around the country were proudly displaying with open palms paper-stuffed Guy Fawkes dummies while eagerly anticipating the evening's bonfires and explosives, the 17th Middlesex were told to ready themselves for their move across the Channel to take part in a continental fireworks show of unimaginable proportions.

Embarking from Tull's hometown of Folkestone in the early hours of 18 November, the bulk of the battalion, now commanded by Captain H. J. Fenwick and part of the 33rd Division, 100th Brigade (New Army), arrived in Boulogne around 3 am. (A division comprised three brigades, each brigade consisting of four battalions.) At the quayside they waited around for a couple of hours in the dark cold and pouring rain until finally ordered to march to Ostrohove Camp, positioned on high ground above the town. For 2nd Lieutenant 'Cosmo' Clark it was not the best of starts to a tour of duty.

> We are in what is known as a 'Rest Camp' and arrived here this morning at three o'clock feeling very tired and fed up. Tramping through the town where we disembarked in the early hours of the morning over frozen cobblestones and up that very steep hill . . . All the place was in darkness and we had a guide with a lantern at the head of the column . . . We are in tents which strange to say I don't find cold. The men are twelve in a tent – we are five and very cosy . . . Within the next day or two we are moving from here to somewhere a bit nearer the trenches. Everybody is excited and keen to get up at least to within sound of the guns.[15]

After a day at the camp, the 17th took a nine-hour train journey to their initial billets at Les Ciseaux, 16 miles from the front line.

Having moved home a couple more times, their accommodation by early December was the 'Collège des Jeune Filles' (Young Women's College) at Béthune, minus the usual occupants! The proximity and duties of extra-ordinarily large numbers of officers and men from a Britain of

> two nations between whom there is no intercourse and sympathy; who are ignorant of each other's habits, thoughts and feelings, as if they were dwellers in different zones, or inhabitants of different planets who are formed by different breeding, are fed by different food, are ordered by different manners, and are not governed by the same laws[16]

caused a privileged few to question their preconceptions.

> I censored about sixty men's letters tonight. It was queer job. Some were very funny and some quite pathetic . . . They all ask for socks and fags – they want both, poor beggars their money all goes on little extra comforts – not beer.[17]

This forced overlap and mixing of the classes would further persuade some officers, such as Tull's Commanding Officer (CO) in the 23rd Middlesex, Alan Haig Brown, that the hithertofore reluctance to commission from the ranks may have had more to do with the maintenance of social hierarchy than military efficiency.

Tull and 2nd Lieutenant Clark, in letters home, wrote of their impatience to get to the Front. Fifty weeks after enlisting and after months and months of training, Lance Sergeant Tull, a member of Major John Pretyman-Newman's 'A' Company and already promoted three times, reached the wet, cold, muddy front line between La Bassée and Loos, near Annequin Fosse on 9 December. Member of Parliament 1910–18 for Tottenham's neighbour constituency Enfield, it would be likely that Pretyman-Newman would have known of Tull prior to commanding him.

The day before taking up their front-line combat position the 17th Middlesex had been transferred to 6th Infantry Brigade, 2nd Division, commanded by Brigadier General Arthur Daly. (It is not known if his batman was Terence McCann!) Other battalions in the Brigade were 13th Essex, 1st King's and 2nd South Staffordshire Regiments. The reallocation was part of a full-scale restructuring of troops that attempted to incorporate fresh New Army divisions into experienced regular battalions. The revision was instigated largely as a consequence of the lessons learned at the Battle of Loos in September 1915 when 60,000 British soldiers had been killed, the majority civilian enlisters.

The War Diary of the 17th Middlesex records the battalion suffering their first casualty on 11 December, 21-year-old Private James MacDonald from Fife, killed by machine gun fire while on sentry duty. Just under two weeks later, 22 December, the 17th Middlesex were relieved out of the front line, taking up billets at Beuvry, a few miles out of the killing zone.

For the next five months it was in and out of the combat zone, usually spending about three weeks at the front line, around the Givenchy/ Béthune/Festubert region of the Pas-de-Calais. Festubert, 'a pestilential part of the line'[18] where Tull spent the best part of February, was particularly disliked because of its marshy terrain, preventing trenches being dug deep. 'Grouse butts' or 'islands' were built of sandbags above ground instead, giving poor protection and security. At some points around Givenchy the German trenches were just 20 yards distant. Tull described his location to the new principal at the NCH, Mr Hodson-Smith: 'The part of France we are in could at no period of the year be termed beautiful & just now it is looking very bleak and desperate, with a super-abundance of mud on all roads'.[19] Over a period of four weeks the troops would usually engage in a cycle between the front line, second line and reserve trenches, and rest.

Action on the BEF section of the Western Front was continuous as both sides attempted to gain ground and supremacy. Between November 1915, when the 17th Middlesex arrived, and the following May, when Tull was shipped back to England, the British forces extended their troop strength and trench lines to cover a distance of over 85 miles. Vivian Woodward, the ex-Spurs forward whose transfer to Chelsea prompted Spurs to sign Tull, was wounded on 22 January 1916 and also hospitalised to the UK. At the end of February, during the Battle of Verdun, in order to help the French move troops to sectors of intense fighting, the 17th Middlesex took over a sector formerly allocated to their Gallic allies around Calonne, quickly replacing French names for the trench system with more homely versions such as Middlesex Walk and Footballers' Avenue.

Soon after, the battalion was visited by its co-founder Joynson-Hicks bringing a goodwill message from King George V. The curiosity of their founding father to see his boys fighting at the Front did not go to plan. Arriving inappropriately dressed in top hat and frock coat, 'Jix' brought a smile to the men's faces.

> Clearly dissatisfied with the view of No Man's Land afforded by a trench periscope, Joynson-Hicks put his head over the parapet. At that moment a shell landed nearby. Fortunately for everyone present the shell was a dud. The next one, which landed a little further away, was not. In the subsequent explosion, parts of a nearby brick wall were tossed high into the air. Maj. Gen. Heath and Col. Fenwick immediately 'began to contemplate what might happen to them, if he were killed, and they put an early end to this part of the tour'.[20]

Also serving round and about were poets Edmund Blunden, Siegfried Sassoon and Robert Graves. In the second verse of *Two Fusiliers*, Graves' few words vividly describe the hostile environment.

By wire and wood and stake we're bound
By Fricourt and by Festubert,
By whipping rain, by the sun's glare,
By all the misery and loud sound,
By a Spring day,
By Picardy clay.

The hazardous geography of this posting, the constant enemy action of gas attacks, sniping and shelling, was a savage, startling induction to an indeterminate reality that, so long in hiatus, contrasted sharply with the tone of relative innocence expressed by Tull writing home early in 1916.

> For the last three weeks my Battalion has been resting some miles distant from the firing line but we are now going up to the trenches for a month or so. Afterwards we shall begin to think about coming home on leave. It is a very monotonous life out here when one is supposed to be resting and most of the boys prefer the excitement of the trenches to the comparative inaction whilst in reserve.[21]

'The excitement of the trenches'! This was written before the Somme, still some months off but being planned. His letter illustrates the naïve optimism characteristic of the pre-July 1916 BEF Tommy, an emotion soon extinguished in many through brutal experience.

The War Diary of the 17th Middlesex, written by officers in the field for the benefit of the War Office in London, provides a daily snapshot of life and death. Away from the survivalist intensity of the front-line trenches, the 17th participated in numerous football matches, tugs-of-war and other athletic competitions and military training. Sometimes there would be football matches on consecutive days. In April the battalion won the prestigious Divisional Cup, beating to embarrassment the 34th Brigade Royal Field Artillery, 11–0. Tull did not play.

Officially, at least, life off the front line was full-on and being redefined, reappearing as a fantastical chimera amidst the slaughter. Yet reminders of the latter were never far away. During early April, the battalion was detailed to repair damaged trench lines in the vicinity of Souchez, a location littered with decomposing cadavers after heavy fighting between French and German troops. Time in the trenches was a mixture of monotony, terror, routine, sleeplessness, fatigue, humour, camaraderie, vermin infestation, wet feet, bully beef and biscuits, letter writing, death, hope and despair. For both sides the day would begin before dawn with 'Stand To' and a wake up call to their adversaries across No Man's Land, usually shelling, often a volley of bullets, known as 'morning hate'. Thus begun, the subsequent repertoire of exchanges would expand, taking many forms: bullets, shells, gas, explosions, mortars and shrapnel. In between, or simultaneously, depending upon the intensity of fighting in the sector, troops would clean their weapons and attend to trench repairs, such as filling sandbags, strengthening walls and supports. Ferrying in food and munitions, troop rotation, enemy trench raids and laying explosives under and alongside these trenches would usually take place at night.

Perhaps in hindsight Tull would have accepted the 'monotony' because 'the excitement of the trenches' within a couple of months paralysed him with 'acute mania'[22] (shell shock/trench fever), or what today would be diagnosed as post-traumatic stress syndrome. Admitted to Lady Hadfield's Anglo-American Hospital at Wimereux on 28 April – his birthday – he was transferred back to England on hospital ship *St. Denis* on 9 May 1916. His 28th birthday 'celebrated' nine continuous days on the front line. He had served nearly seven months in cold, snowy, wet France without leave.

Another soldier of the 17th Middlesex, Private Allen Foster, writing to his spouse, recognised war was

> very trying on the nerves, and lots of fellows get what they call shell shock. What with the continual bursting of shells etc. and the thundering of the guns, they seem to go all to pieces. So I am afraid you won't last long out here.[23]

There was a military hospital at Sandgate, Folkestone. It's not known if Tull was a patient there. Presumably it would have helped his recovery if he was, because his elder brother William, who lived in Dover, would have been able to visit. However, as a sapper in the Royal Engineers, he may have been actively assisting the war effort elsewhere.

While there are no documents – letters, diary, notes, medical reports – recording Tull's confinement, another soldier, Bombardier Bertram Spires, for a while spent time in the same hospital (at Wimereux) as Tull, also suffering from shattered nerves and emotional exhaustion. His diary entries provide an illuminating and informative insight into the cause and symptoms of his illness, as well as the conditions and daily routine within the military hospital:

On 21st/22nd [August 1917] I was on duty from 22.30 to 02.30. Fritz started to gas us at 23.00 and continued the caper until 02.00. Frank Heys relieved me at 02.35. At 03.30 shell hit corner of telephone pit killing Heys and Lt Collins, both in pit, and severely wounding the Major, Lt Worth, Bdr Lovall and Sigmn Reid. Stunt started at 4 am. Lt Jones, Howard and self sorted out the mess. Up to the elbows in blood and felt a bit 'done up' by breakfast.

Poperinghe 26th August 1917
Arrived hospital. High temperature and horrible dreams of various messes up the line. What a treat to be able to lie out full length on a bed of wire netting. Diet condensed milk and water 3 times a day. August 27th loaded up in Red Cross motor and taken to clearing station and then to No. 12 CCS [Casualty Clearing Station] Proven. Carried about on stretcher as though I was a serious case. Finally passed on to No. 10 ward Medical. Fritz bombed locality during the night.

Proven 28th August 1917
Arrived No. 12 CCS. What a treat: Double marquee chrome lined and electric light. Stretcher beds on trestles. Canadian nurse. Sponge down and back to bed once more. Splendid camp near railway. Food good. Sardines or ham for breakfast. Beef and veg for dinner followed by rice pudding. Tea; jam, jellies and tinned fruit. Supper cheese and cocoa. Bread and butter each meal. Up 2nd Sept and started to make myself useful. Barber for the ward. West Indian's hair some stuff to cut. Snowball a great case for possy and tales of Jamaica. Made beds and assisted in pantry.

Wimereux 5th September 1917
Red Cross train from Proven. Motor from train to hospital (14 General). Raining. Had vapour bath and supper then bed No. 12 ward, which in peace time was the servants quarters over the garage of

Hotel Splendid near the Casino. Two mins from beach. Lovely view from ward window of sea and coast up to Cap Gris Nez. Camp on cliff.

Boulogne 12th September 1917
Arrived by motor from Wimereux (5k) No. 1 Con camp (2k from Boulogne). Camp of marquees surrounded by gardens. Met Baxter. Had to return to Wimereux on foot with three others for cap comforters. What a gag. Took road along cliffs and returned via 53 Cen hospital so that Canada could get his clobber.[24]

Spires' reference to fellow patient Snowball also supports anecdotal and other rediscovered evidence that larger numbers of Black soldiers served on the front line than was previously accepted.

While Spires had less than three weeks to recover, without a ticket home to 'Blighty', Tull had the relative luxury of five months across the Channel without bullets, bombs, gas vapours or shells terrorising his waking moments.

Recent research into the treatment of soldiers in military hospital during the First World War by Dr Ana Carden-Coyne, *Men in Pain* (2008), found that the wards of the wounded were far from havens of care and recuperation. Using soldiers' diaries and letters she cites references to brutal and insensitive treatment by doctors, surgeons, nurses and physiotherapists. Surgeons and physiotherapists seem to have been most feared, the former referred to as Captain Hack or Captain Scalpel, while some physios believed if pain wasn't inflicted their treatment wasn't working. The medical staff worked in a conveyor belt environment where their primary duty was making their patients soldiers-fit-for-the-Front as speedily as possible. Mental and emotional breakdown owing to war fatigue and experience was treated seriously as a military, rather than a medical, problem.

Writer Elaine Showalter regards shell shock/acute mania – male war neurosis – as disguised reaction to the unbearable pressure of assuming a martial identity in which 'being bloodthirsty, and forever thinking how to kill the enemy'[25] was a rule.

In an interview with poet laureate Andrew Motion in the *Guardian G2*, 5 November 2008, the oldest British survivor of the trenches of the Western Front, Harry Patch, a Lewis gunner with the Duke of Cornwall's

Light Infantry, recalled how, in the relentless carnage of Passchendaele, he would not shoot above the legs unless he felt his life was directly threatened. In this small, persistent but profound abrogation of his duty Patch circumvented military destruction of his civilian compassion and humanity.

Private Cox, like Patch, survived Passchendaele, the only member of his platoon to do so. And like Patch, held firm his compassion and respect for life. In Italy for the Battle of Piave, October 1918, he

> saw a young German coming towards me and at that moment I just could not murder him and lowered my gun, he saw me do so and he followed suit, shouting 'what the h. . . do you want to kill me for, I don't want to kill you'. He walked back with me and asked if I had anything to eat? At once the relief inside was unspeakable, and I gave him my army rations and my army biscuit.[26]

This humane behaviour, the polar opposite response to what was being taught to new recruits, was certainly not an example of the 'bloodlust' that was meant to be instilled in induction training. Yet, in the civilian army of the BEF of 1918, it was not as irrational and life threatening as it seems. All combatant armies – with the possible exception of the United States – were institutionally war weary and peopled with soldiers, usually conscripted, increasingly willing to take the law into their own hands through disobedience, refusing orders, self-harm, mutiny and desertion.

Ben Shephard (2002) argues that as many as 50,000 men were treated for nervous complaints during the second half of 1916, a period roughly corresponding with the First Battle of the Somme. Richard Smith (2004) notes that approximately 200,000 soldiers were discharged from the Army on psychiatric grounds during the war, by the end of which there were 20 specialist Army hospitals dealing with shell shock compared to one in 1915.

Medical staff didn't fully understand the cause, effect or treatment of the epidemic of neuroses witnessed during the conflict. Writing to a friend in 1915, the Oxford Professor of Medicine commented 'I wish you could be here in this orgy of neuroses and psychoses and gaits and paralyses. I cannot imagine what has got into the central nervous system of the men'.[27] Various explanations were constructed, ranging from cowardice to damage of the brain caused by nearness to explosions of heavy shells. Treatment often consisted of dismissing individual pain and eradication of symptoms through electric shock, the medical response as brutal as the cause. Siegfried Sassoon was more fortunate. Suffering from neurosis he was sent to the relatively enlightened regime at Craiglockhart, Scotland, where Army psychologist W. H. R. Rivers was using a revolutionary approach: talking to his patients. The relationship between Rivers and Sassoon is brought to vivid life in Pat Barker's novel *Regeneration*.

Some medical staff suggested that nervous complaints were signs of racial degeneracy, the complainants lesser individuals unworthy of equal treatment. This eugenicist view legitimised any medical response, however brutal, because the recipients were defective, not full citizens of the human race. It was a view that chimed with White supremacists' attitudes toward people of colour. We can only hope Tull, a Black man with war neurosis, was not under the care of such doctors and nurses.

After hospitalisation and recuperation, passed fit and able by Army medical staff, Lance Sergeant Tull was posted to the 27th and 6th Battalions of the Middlesex Regiment for three weeks respectively in August and September 1916. These secondments were time fillers while he was stationed at the regiment's depot in Mill Hill, north-west London, before his return to France and posting to the 23rd Middlesex (2nd Football) on 20 September. The 27th in particular acted as a reserve battalion for the 17th and 23rds to which soldiers would be posted while in England before returning across the Channel.

The 23rd was fighting on the Somme. Raised in the capital in June 1915, it was sent to France in May 1916 after 11 months' training. Following on four months later, laden with kit again, Tull's step may have beat time with boyhood memories of happier, peaceful times as he once more embarked from his hometown port. When he and Edward had left, making that difficult unwanted journey to Cannon Street station and the orphanage 18½ years earlier, neither had known what to expect; marching to war, an innocent in November 1915, he had been beaten to breaking point as punishment for his naïvety. Leaving Folkestone now, there was no mystery concerning the future. Stepping ashore at Boulogne later that day in the fading autumn light, at the mid-point of the first Battle of the Somme, his eyes were wide open, his mind aware, his sensitivity hardened, his self scarred.

The emotion that linked the journey to Cannon Street station in 1898 with this 1916 crossing to France was fear. Tull had encountered many sit-uations, legs unsteady, that entailed digging deep, drawing upon hidden reserves of strength: the death of his mother at 7, the death of his father at 9, the loss of Edward aged 11, the brutal hostility of the crowd at Bristol a few months after his League debut at Spurs as a 21-year-old. Succumb-ing to 'acute mania' was, perhaps, not the result of his inability to face the unprecedented horror of the front-line trenches but an accumulation of the emotional trauma he had witnessed and attempted to deal with during the previous 19 years. And on this list of debits we have not included the tension brought about by the common, day-to-day racism, a fixture of life in the UK from which there was no escape.

Lance Sergeant Tull joined his battalion in the field on 29 October 1916. From his arrival in France on 20 September it is probable he was undergoing further training. Fortunately, he appears to have spent just three weeks engaged in a battle that, today, still has a ghostly resonance whenever 'Somme' is spoken, heard or read. It recalls, echoes and reverberates death. It is not first and foremost a region of Picardy. It is a collection of letters emblematic of pointless slaughter.

Tull's original battalion, the 17th Middlesex, began their first period on the Somme front line at the end of July. In their last major action in that conflict, at the Battle of Ancre, November 1916, the battalion was ordered to attack the German defences on the Redan Ridge. Prior to the men going over the top, the attack had been postponed a number of times because of unfavourable weather. Some officers believed it should not go ahead at all. However, General Sir Douglas Haig thought success would help morale at home and alleviate pressure on the Russian and Romanian fronts. General Gough gave the order to proceed. At 5.15 am on 13 November, with vis-ibility down to 30 yards because of dense fog, in the cold dark the men climbed up and out into No Man's Land. According to the War Diary entry

> All ranks were extremely cheerful and success seemed inevitable.
> [They] went over in waves, 'B' and 'D' Companies playing mouth
> organs. [By 7.20 am] a certain amount of confusion existed . . .
> various units were all mixed up in 'No Man's Land' . . . [and] the
> machine guns were causing a lot of trouble . . . The enemy killed
> heavily various parts of our line. [28]

Their attack failed, with the battalion suffering nearly 300 casualties. Only 79 men returned from over 400. In his War Diary entry the commanding officer of the 17th Middlesex put the near decimation down to 'fog' and 'uncut wire' and the added disorientation caused by the movements of the Royal Scots and East Yorkshire Regiments, which confused his men. Some casualties were almost certainly the result of fire from the battalion's own machine-gunners and those of the Scots and Yorkshire Regiments. Thankfully, the writer didn't use the terms 'friendly fire' and 'collateral damage'.

It wasn't until mid-September that the 23rd Middlesex first saw action on the Somme, at the Battle of Flers-Courcelette. The battle was notable for the first use of tanks in the history of warfare. (They were so called because of their similarity to metal water containers.) The British committed to the offensive every one they possessed, 49. It was a daring and costly experiment. Technology was basic: communication was by carrier pigeon, top speed half a mile per hour and mechanical breakdown frequent. Only 32 got into action; just 15 were utilised in the battle itself. Fortunately, the infantry, including the 23rd Middlesex, achieved its target of capturing the villages of Martinpuich, Flers and Courcelette, as well as High Wood. These possessions came at a terrible price, the 23rd Middlesex losing half its men including their commanding officer, Lieutenant Colonel William Ash. It was a savage de-flowering of the virgin battalion.

It suffered further casualties at the beginning of the following month in the opening stages of the Battle of Le Transloy Ridges, the British making painful progress in the face of worsening weather, glutinous mud and determined German resistance.

In common with other Middlesex Regiment battalions both the 17th and 23rd had been culled of great numbers fighting on the Somme. Military historian Everard Wyrall, writing in 1926, noted 'In no other series of battles fought on the Western Front were more Battalions of the Middlesex Regiment engaged than in the operations on the Somme in 1916'.[29]

At the close of the battle in Picardy, northern France in mid-November, the slaughter of young men of all combatants stood at 1,115,000. There isn't a comparison against which we can scale this contrived catastrophe. Perhaps the nearest, in terms of the numbers of people killed, is the Asian Tsunami of 2004, a disaster of apocalyptic proportions, in which 300,000 were drowned, buried or battered to death by the machinations of nature.

This long, unprecedented, planned battle quickened a change in class relations within this new, predominantly civilian British Army. Front-line ranks and officers shared the depravities of prolonged trench fighting. War poet Siegfried Sassoon commented that 'social incompatibilities were now merged in communal discomfort'.[30] Fighting in the hellish opening days of the Somme, during which the British Army lost full football stadia of men, Rex Gee recorded in his diary that he

> Scrambled from shell hole to shell hole, through wire and craters and *awful* havoc, *terrible* sights. Terrible slaughter by the hun artillery and machine guns . . . Hun trenches simply myriads of shell holes . . . Stopped bullet on my head about 8 am, dazed for an hour or so, steel helmet saved my life without a doubt . . . Was only survivor from second charge . . . Cannot understand how anyone escaped alive . . . Thus the 1st stage in the battle of Fricourt . . . Haven't got much left in the way of nerves. Had no sleep for 50 hours and no proper meals or rest . . . Everything was *horrible ghastly* and *awful*. May I never experience the same again . . . Words cannot express the horror of it all.[31]

Twelve years later Gee's great-nephew Geoffrey Streetfield was indeed trying to 'express the horror of it all' as an original cast member of R. C. Sherriff's controversial anti-war play, *Journey's End*, performed at the Apollo Theatre in December 1928. The play, drawing on the author's experiences of the conflict was a great success, and still is, having recently had an extended West End run.

What, then, should we make of the carnage in Picardy in the summer and autumn of 1916? The death toll was unprecedented in its swift, exponential rise where each dawn lit upon a mangled array of corpses. The following year another five-month long, set-piece battle of attrition took place at Ypres, known as Passchendaele. Three-quarters of a million men lost their lives, limbs and sanity. Such was the industrial scale of killing that the First World War came to be known for a short optimistic period after the Armistice as the 'war to end all wars'. (Because there were not enough men to fight another?)

Battle plans are usually thought-out, strategic designs where luck and other phenomena associated with the high street bookies are not supposed to feature. However, ego and gambling seem to have been the two primary characteristics of much decision-making by commanding officers at the highest level. Feeling let down, angry and frustrated, soldiers in all armies mutinied, individually and collectively, in the latter stages of the war.

> The real explanation of the fury felt by the soldiers, which invested the war with a more savage character, is to be sought elsewhere. In the face of gas, without protection, individuality was annihilated; the soldier in the trench became a mere passive recipient of torture and death. A final stage seemed to be reached in the whole tendency of modern scientific warfare to depress and make of no effect individual bravery, enterprise and skill.[32]

If the barbarism of war had reached its apogee in 1914–18 with the mass-kill power of the weapons used, such as the various types of deadly gasses – the first gas masks issued were socks soaked in urine! – aeroplane bombing and the accuracy and potency of heavy artillery shelling, this new-fangled, machine warfare still needed to re-condition the mind of the ordinary soldier. Brigadier General Crozier describes the mentality wanted in his men.

> Blood lust is taught for the purpose of war . . . by doping their minds with all propagandic poison . . . to bring out the brute-like bestiality which is necessary for victory. The Christian churches are the finest 'blood-lust' creators which we have, and of them we must make full use.[33]

Having, against the odds, survived the year, Tull arrived back in England on Boxing Day, 1916, his first official leave. How beautiful it must have seemed compared to the mud, bones and trauma of France and Belgium. He had made it through, and the fairy on top of the tree for the 28-year-old was his recommendation for a temporary commission by his commanding officer, Lieutenant Colonel A. R. Haig Brown, a respected soldier, sportsman (friend?) and military theorist. His endorsement is significant; it would have carried a great deal of weight higher up the military line in France and at the War Office in London. It may have been at Haig Brown's suggestion that Tull applied, given the rules prohibiting men of colour from 'exercising any actual command or power'.[34] Having this particular commanding officer's name on his MT 393 application form was an important factor in Tull being accepted for training.

War poet Robert Graves believed the ingredients above all others that delivered respect from superiors were courage and bravery. An overabundance of both almost ensured promotion from the ranks and in Tull these qualities were not lacking.

Alan Haig Brown had been a pupil at Charterhouse, excelling in sports rather than studies. The headmaster was his father, Reverend Dr W. B. Haig Brown, who had moved the school from the Smithfield area of London to its present site in rural Surrey. Sport was an important feature of the curriculum and one of the deciding factors, no doubt, in the reverend's pressure upon the governors of the school for a move to a site surrounded by green fields. The relocation paid off handsomely, personally and collectively: Alan Haig Brown developed into an all-round athlete, playing football, cycling, sprinting and long jumping; the alumni team, Old Carthusians FC, won the FA Cup in 1881. Despite his predilection for strenuous sport over concentrated study, Alan Haig Brown followed his father's footsteps and graduated with an MA in Classics from Pembroke College, Cambridge.

While assistant master at Lancing College, 1899–1915, in June 1907 he married Violet Mary Pope, the second daughter of a wealthy Dorset brewer. His favourite sports were hunting, shooting and fishing, writing (published) prose and poetry on these pursuits. He encouraged his pupils in field sports rather than football, to which his attitude was pragmatic and utilitarian. The latter was a means to an end – fitness – rather than an end in itself – getting in touch with one's primeval essence – which field sports facilitated.

> The first two years of my public school career were spent among dogs and ferrets when the classrooms were closed, then I was kicked (literally) on to the football and cricket grounds and did not escape again for nearly ten years. Unpleasant but good for me, of course – the two things always go together.[35]

A friend of England cricket legend Prince Ranjitsinhji, 'a wonderful shot and billiard player', Haig Brown was a very good footballer and played as an amateur for a number of first class football teams, including Corinthians, Spurs, Clapton Orient, Brighton and Old Carthusians, but his attitude, noted above, to team sports was ambivalent and contradictory. He felt competition hindered sportsmanship, winning being more important than the pleasure of taking part. Yet he writes in *My Game Book* (1903) of his Christmas excursion to Glasgow with the successful, accomplished and almost exclusively public school and Oxbridge Corinthians FC. Published in the same year, his collection of poetry on the theme of sport, *Sporting Sonnets*, acknowledges the low opinion many other scribes had of the national pastime while eulogising the physical benefits of playing football.

> O let the poet in scornful verses weep
> The lesser joys that captivate our race,
> Proclaiming thee as useless for the fight:
> Thy sons and thy son's sons shall surely reap
> The harvest of thy strength, thy speed, thy grace,
> And garner it in limbs of iron might.[36]

At Lancing Haig Brown commanded the Officer Training Corps (OTC) while serving, from 1906, as Lieutenant, 2nd Volunteer Battalion, Royal Sussex Regiment, Territorial Army. Instrumental in the development of the Officer Training Corps in public schools, universities and the Inns of Court, in 1915 he published his views on what training should and should not consist of, especially in time of war. A firm believer in the healthy body, healthy mind philosophy of the Muscular Christians, an ethos practised at Tull's orphanage, he suggested public schools and universities should include integrated military and physical training as a compulsory part of their curriculum.

> The physical training that is so important a feature in the training of our Armies would do an incredible amount of good to Public School boys. Many of our Schools dabble in physical training, none take it seriously, some neglect it altogether. A definite feature of future OTC work should be that every single boy in the school must have twenty minutes to half-an-hour a day of such training under proper instruction and discipline. If this exercise is allowed for out of the overcrowded time-table of work, both brain and body will be the richer for it, but it will be of no benefit if it is not regular and daily.[37]

It is not surprising, then, that Tull's qualities as a patriotic soldier (enlisted rather than conscripted), athlete and man appealed to Haig Brown's sensitivities, personifying excellent officer material. (Another poem in *Sporting Sonnets* lambasted Irish MPs at Westminster who had been disloyal during the South African War, 1899–1902.) To Haig Brown, an experienced trainer of young soldiers and attuned to recognising leadership qualities, Tull embodied those traits that would see the British Empire successfully through the war: loyalty to king and country; a Muscular Christian education; and the emotional steel and physical tenacity of the sportsman.

A battalion's commanding officer shaped its character. A rigid disciplinarian using punishment and fear to maintain order ruled without respect; a lax leader, susceptible to persuasion and indecision, would be equally derided. Achieving respect and authority was a difficult and fine balance. Haig Brown achieved this. Recommending Tull he was aware of the close relationship the two were expected to have. The ex-schoolmaster was, as an overtly God-fearing soldier, pulling closer another of similar mind and belief. Surprisingly, given their different histories, their trajectories had been remarkably alike in some respects: both excelled at sport; both were patriotic enlisters; both had been guided by Muscular Christian principles in their moral pathways. As head of the battalion, Haig Brown would play the role of older brother to his new subaltern, keeping a watchful eye, sensitive to his inexperience and unique tribulations. Roderick Haig Brown describes his father as 'an Edwardian: one of the young, the strong, the brave and the fair who had faith in their nation, their world and themselves'.[38]

On his death those who had served with this 'brave Edwardian' wrote of their respect and fondness. His first Adjutant stated 'never was a CO so entirely beloved by all who knew him; I am sure it will help you to know in what affection, and almost reverence, everyone who served in the 23rd holds Colonel Haig Brown's memory'. 'Nor did he, like some COs, consider his men at the expense of his officers. 'None of us subalterns ever wished to serve under a finer man',[39] wrote one of his officers. Major General Sidney Lawford, commanding the 41st Division, noted he 'was one of the very best commanding officers, always ready for whatever was to be done, cheerful under the hardest conditions and was ever ready for the welfare of his men'.[40]

In each formative era and dimension of his life, as a child, footballer and soldier, Tull had attracted the affection of influential men: Stephenson,

Chapman and now Haig Brown. For reasons known only to themselves but at which we can guess, they chose to champion his cause. Without these figures rooting for him, Tull's life experiences would have been less rewarding and his achievements more difficult to attain. Indeed, without Haig Brown's support it is probable that his application for a commission would not have been submitted, accepted and realised in a regular British Army regiment. However, while Tull and his supporters were changing the world from within, wider society was also changing – none more so than the Army, an institution hitherto rigidly structured by class.

Recruitment pressure after the losses of men in the battles of 1914 impelled the Army, by early 1915, to relax its rule that a candidate for a temporary commission have post-elementary education. Attention now would also be given to the abilities and service records of men in the field. This opened the way for men such as Tull who had not studied beyond their first school but who could nevertheless get someone to vouch for their educational capability. To illustrate the change that occurred, Chang-boo Kang's study of the Royal Warwickshire Regiment (RWR) found no officers educated in state school prior to 1914. By 1918 the proportion of commissioned men from working-class backgrounds was greater than it had ever been. Over 50 per cent of RWR officers had attended state institutions, one of whom – 2nd Lieutenant J. Critchley – was an ex-pupil of Wolverhampton Orphanage School. Commissioned in March 1915, he was killed on the first day of the Battle of the Somme, 1 July 1916. The 17th Middlesex also had a commissioned officer from an orphanage background, 2nd Lieutenant Frank Bonathan, who was killed in action at the Battle of Arleux on 28 April 1917. Bonathan had been promoted while serving with the 23rd Middlesex. He died on Tull's birthday.

The officer corps expanded exponentially during the war. In August 1914 the British Army had 28,060 officers. Between then and December 1918 approaching 230,000 soldiers were commissioned as combatant officers, just over 16,500 of these into the Regular Army. The rest – the vast majority – were appointed to temporary commissions in the BEF. Chang estimates that 14.6 per cent of officers lost their lives, a proportion of one officer to every other rank. As the war progressed, the number of officers per month killed or injured increased, with 1918 seeing the greatest number of battle casualties. 2nd Lieutenants and Lieutenants comprised the largest proportion, not surprisingly given their growing importance and responsibility in

the field for combatant operations. And the first year was the most dangerous, as Tull's experience testifies.

In his signed application form MT 393 dated 25 November 1916, one
week after the cessation of the Battle of the Somme and its 400,000 British
casualties, Tull states he wants to serve in the infantry or Royal Flying
Corps wireless equipment department. His 'good moral character' is cer-
tified by solicitor A. J. Darnell, founder of Northampton Town Football
Club. A. Jones, the club secretary, who gives his occupation as chief assistant at Stimpson Avenue School, testifies Walter has attained a good
standard of education.

Darnell is an iconic figure in the history of Northampton Town, a solicitor with town centre offices in St Giles Square. It is an indication of the
esteem in which Tull was held that Darnell was willing officially to confirm
his trust in his former employee's moral character. Mr Jones' input is a little
more unclear. He gives the impression that Tull had reached a decent grade
of education at Stimpson Avenue School! What is completely transparent,
however, is the willingness of both to assist Tull.

The six weeks of leave before training commenced at Gailes were
a period of grace in which Tull could push from his mind, temporarily,
his memory of Hell – to forget would have been impossible – and catch
up with William, his wife Gertrude and daughter Gladys at 59 Greenfield Road, Folkestone, visit Edward in Glasgow and attend the Wesleyan
Church in Claremont Street before catching a train to the Ayrshire coast
to spend time with 'Mater' Warnock, Clara and Bill Beer and his sisters in
Girvan.

It was during this period of leave and officer training, according to the
Glasgow Evening Times, 12 February 1940, that Tull signed for Rangers of
Glasgow.

He could also have spent time with his Rushden landlady Miss Annie
Williams at 26 Queen Street. We do not know if she and Walter were lovers,
but the physical and emotional affection of a woman, the comfort of her
arms, the feel of her skin, the sight of her bare back, her warm breath on
his neck, could never have been more deserved. Not to have someone with
whom to share intimate longings and pleasures would have been a further
deprivation. While the camaraderie and loving friendships of soldiering
were compensation, for most this only accentuated desire for the opposite
sex.

On 6 February 1917, reporting to No. 10 Officer Cadet Battalion, Gailes, Ayrshire, Scotland Tull began his four-month training course, opening a new chapter in British military history. In peacetime, officer training at the Royal Military Academy at Woolwich or Royal Military College Sandhurst usually lasted between one and a half and two years. This was condensed to three and six months once the pressing need for commissioned men was felt during the summer recruitment drive of 1914.

Second Lieutenant W. Paterson was also a cadet at Gailes, having reported for training to the remote collection of Nissen huts and assault courses on the coast between Troon and Irvine exactly one month earlier, on 6 January. Also near Kilmarnock and Ayr – places of leisure cadets would visit in their time off – he describes 'a rather barren spot near to the sea coast . . . [and] some of the finest golf courses in Scotland'. (One of which, Turnberry, Edward Tull was a member of. It's possible he and Walter played during the latter's spell at Gailes.) Though the weather was generally 'cold and bleak' it had beautiful views. Out to sea the 'Isle of Arran or "Paddy's Milestone" was visible with its snow covered peaks'.[41] Paterson was not being dramatic in his description of the climate.

The winter of 1916–17 was the coldest for many years, the beginning of February particularly so. An anticyclone developed over the UK sucking down Arctic northerlies. Clear night skies and snow cover contributed to the coldest spell of the winter, with temperatures dropping to –10 degrees C and below in various exposed parts of the UK.

Despite the brutal weather, Paterson's (and Tull's) 'four months of varied and strenuous [but] . . . very enjoyable . . . training'[42] consisted of, among other things, practical infantry work, including rifle practice, Mills bomb throwing, trench planning and building, map reading and other essentials of warfare.

In order to graduate, candidates were expected to be self-confident; show initiative and leadership; be competent in training and commanding a platoon of men, attacking and defending, drilling and discipline, and map reading; and, importantly, demonstrate a thorough knowledge of the King's Regulations as contained in the *Manual of Military Law*. Classes examining the rules governing eligibility to officer cadet battalions would have been interesting, surreal even, had the instructor scrutinised pages 198 and 471 of the 1914 edition dealing with soldiers not of 'pure European descent', who were categorised as *aliens*, 'negroes and persons of colour'.

To cope with the ever increasing need for new officers and to replenish the culled stock, officer cadet battalions were created in February 1916, facilitating the greater variation in the class background of men becoming officers. More lower-middle-class and working-class candidates were accepted for commissions from the ranks of both volunteers and conscripts, conscription having been introduced in January 1916 with the enactment of the Military Service Bill. All men from their teens to their 40s could be called up. Despite the buds of an imperfect, restricted meritocracy briefly showing themselves, the chance of attaining a commission was still primarily influenced by class more than any other factor. Changboo Kang, in his study of the British infantry soldier during the First World War, found that over a quarter of officers in the Royal Warwickshire Regiment were commissioned before reaching the age of maturity at 21. To be appointed at such a young age, with all the responsibility attached but without the time to accumulate the necessary experience in the field, officers would have to have had post-elementary education, a requisite not in the CV of most working-class recruits. Tull, for instance, was 28 when he applied for his commission.

On passing his practical tests and 'none too easy'[43] exam, Tull graduated on 29 May and was appointed to a commission as 2nd Lieutenant in the Special Reserve of Officers on 30 May, becoming the first Black infantry officer in the British Army. Though formally attached to the 5th Battalion Middlesex Regiment, he was posted back to the 23rd Battalion, joining them on 4 August and serving with them until his death.

Returning an officer, Tull would have immediate power and influence. This would be utilised, broadly, toward the twin, connected aims of raising morale and maintaining firm discipline. Second Lieutenants usually commanded platoons, assisted by a Platoon Sergeant. Important duties were the physical and emotional welfare of his men and implementing orders received from his superiors. In relation to some of the youngest conscripts and volunteers, this included being in loco parentis. Generalising this duty of care to his men, among the more onerous tasks would be monitoring by frequent inspection the condition of their feet – unwashed and imprisoned in wet socks and sodden boots for days on end!

> We have to know all there is to know about the feet, socks, food, cleanliness and health of each one of our men, and it has been

made part of our religion that an officer must never, never, never, eat, sleep or rest until he has personally seen to it that each man in his command is provided for in these respects.[44]

Commissioned in the second half of the war, Tull would have had more freedom to act upon his initiative, a licence less available to 2nd Lieutenants appointed prior to the First Battle of the Somme. The officer's bible, the ss 143 training manual, published in 1917, recognised and reflected the change in social relations that had taken place during the war with the practical devolution of officer power toward the commander in the field. Subalterns were expected to be 'quick to act, taking real command on all occasions, issuing clear orders, and not forgetting to see them carried out'.[45] The character, confidence and respect of the platoon commander should be stamped all over his men. This would show itself in their fighting capabilities. The driving force in creating a fighting spirit, an esprit de platoon, he would be 'blood thirsty, and forever thinking how to kill the enemy, and helping his men to do so'.[46] The daily routine of a platoon commander was determined by his battlefield position. If he and his men were in the front line, daylight duties would be focussed upon repairing and strengthening trench fortifications and maintaining equipment. At night, intelligence gathering, raiding and supplies were the primary concerns. Officers had access to wartime luxuries such as a wider range of foods and alcoholic drinks, freedom of movement, brothels and other creature comforts largely unavailable to the men.

> Lieutenant B. Lawrence (1st Grenadier Guards) and his brother officers had a dinner in their dug-outs in the front at Trones Wood, Somme, in November 1916 and praised their servants for the quite wonderful dinner prepared despite the circumstances: 'This was quite a wonderful performance consisting of soup, stew with vegetables, stewed fruit and sardines on toast, and drinks and coffee. It is amazing how well, and what a quantity of courses, our servants manage to cook on a coke brazier, in a dug-out where there is hardly room to turn around.'[47]

These privileges, alongside the statutory conditions attached to their status – four meals a day instead of three, more power, pay, leave, obedience and deference – also held a negative charge as a source of friction with the rank and file – in turn damaging morale and fighting ability – if not handled with diplomatic sensitivity. (Kang argues officers violating military law were also treated more leniently at courts-martial.)

Tull's battalion was in action at the Battle of Messines, 7–15 June, a prelude to the Flanders offensive. The objective of General Plumer's 2nd Army was to capture the village of Messines and with it the strategically advantageous ridge from which the Germans were able to overlook British lines. The plan was to blow the Germans away with the detonation of 19 mines under their positions: 'Burrowing by British soldier-miners and uniformed navvies had been going on for eighteen months. The longest tunnel was over 700 yards, the deepest more than one hundred feet'.[48]

The 23rd Middlesex were detailed to advance to within 75 yards of enemy trenches at 2.45 am and lie down. A heavy barrage would be saturating German positions; at 3.05 am a rocket would be fired giving the signal for the detonation of the 19 mines two minutes later: 'Many of the explosions had a radius of destruction of 200 feet. Thousands of German soldiers were killed. Many went mad. Thousands more were taken prisoner. And one more ridge was captured'.[49] Four days later, having secured 80 of those prisoners and lost half its strength (again), the battalion was relieved out of the line taking no further part.

At the end of July the 23rd Middlesex, part of 123rd Brigade, 41st Division, commanded by Major General Sidney Lawford – 'Swanky Sid' to his men because of his habit of wearing full dress uniform and medals – was thrown into the Third Battle of Ypres, better known as Passchendaele. This offensive by British, Australian and Canadian troops sought to take control of Belgian coastal ports.

A major push by the British, the Battle of Pilkem Ridge, began before dawn, 31 July, after ten days of heavy bombardment of German trench lines. The 41st Division captured Hollebeke, consolidating their position around the Ypres–Comines canal. At various points the front line had advanced between 200 and 800 yards. The 23rd were relieved on Friday 3 August, after sustaining yet more casualties: 17 killed, 122 wounded and 4 missing. However, enemy resistance and the unusually heavy rains prevented an immediate and decisive breakthrough. The battle for, and human fertilisation of, the soil continued until November.

Fortuitously linking up with his (unrecognisable?) battalion one day after they had come out of the line, Tull shares his feelings with his brother, writing on 10 August from the YMCA, Officers' Rest House, France. His revealing thoughts are quoted in full.

Dear Eddie. I'm once more enjoying life some miles distant from the front line & if that jade 'rumour' doesn't err, we shall be a few miles still further away by this time next week. Our crush are expecting some weeks rest to re-organize, so if that comes off I shall be very lucky.

I joined the Battalion on Saturday when they came back from the line & was posted to 'D' Coy.

On Monday at noon my Coy. Cmndr detailed me to go up & inspect the portion of the trench 'D' Coy were to hold as we were to go up that night. Three other subs & myself started off about 1.30 but Fritz was shelling the back areas like a demon & after dodging about from trench to trench we got fed up & struck across country. We were lucky & got to a tunnel which would help us on our way considerably. Unfortunately the outlet was flooded & we got soaked up to our hips, but H_2O is less dangerous than shrapnel or HE. From the flooded place we had to go along a track knee deep in mud, but Fritz let us alone & we reached retired HQ safely, where the Adj't of the Batt. to be relieved made us welcome & gave us tea. From there our way lay across open ground formerly no man's land, now one mass of shell holes. It was impossible to proceed in a straight line anywhere of more than one to two yards. Our guide did his best & after being on our way about 5 hours from the time we left camp, we reached our destination a distance of about 3 miles taking a direct line. My Coy. arrived soon after 1 am & then I was informed I would not be wanted. You can guess I wasn't long in getting a move on, but by the time I was back in the tunnel I was well knocked & begged a seat amongst some RE Signallers. I found they were all from Scotland. Didn't Glasgow Corporation form a Coy? This was the crowd. Anyway the Serg't was from Burntisland & had been at school with Manning of Northampton. They refreshed me with a good tot of rum, & sat talking until nearly 5 am when I pushed on for the nearest village. I must have been within 200 yards of the place when I nearly collapsed, & suddenly realised I'd had nothing to eat since lunch, about 17 hours since. A YMCA Canteen was my salvation & I succeeded in persuading the orderly to cook some sausages & make a cup of tea. The meal revived me & after a rest I proceeded on my journey, reaching the transport lines about 8 o'clock. I had a good tub and got into bed, but couldn't sleep, so dressed again & walked into a small town nearby for lunch. Didn't I sleep that night through! All the guns in France couldn't wake me.

This morning one of our chaps arrived from the line after taking part in a good piece of work. Keep your eyes on the papers & perhaps you will read about it. Anyway, he's bound to get a decoration. Enclosed is a 1 mark note which he gave me as a souvenir. You can guess where it came from. I'm also sending a label which I cut from a box. Note the date!

Cannot stop to write more now. Have had all your letters. Love to all. Yours affectionately, Walter.

PS I am applying for transfer to the BWI when the Batt. come out tomorrow.

This understated letter is one of two surviving Tull wrote from the Front. His first in 1916, discussed earlier, was optimistic and lacking information about action. In this YMCA missive he recounts a dangerous assignment and talks of 'reorganisation' after the decimation of his battalion in the Battle of Messines. In letters written to his sister Cecilia, Jean Finlayson (Tull's niece) believed her uncle had, by this time, developed a hatred for the war.

The 'inspection', a mission undertaken with the other subalterns – 'subs' (2nd Lieutenants) – was life-threatening and extremely tiring, not to mention uncomfortably wet. After his nostalgic drink and chat with the Scots signallers, his lack of food and rest began to bite hard but still he had to *persuade* a cook to knock something together for him. Attempting sleep he finds he is in that post-exhaustive state where the body utilises its adrenalin for fuel. A day and a half after he had set out to assess the trench to be used by his Company, having eaten one snack and one meal, he eventually laid his head on a pillow and slept. 'All the guns in France couldn't wake' him.

He also alludes to another mission with his reference to the (German) label from a box, presumably taken while in a captured German trench.

In a letter to Edward by Major Poole, after Tull's death, his commanding officer eulogises about his qualities.

> [Tull] was very cool in moments of danger & always volunteered
> for any enterprise that might be of service. He was recommended
> recently for a Military Cross. He had taken part in many raids.
> His courage was of a high order and was combined with a quiet &
> unassuming manner.[50]

Tull's YMCA letter reflects his 'quiet and unassuming manner'. He talks of life-threatening experiences as if they were expected daily occurrences, which, of course, they were. But then we are told, posthumously, that he was putting himself forward for such missions. In light of this knowledge it does not come as a surprise that his superior officers were willing to ignore Army rules and regulations in recommending and enabling his commission. He literally led his men from the front.

The 23rd Middlesex took an active part in the Battle of Menin Ridge Road, 20–25 September, part of the Passchendaele offensive. Like Messines, they were involved in the opening action. Unlike Messines, radically new battle tactics of 'bite and hold' were to be utilised. This entailed attacking a particular section of the enemy line and holding onto it, rather than a mass attack on a broad front. It succeeded spectacularly, with the majority of the objectives achieved early on. This achievement is more remarkable when we consider the conditions in which the men were living and fighting.

> That the troops could endure and yet be fit in such awful sur-
> roundings – mud, and gaping shell holes and craters full of filthy,
> putrid water, the whole countryside waterlogged and with scarce
> a dry rag to their bodies, or an inch of dry ground anywhere –
> speaks volumes for their grit, determination and endurance.[51]

The physical cost to the 23rd Middlesex was 15 killed, 121 wounded and 23 missing; the emotional cost incalculable, continuing long after the guns had quietened. For some of these victims the war ended only at death.

Four days into the battle the depleted battalion were relieved out of the front line, taking rest and shelter at Micmac Camp. They would not see action again until they took over from the Durham Light Infantry at

Nieuport Bains on 11 October. Here they engaged in active patrol work across the canal that fed into this coastal town, reconnoitring German positions. Unbeknown to those involved, the night patrols and raiding parties would be ideal practice for what was to come. The 23rd Middlesex left the Western Front for the last time in 1917, on 15 October.

The Third Battle of Ypres – Passchendaele – lasted over three months. Eight kilometres of territory was gained at a cost of 37,500 casualties per kilometre. Earl Haig, the British commander in chief, considered the campaign a victory. All ground won was lost in the German spring offensive begun in March 1918.

After the killing fields of Flanders, five divisions of General Plumer's 2nd Army – including what was left of the 23rd Middlesex – comprising 14 Corps was posted to the less frenetic beauty of alpine northern Italy. The fresh young conscripts, filling spaces left by names that would, once the guns had fallen silent, feature in roll-calls upon stone-chiselled memorials the length and breadth of the UK, could comfort themselves that the casualty rate in this theatre of war was 1 in 21, compared to 5 out of 9 on the Western Front. And comfort had to be taken from wherever it could be found.

The British troops, along with six French army divisions, were to help the Italians stem the advance of Austrian and German troops which had broken through, at the end of October, at the Battle of Caporetto pushing the front line back to the River Piave, threatening Venice, Padua and Rome. Leaving Esquelbecq, France by train on 15 November, the 23rd Middlesex crossed the Italian border four days later as an unsuccessful attack by the Austro-Hungarians on Trentino was petering out.

Captain Phillips, 10th Battalion, Duke of Wellington's Regiment, while captivated by the unspoilt attractiveness of rural southern France as the troop train progressed toward Italy, was mesmerised by Italy: 'By the country we were greatly impressed, its grandeur and beauty being quite equal to that of France. Italy's people were full of hospitality and could not do more for us'.[52] After detraining at Isola Della Scala, on 22 November, the 23rd Middlesex marched the 105 miles to Giavera in their allotted sector around Montello, a hill in the lower Dolomites that overlooked the 800-metre-wide River Piave.

Conscript Private Cox, the only surviving member of his platoon at Passchendaele, did not remember Italy with affection. On disembarkation, after being pelted with rotten eggs and tomatoes, he was 'force marched'

100 miles upon feet bleeding with broken blisters. 'The Colonel sat on his horse-back and shouted "fall out you forage men, see to the horses first – they cost £50 each, you men cost nothing".'[53]

Captain Phillips and Private Cox both arrived by train but that is where the similarity ends. The officer would have travelled in a carriage, possibly first class; the private in a goods or cattle truck along with at least 20 others, sleeping head to feet, toileting at halts along the way where they could also stretch their legs.

Lieutenant General A. N. Floyer-Acland who served in Italy with the Duke of Cornwall's Light Infantry described the terrain of the British sector in his diary.

> An oval, hog backed hill some eight miles long from east to west and three and a half to four miles from north to south. It rises sharply out of the plains to a maximum of about 650 feet . . . On its north eastern and northern faces it is bounded by the river Piave, the river varying in breadth from about a mile to 300 yards. Under the south face of the Montello runs the Brentello stream . . . Traversing . . . north and south, parallel to one another, are twenty roads, little more than cart tracks . . . all of which lead out . . . to the big, well made road which completely encircles the hill.[54]

Floyer-Acland preferred the infinite charm of Montello, a glorious rest after Flanders.[55] The continuous arrival of reinforcements to the Italian Front during November was heralded in *The New York Times*:

> So many French and British troops are now in Northern Italy that the novelty of their presence has worn off, although the sight of their regiment marching toward the front or to their cantonments evokes the same tremendous enthusiasm as when they first arrived.[56]

The objective of the combined Italian, British and French forces was to hold the western bank of the River Piave and, if possible, sabotage enemy manoeuvres designed to consolidate and further their foothold on the eastern bank. The Montello sector acted as a linkage point of the Italian front line, joining the northern portion from Mount Tomba to Lake Garda with the defensive line of the river close to Venice, defended by the Italian 3rd Army.

(Down in the south of the country, at Taranto, the British West Indies Regiment were working as labourers. It was a posting that would eventually erupt into mutiny and rebellion over their status and treatment.)

It was more difficult to build Western Front-style trenches on the Montello owing to the rocky ground. Shelter and protection was given by dug-outs and the natural cover of woods and shrubs. It was only by the riverbank that troops were relatively more exposed to fire and shelling. The inability to get solidly entrenched did not produce unbearable additional risks because German and Austrian front-line positions were much farther away than was usual on the Western Front, between 1,000 and 2,000 yards. However, because of the hilly topography the enemy did have an uninterrupted view of the British, French and Italian lines and back areas from a distance of four miles.

The real, indefatigable enemy, though, was the inclement weather. With the ice-cold River Piave as the front line, this natural foe was ever present. Holding the line aganst the German and Austrian forces on the eastern bank necessitated reconnaissance and raiding parties, designed to capture prisoners and intelligence. Missions, more often than not led by subalterns, meant wading across the fast-flowing series of waist- to chest-high streams that constituted the Piave, usually at night, very often bare-chested with a smothering of whale oil or thick grease. Wearing minimal clothing and kit, various methods were used to ford the river, including ropes, linking arms, piggy back, thumb-sticks with wrist loops and long sticks. Boats and rafts were tried but found to be unsuitable or unmanageable. Wading tended to be the preferred option. Francis Mackay feels 'these river crossings were a new and unwelcome experience for the British troops, perhaps the worst many experienced during the war'.[57]

To pre-empt hypothermia and frostbite, sodden soldiers returning from missions would be wrapped in warm blankets or hauled into barrels of hot water in specially constructed steam rooms resembling Turkish baths. Norman Gladden of the Northumberland Fusiliers describes a raid on 8 January 1918. His 15-man patrol, on an intensely cold night, each wearing white overalls, underwear, socks and boots, carrying a rifle and one bandolier of ammunition,

> waded the first stream, a gliding torrent of icy water not more
> than a foot deep. Hitherto the scrunchy snow had struck a deep

chilliness through my boots; now the icy bath penetrated to my skin and took away all feelings from my legs . . . a much bigger stream, some thirty yards or so across, now obstructed our progress, and we began with little thought to wade across. It was shallow at first, like the previous streams, but deepened towards the middle. The water was now swirling nearly to our waists. Now surely it would get shallower, but as we approached the opposite bank the waters continued to rise and the current to rush upon us with terrific spate. Taken by surprise, I found myself struggling up to my neck . . . For a few moments I completely lost my balance and felt myself swirling along hopelessly like a cork. It was touch and go for I was no great swimmer. I saw the bank coming up towards me and then, when right in the grip of the eddy, a hand shot out and I found myself scrambling up the shingle to safety . . . [T]he officer, accompanied by an NCO and a runner, went forward to reconnoitre.[58]

Two weeks previously, at 7 pm on Christmas Eve 1917, Tull led a raid through the numbing rapids under cover of darkness. The 23rd Middlesex War Diary entry for that day reads: '2/Lt Tull & fighting patrol cross river, short reconnaissance raids, no sign of enemy'.[59] This is the first known, documented occurrence of a Black officer leading White, British Army infantry troops on a wartime mission.

On New Year's Day, at ten past six in the evening, under the stars Tull once more commanded troops on a life-threatening mission into enemy territory. He and 26 men from his 'C' Company crossed the Piave to attack and destroy any forward positions of Austrian and German soldiers. After his party had waded through and given the all-clear behind them, some 30–50 minutes later, would come 327 of their 23rd Middlesex Battalion colleagues, led by 2nd Lieutenant Pickard, intent on throwing a pontoon bridge across the river, laying telephone wires, raiding enemy positions in the village of Fontigo, capturing prisoners for intelligence gathering and attending to and recovering any wounded or dead.

Tull and his men were the advance guard, the bush clearers, the risk takers. Any opposition to the 23rds' operation would be met first by them. Bombardier Charles Bertram Spires, who also served in the Montello sector, mentions the raid in his diary entry for New Year's Day, 1918:

Beautiful day of sunshine, sharp frost and deep snow. Erskine and I completed the metallic circuits on both OP lines. Saw Fritz plane come down after scrap in clouds struck mountainside and rolled down. Spent from 17.30 to 23.00 on top of mountain on look-out and to signal A' & 'B' batteries when rocket went up to let us know that the boys had crossed the Piave and required the assistance of our artillery. Cold job too. Fritz didn't show much fight and we were not called upon. Have heard since we captured 3 prisoners one was stupid so was drowned.[60]

Tull returned with his party intact. Major General Lawford, commanding the 41st Division, visited the battalion two days later to congratulate them on this mass incursion and capture of prisoners, officially citing the Black 2nd Lieutenant for his bravery.

I wish to place on record my appreciation of your gallantry and coolness. You were one of the first to cross the river prior to the raid on 1/2 Jan. 1918 & during the raid you took the covering party of the main body across and brought them back without a casualty in spite of heavy fire.[61]

In so doing, Lawford acquiesced in formally defying Army regulations which barred men of colour from 'exercising any actual command or power'.[62] The Major General was not the archetypal First World War 'donkey'. He was liked by his colleagues, and the nickname Swanky Sid seems to have been attached with affection by his men rather than mockery. On inspecting his front-line troops 'at one trench the parapets were too low, they would not allow General Lawford to go down the front line as it was too dangerous'. In the same diary from which this quote is taken Major General L. H. R. Pope-Hennessy who, in 1916, served under Lawford as a General Staff officer grade 2 at 41st Division HQ, wrote 'My General is a splendid person. Everyday he is in the front line trenches . . . very different to some Divisional commanders who never go into the trenches and trust the reports that all is well'.[63]

After the war Lawford settled in Florida with his wife and their only child, Peter, who was never formally educated. The latter became an actor starring in many box-office hits and was a boyfriend of Marilyn Monroe and various other household-name screen stars, as well marrying a Kennedy and becoming brother-in-law to John. In Hollywood he was part of the legendary Rat Pack of Frank Sinatra, Dean Martin, Sammy Davis Jr and Joey Bishop.

Peter Lawford's fourth and last wife, Patricia Seaton, after his death in 1984 wrote a biography of her husband in which she tells of his close attachment to his father. In discussing his adolescence she recalled an episode which highlights an example of Sir Sidney Lawford's benign influence upon his son: 'Peter teamed up with some local Black teenagers, hanging around a car park where, to earn pocket money, they would offer to wash cars. Friends of the Lawfords warned Peter and his parents against such associations, emphasising it would damage his prospects as an aspiring actor.'[64] The story illustrates his (English) parents' progressive attitudes to questions of colour, a stance that did not go down well in the more overtly racist culture of the 1930s USA, providing a clue to understanding the Major General's positive attitude to Tull.

It is probable that it was to the 1 January mission that Major Poole and 2nd Lieutenant Pickard were referring when they informed Edward that his brother had been recommended for the Military Cross.

A secret report of the raid was written for General Headquarters by Lieutenant Colonel Haig Brown, commanding officer of the 23rd Middlesex, in which he praised the work of Tull's group: 'The covering party established themselves in a forward position 300 yards after crossing without any opposition, and did excellent work until withdrawn'.[65]

Haig Brown's account would have provided the substance for 14 Corps' GHQ Intelligence Summary for 2 January 1918 which reiterated the overall success of all elements of the raid:

> Our patrols crossed the Piave . . . opposite Fontigo without difficulty. On the far bank hostile patrols were met with and considerable rifle and machine gun fire encountered. Our patrols withdrew after inflicting casualties on the enemy . . . Our casualties were insignificant.[66]

This dent in the enemy's defences was much publicised by the British government which was eager to propagandise early British successes in their assistance of the Italians. A *New York Times* article, 8 January 1918, was headlined 'British Are Active on the Piave Front': 'British patrols have once again crossed the Piave River, the War Office announces. They forced passages at various points, causing alarm in the enemy lines'.

Military historian Everard Wyrall wrote of the 'well organised raid on the Austrian trenches'[67] in his two-volume history of the Middlesex Regiment. General Plumer, commander of British forces in Italy, made special mention of the action in his quarterly report published in the *London Gazette* on 9 April 1918.

> On 1st January our biggest raid was carried out by the Middlesex Regiment. This was a most difficult and well planned operation, which had for its objective the capture and surrounding of several buildings held by the enemy to a depth of 2,000 yards inland . . . The recrossing of the river was successfully effected, and our casualties were very few.

Both sides continued to shell, bomb and raid over the winter.

Throughout January and February British, Italian and French forces harassed the German and Austrian positions on the east bank of the river, constantly sending out raiding parties. During January, the British tried 26 times to cross, only nine being successful. It isn't known how many, in total, Tull was involved in.

After making headlines in the Alps, Tull and the 23rds returned to France, arriving on 8 March. They found a (youngish) civilian army with plenty of attitude that was 'above all, an army of trade unionists, less malleable than their regular [army] forebears'.[68] This wasn't a surprise. The growing discontent with the war, the dwindling number of regular soldiers and the ever-increasing number of working men from the industrial cities and organised workplaces involved in the period of the Great Unrest immediately prior to the war, speeded a momentum recognisable before Tull and his battalion left for Italy. However, by 1918 the widespread disillusionment – among all the armies involved in the conflict – was increasingly obvious.

> The future seemed to be an endless vista of battles, each one worse than the last . . . the morale of the army had settled onto a bottom of fatalistic despair, in which the majority carried on mechanically, waiting for their next wound, while the weaker members went under, either to lunacy, desertion, or self-inflicted wounds.[69]

Within a fortnight, on 21 March, the Germans launched the first phase of their big push, Operation Michael. The aim of this spring offensive – the Second Battle of the Somme – was a decisive, final, war-ending victory.

On 23 March, in the front line at Beugny, the 23rd Middlesex came under heavy bombardment in the morning, suffering large numbers of casualties, before being attacked by incessant waves of determined German infantry. Severely weakened, the battalion retreated, taking up a new line astride the Beugny–Frémicourt road. With the German advance gathering pace they bivouacked the night at Favreuil aerodrome, a village British troops had held since the previous March. The day's losses amounted to four killed, 39 wounded and 12 missing.

The aerodrome fell the next day and a further retreat took the 23rd Middlesex back to Monument sector, on the Bapaume–Sapignes road. Again casualties were high: 13 killed, 57 wounded, six missing, six missing believed killed and 22 missing believed wounded. On 25 March, after two days and nights of bloody hell, they woke – if sleep was at all possible – once more to the sound and impact of shellfire, followed by further surges of grey-clad soldiers. Abandoning their position, they withdrew across the Arras–Bapaume road, taking up positions behind a railway embankment at Bihoucourt and Aichet-le-Petit. The day was characterised by chaotic retreat, compounded by the abandonment of the 41st Division HQ at Achiet-le-Grand. By midday 'Our Brigades and Battalions were very mixed up and, in addition, troops of many other units, including old Labour Company men and other oddments of that sort were intermingled in the constant stream which poured through'.[70]

It was in this defensive action that 2nd Lieutenant Walter Daniel John Tull lost his life. His death is officially recorded as somewhere 'in France or Belgium'. The Black Briton had been in action since November 1915. Lieutenant Colonel Alan Haig Brown, commander of the 23rd Battalion, who recommended him for his commission, was also killed. The War Diary entry reads:

Monument [sector] March 25 8 am: Shelling of our line commenced. Enemy attacked shortly afterwards compelling the troops to withdraw . . . The enemy continued to push forward in massed formation. It was not until the units on both the left and right had retired that the Battn commenced an orderly withdrawal by platoons. Casualties were heavy and the enemy reached the trenches in considerable numbers . . . The Battalion assembled at GOMMECOURT 25/26th. 13 Killed. 61 Wounded. 30 Missing. 1 Missing believed Killed. 7 Missing believed Wounded.

Killed – 2nd Lt W. D. Tull, 2nd Lt T. J. Petty.

Wounded – a/Capt W. Hammond MC, Lt R. A. Green, 2nd Lt G. Barton.

Missing believed Killed – Lt Col. A. R. Haig-Brown DSO.

Missing – a/Capt. B. T. Foss MC.

Evacuated Sick – 2nd Lt J. Jennings.

The 23rd Middlesex, along with the other battalions of the 41st Division, were relieved out of the front line that evening. 2nd Lieutenant Pickard, commanding 'C' Company, in a letter of commiseration written to Tull's brother and next of kin, Edward, three weeks after death, stated his battalion's soldiers had been ready to follow their Black officer.

Allow me to say how popular he was throughout the Battalion. He was brave and conscientious; he had been recommended for the Military Cross & had certainly earned it; the commanding officer had every confidence in him & he was liked by his men. Now he has paid the supreme sacrifice pro patria; the Battalion & Company have lost a faithful officer; personally I have lost a friend. Can I say more! Except that I hope that those who remain may be as true & faithful as he.

Leicester Fosse goalkeeper, Private T. Billingham, ears ringing from the incessant whistle and crescendo of enemy shelling, mouth dry with fear, struggled heroically in retreat to carry the deadweight of his platoon commander, shot through the head, to their reserve trench line. Honoured by his burden, desperate to ensure a respectful, mournful burial, breathless he risked sacrifice. Advancing German soldiers closed ground, their voices audible. Billingham's instinct for self-preservation kicked in. With tears of regret he discarded the former Spurs and Northampton Town star to the swamp-mud, concave-cratered battlefield. Ducking and weaving like a spinning top, Billingham fled for his life. Tull's prone, bulleted, blackening, bloated body, riddled with maggots, reeking of nauseous decomposition, lay abandoned amid uncounted others.

Up to his death the lone Black 2nd Lieutenant in the British Expeditionary Force had spent eight months at the Front without leave, firing bullets, dodging them and more. Never had his neat footwork, applauded as a player, been more crucial . . . or ultimately pointless.

Most inhabitants and soldiers of the fighting zones had not experienced or witnessed industrial death on such a scale as occurred in the First World War. Alan Sillitoe in *Raw Material*, a book described on its cover as 'part novel, part autobiography', tells of his family's involvement in the 1914–18 conflict, in particular the First Battle of the Somme into which the British military chiefs of staff allocated four armies comprising 1,500,000 men. Of these around 60,000 were killed or injured on the opening day, 1 July.

> The English war machine had spent nearly the whole of the nineteenth century limbering up for the super-butchery of the Great War . . . But not until 1914 did the military hone up their ineptness, and sniff the possibility of real home-brewed slaughter.[71]

For many working-class soldiers and their families, the Somme was confirmation of a reality they hadn't wanted to recognise: they were expendable. Had the deaths of the Somme Tommies, mown down by German machine gunners with a clear field of fire, been the result of glorious failure, outwitted and overcome by a superior enemy, their loss might have been assuaged. Sillitoe, condemning the military establishment with brutal clarity, rages the slaughter was the inevitable outcome of conceited complacency and incompetent planning, the mother of all balls-ups.

To illustrate, he cites the case of Meaulte, adjacent to the Somme front line. In February 1916, the village residents were told to clear out. Instead of wrapping some brie and bread in a hanky, tying it to a stick and getting their marching boots on, they sent a petition to George V communicating a collective *non*! The monarch passed the buck. Sir Douglas Haig, commander of the BEF, was ordered to make a decision. With uncharacteristic conciliation he allowed the inhabitants to stay put with the proviso they remain in their houses for three days from 1 July! (With the thank you note from the citizens of Meaulte came one from Erich von Falkenhayn, commander of German forces?)

If the horrific cull of young British men marked the symbolic death of the UK as a world power, as Sillitoe argues, it also speeded social change in which the organised working class no longer accepted their collective function as a source of profit for the great and the good.

The date of Tull's death is given as 25 March 1918. Aged 29, he was at the peak of his physical prowess. He has no known grave. His name is inscribed on Bay 7 of the Arras Memorial to the Missing, Faubourg d'Amiens War Cemetery, Arras, France. It commemorates some 35,000 servicemen from the United Kingdom, South Africa and New Zealand who died in the vicinity of Arras between the spring of 1916 and 7 August 1918 whose bodies were not recovered. It also has 2,650 graves, including soldiers from the West Indies Regiment and German army.

His obituary in the *Rushden Echo*, 12 April 1918, entitled 'Famous Footballer Killed', included a side-profile photograph of the handsome, smiling officer in military fatigues. It recalled his transfer to Southern League Northampton Town from first division Spurs for 'a heavy transfer fee', his 'fine physique', his commission and (incorrectly) his 'mention in despatches' (possibly confusing the honour with Lawford's citation). The closing sentence read: 'The deceased sportsman was an officer and a gentleman every inch of him, and the news of his death will come as a great shock to his many Rushden friends'. His death was reported in regional and national sporting and football newspapers from west to east, Glasgow to Folkestone.

His next of kin, brother Edward, was devastated. His daughter, Jean, told of the day, 17 April 1918, her watery-eyed father recalled receiving the dreaded telegram from the War Office 'regretting the loss . . .'. 'The worst moment of my life', he tearfully sighed, continuing 'I just couldn't believe it . . . the thought kept going through my head, Walter is dead, Walter is dead'.[72]

As well as at Arras, Walter's name is also inscribed on the Folkestone, River and Dover War Memorials, Kent.

9

'Not of pure European descent'

The policy of restricting the entry of recruits of darker pigmentation into the British Army in the First World War, as outlined in the 1914 *Manual of Military Law*, was a legacy of debates within the Establishment during the latter half of the 19th century over the desired ethnic composition of the armed forces. Fortunately, a coincidence of history has allowed a glimpse into the mindset and culture of the British military elite of that century in its thinking on questions of 'race'.

The first Black man appointed a Wesleyan missionary in West Africa was Grenada-born Henry Wharton, who was in fact of mixed heritage. The father of Arthur, the world's first Black professional footballer, he was appointed, in 1873, Wesleyan chaplain to General Garnet Wolseley's Asante invasion force during Britain's imperial conquest of the Gold Coast, now Ghana. Many of these soldiers would have been locally born and trained.

As spiritual guide to Wolseley's Methodist troops, Henry Wharton, of Scottish and African-Caribbean heritage, came into daily contact with the men in his pastoral care. What they thought of him, and he them, we can only guess. If many of these rank-and-file soldiers of the British Army had the same kinds of views about people, colour and 'race' as typically enunciated by the officer class, Wharton's ministrations would not have been easy. However, that would be an easy and unfair generalisation, given many would not have been White or necessarily robotic in their thinking. In his biography of Henry, William Moister makes the point that his subject inhabited two parallel universes in which he was an outsider: to Africans he was a European because of his light skin and European style of dress and manners; to Europeans he was a Black man because of his brown skin.

General Wolseley, who was to receive honorary degrees from Oxford and Cambridge for overseeing the 'most horrible war I ever took part in',[1] argued that Africans were intended to be White men's slaves. 'The Negroes are like so many monkeys; they are a lazy good-for-nothing race.'[2] At the War Office, he pleaded in 1886 'let us keep our British Regiments strictly British . . . If ever we begin to fill our ranks with alien races our downfall will most surely follow'.[3] Such opinion, informed as it was by the development of ideas about 'race' and a universal pigmentocracy, a wild distortion of Darwin's thesis on evolution, denied the British Army's historical experience. As J. D. Ellis has noted, Black soldiers had fought at Waterloo and before.

> During the eighteenth century the 29th's [Worcestershire Regiment of Foot] black soldiers were present as drummers at every major action the Regiment fought, from the infamous 'Boston Massacre' of 1770 to Saratoga in 1777, and as marines at 'The Glorious First of June' in 1794. In the nineteenth century [they] accompanied the Regiment to the Peninsula . . . serving at Albuera in 1811, an action in which over half the Regiment was wounded or killed . . . In other regiments black soldiers can be found serving alongside their white peers in prominent battles, including Assaye, Badajoz and Waterloo.[4]

In 1858, the young Garnet Wolseley, writing candidly to his mother from a posting in India, tells of his sexual attraction to a local woman, an 'eastern princess [serving] all the purposes of a wife without all the bother [of] some [European] bitch'.[5] This selective gradation of people of colour – Asians, acceptable; Africans not – is a frequent characteristic of British imperial culture and is noticed elsewhere, in sport, for instance where Prince Ranjitsinhji is remembered and revered as a cricketer, while African athlete and footballer Arthur Wharton, also of royal stock on his mother's side, was quickly forgotten. In this sense Wolseley is fairly typical of his age in his acceptance of fraternisation between South Asian and British, while turning his face against any such collaboration between British and African. However, in relation to both Indians and West Africans, his personal relationship is one of power and dominance. He wants the 'eastern princess' to satisfy his sexual desires; he uses Black soldiers in his campaigns.

Wolseley's mediated version of classic 'scientific' racism played itself out in a curious form. The fearful reputation of the Gold Coast climate was such that the British government was reluctant to commit White troops from the UK. A surgeon general of the Army had put life expectancy of the British soldier in the tropics at one month. Wolseley was therefore forced to recruit both African-Caribbean troops and local Fante and Hausa men and women for the West India Regiment. In so doing, a large proportion of his conquistadores were mercenary or press-ganged.

Imperial military campaigns, like that of Wolseley, had oppressive social repercussions for the place of Euro-Africans in West Africa. As the presence of Europeans grew and became hegemonic, the metaphorical size of the African decreased. They and their history diminished, except of course in two respects: as tools of labour and as a comparative yardstick by which the superiority of European culture and civilisation could be measured.

Henry Wharton, for his part, seemed to accept much of this Eurocentric arrogance. He was an active agent in the attempted Europeanisation of the African through religious conversion; and went along with their proletarianisation. Yet he was deeply conscious of the 'pernicious' and 'immoral' side effects of this latter process if it was guided solely by the invisible hand of the market, untempered by God's intervention. Moister, Henry's biographer, also commented upon the 'demoralising and ungodly'[6] behaviour of many European traders in Africa and how the job of conversion had been made harder by the merchants' acts in Africa.

The variation of Anglo-Saxon cultural attitudes and practices towards ethnicity and race experienced by the cosmopolitan Euro-African travelling between the metropolitan centre of empire and peripheral colonies created a limbo world of moving and changing reference points: in the Africa of the African, cultural distinctions were more important than an individual's colour; in the Africa of the European, colour and culture in that order become significant as determinants of social status. In the Europe of the European, class – one's social relation to the means of production – was the primary determinant of political power and social status; in the Europe of the Black, colour was all, few distinctions being made between different ethnic groups of darker hue. The vast majority were tarred with the same brush as 'darkies', 'niggers' and, if the categoriser was feeling benevolent, 'noble savages'.

The colour bar on non-regular officers in the armed forces, designed and imposed by the political and military elite, is explicit in the *Short Guide to Obtaining a Commission in the Special Reserve of Officers*, published by His Majesty's Stationery Office in 1912. It confirms that, to qualify for a commission, 'a candidate must be of pure European descent, and a British born or naturalised British subject.'[7] This unambiguous regulation that stated ethnicity was more important than natality was not officially lifted until the Second World War, when Charles Arundel Moody was allowed a commission in the Queen's Own Royal West Kent Regiment. His father, Harold Moody, President of the UK-based League of Coloured Peoples, had campaigned against the restriction, complaining to the Colonial Secretary. On success, he claimed that his son was the first Black officer, until corrected in the *League of Coloured Peoples Newsletter* by another member and acquaintance, Edward Tull-Warnock, who reminded Moody and readers of Walter's commission in 1917! Edward also managed to persuade the *Glasgow Evening Times* to publicise his claim on behalf of his brother. Alongside a photo of Tull as a smiling Officer Cadet, the headline described him as the 'First Coloured Officer in the British Army', claiming this honour for Walter, the Tull family and the city of Glasgow.[8]

While Section 95 (2) of the Army Act allowed people of colour to enlist, the consensus of opinion among military chiefs of staff and those within government with responsibility for military recruitment was that White morale would suffer by serving alongside soldiers of colour. Consequently, it was not desirable to have numerous Black soldiers alongside Whites on the front line. Further, White soldiers would not readily accept orders issued by men of colour. *The Manual of Military Law* (1914) authorised 'alien' soldiers, including 'any negro or person of colour to hold honorary rank but they must not exercise any actual command or power'.[9] This seemingly nonsensical rule created a contradiction because the British Nationality and Status of Aliens Act 1914 affirmed 'the status of all those born within the British Empire' as 'natural born British subjects'.[10] The act gave all peoples of Empire equivalent legal status to those born within the UK. However, if there was ambiguity as to the ethnic criteria needed to become an officer, this was spelled out on page 198 of the *Manual*, confirming the regulation contained in the *Short Guide* of 1912, governing the Special Reserve of Officers (to which Tull was appointed to a commission in 1917): 'Commissions in the Special Reserve of Officers are given to qualified candidates who are natural born or naturalised British subjects of pure European descent'.[11] Quite simply, it didn't matter where you were born within the Empire but it did matter what colour you were.

The debate continued throughout the war. Charles Messenger in *Call to Arms* cites the career trajectory of another Black soldier who was appointed to a commission. In April 1917

the War Office conceded that temporary commissions might be granted to 'slightly coloured gentlemen' in the West Indies contingents, which by now were making a sizeable contribution to the labour forces in France. The precedent had been set by Reginald Emmanuel Collins, a civil servant in the West Indies who had enlisted in the Royal Fusiliers in August 1915. He successfully applied for a commission and was posted to No. 6 OC [Officer Cadet] Battalion. Its CO was unhappy about this, however, baldly asserting that Collins was 'not suitable to be an officer owing to his colour'. A debate followed over whether he should be discharged from the army and sent back to the West Indies or returned to the Royal Fusiliers. In the end, Collins was granted a commission in the British West Indies Regiment at the end of March 1917. Three months later, the Army Council agreed that any candidate 'not of pure European descent' could put himself forward for a temporary commission if recommended by his CO 'after serving with credit in the ranks of an Expeditionary Force'.[12]

Messenger then goes on to say that Tull took advantage of this relaxation by applying for a commission. Yet Tull had, in fact, been appointed to a commission in a regular British Army regiment one month before this decision by the Army Council, for which Messenger offers no supporting evidence, illustrating clearly that in Tull's case – and in his case only – they threw away the rule book.

Opening Emmanuel Collins' file held at the National Archives reveals how divisions of class, rank and the maintenance of racial purity within the officer ranks obsessed and vexed the collective minds of the Army Council,

War Office and Colonial Office. While training at No. 6 Officer Cadet Battalion, Balliol College, Oxford, the Jamaican's future was being discussed by his superiors. 'This man in not suitable to be an officer owing to his colour; cannot you consider him for appointment to the BWIR [British West Indies Regiment]?; Officers in the BWIR are white!'[13]

A little over a year earlier the Army Council had made clear its opposition to Black officers: 'the Army Council are averse from appointing to the West Indies Contingent [British West Indies Regiment] any officers other than those of unmixed European blood'.[14] This statement from December 1915 remained the consensus opinion within the Army Council on all commissions, whether they were in colonial forces or the British Army. Officially and in practice the colour bar remained in force. The *Manual of Military Law*, prohibiting men of colour to commissions, was not altered. While the Army Council did eventually allow 'slightly coloured' men to officer Black troops of the British West Indies Regiment, its relaxation of the rules remained secret for fear of raising the colour question in the colonies and poisoning the loyalty of the ordinary people, in particular adult males!

In the British Army, as we know, Tull seems to have been the only Black infantry officer. While, during the 19th century, there had been Black medical officers, during the First World War the Army Council did their best to prevent Blacks trained in medicine from joining the Royal Army Medical Corps (RAMC) or enlisting as vets. Dr W. S. Mitchell of Grenada wanted to assist the RAMC in 1915. One of the top surgeons on the island, he was rejected by the War Office because he was not of pure European descent. This caused a row between the Governor of Grenada, the Colonial Office and the War Office, not because of the decision but for the public exposure of the reasons for Mitchell's rejection. He eventually joined the BWIR.

Dr A. J. Allwood from Jamaica had a similar experience when he offered his medical skills to the RAMC. He was told by the Colonial Office to apply instead to the CO of the Jamaica Contingent (of the BWIR).[15] On 26 March 1918, as 2nd Lieutenant Tull's body was decomposing on a battlefield somewhere in 'France or Belgium',[16] the War Office, on behalf of the Army Council, was writing to the Colonial Office rejecting Kenneth Oehler's application to enlist. A 'coloured subject' from the Straits Settlement – Singapore, Penang and Malacca – he was recommended by the Governor of the Straits.

The [Army] Council regret that no exception can be made in this case, there being no suitable unit to which this man this could be posted, as it is not considered desirable to post coloured men to regular British Units.

The Council request therefore that Mr Secretary Long will be good enough to inform the Governor of the Straits Settlements that coloured subjects should not in future be sent to this country for enlistment, and suggest further that this information be conveyed confidentially to the Governors of other colonies with coloured populations.[17]

From the outset of the war, the Army Council – the political executive of the army – resisted Black recruitment and the use of Black troops. The Earl of Dundonald, who had commanded troops in Africa, in November 1914 wrote to the Colonial Office on behalf of West Indian Mr Moore of 70 Addison Gardens, Kensington.

A fine specimen of a man, Mr Moore, has just called upon me, colour black, holding a good position in the West Indies . . . who cannot get accepted by the recruiting authorities. I said 'why cannot you get taken?'. He said 'well I have a suspicion it is a colour question, but when I paid £25 for my passage I had not the least idea there was any colour question in England'.[18]

The Colonial Office believed two interconnected concerns had been raised by the Moore case: preventing other 'coloured people' from coming to the UK to enlist and what to do with such patriots in the West Indies. Their solution was to send a coded telegram to Governors in the Caribbean asking they do all in their power to 'discourage persons not of European descent' from travelling 'without raising the colour question'. It also wrote to the War Office asking if the Army Council could find a way of using West Indians

for the purposes of the war . . . Mr Harcourt [Secretary of State at the Colonial Office] is well aware that it is not possible to enlist black or coloured people in British Regiments . . . Could they be used in Turkey, Egypt or Sierra Leone?[19]

In April 1915 George V entered into this internal, secret exchange of opinion between government ministers, their departmental civil servants and interested individuals such as Dundonald over what to do with men of colour who were offering to fight for Britain and its Empire. Via his secretary Lord Stamfordham he asked something be done to satisfy the patriotic aspirations of his colonial subjects. The king was worried about the political consequences of stopping Caribbean men enlisting in Kitchener's BEF. The atmosphere in Whitehall became even hotter as the latter also weighed in, suggesting to the king he had no problem using Black troops. 'But you said the opposite to me', wrote a furious Lewis Harcourt from the Colonial Office.[20]

The British West Indies Regiment, designed to absorb those from the Caribbean and Black Britons who wanted to enlist, was eventually formed in the summer of 1915. While Secretary of State for War Lord Kitchener and the Army Council reluctantly agreed to use BWIR troops as labourers out of the front line, in so doing their rationale for not wanting Black soldiers in regular units of the British Army was undermined.

The Army Council was adamant that the newly formed BWIR should be officered by men of 'pure European descent'. However, in the context of the BWIR, it would be difficult to use their historic justification of the colour bar: that White troops would not take orders from a Black officer. This was now rendered nonsensical as the majority of troops would be Black. It exposed their stance as irrational, naked prejudice.

Colour-coded entry was also practised in the Royal Air Force and Navy. While the Air Force (Constitution) Act, 1917, allowed, in exceptional circumstances such as war, brown-skinned volunteers, these would not be allowed commissions. The Navy, similarly, did permit 'Maltese and Men of Colour who are the sons of British-born subjects' as ratings but not as officers.[21]

Forty-four years earlier the War Office argued that the Army should be wholly White, despite the presence of Blacks in the Army since at least the 16th century, an African trumpeter being part of the court of Henry VII in 1507. Peter Fryer argues that Black drummers were recruited, enslaved and press-ganged into British Army regiments serving in the Caribbean in the 17th century. Sir Walter Scott, says Fryer, describes six Black drummers in the Scottish Life Guards of 1679 as clothed in 'white dresses richly laced [with] massive silver collars and armlets'.[22] By the 1700s Black drummers were fashionable and numerous. Even prestigious regiments which persisted with a colour bar until the late 20th century are recorded as having Black musicians: the Household Cavalry, by 1720, had Black trumpeters; and a Black trumpeter is illustrated in a 1730s portrayal of Captain Gifford of the Life Guards.

Musicians were officially embedded into British regiments in 1757 when central funds were allocated for six enlisted bandsmen in each regiment, speeding the recruitment of Black musicians. Some officers felt their rank and file marched more precisely to drumbeat. Additionally, these musicians provided an element of performance to their playing which was often extravagant, dexterous and showy in style. A cymbalist of the 3rd Foot Guards, John Baptist, embodied these characteristics to such an extent that he was depicted on canvas by Dubois-Drahoneti.

Alongside this theatrical dimension, until the second quarter of the 19th century, drummers were an integral part of the Army's disciplinary process, having responsibility for administering floggings, under the supervision of the Drum-Major Sergeant. The timing of each lash would be set by a fellow drummer beating his stretched hide in slow time. Surprisingly, this role of rhythm leader does not seem to have attracted the anger of the flogged. It did upset some, however. When practised by the 29th (Worcester) Regiment of Foot in pre-revolution North America the *Boston Evening Post* was outraged: 'To behold Britons scourged by Negro drummers was a new and disagreeable spectacle'.[23]

This habit of using force to correct behaviour was also utilised outside the barracks. Fryer concludes his chapter on Black musicians with a telling and humorous anecdote of bandsman Francis of the Grenadier Guards walking The Strand. Asked by an anonymous passer-by, 'Well, blackie, what news from the devil?' he floored the interrogator, replying 'He send you dat, how you like it?'[24]

If not all Black personnel in the 18th- and early 19th-century British Army were musicians on entry, stereotypical attitudes towards them entailed ascribing that status to them. Recruiting in Cork on the west coast of Ireland in January 1815, after loss of manpower in the Peninsular War, the 71st (Highland Light Infantry) Regiment incorporated Samuel Peters, originally from San Domingo – Haiti – into their ranks. Serving at the Battle of Waterloo in June 1815, Peters eventually asked for a transfer to the 2nd West India Regiment (2nd WIR), reaching the rank of Drum-Major Sergeant.

It will probably never be known why Peters left the 71st. Certainly 'racial' attitudes were changing towards Black people in Britain, with the rise of 'scientific racism'. However, the Black presence in 'white' British and Irish-raised regiments continued until the mid-1840s – this proving if nothing else that the old adage of 'the army being years behind civilian society' was not necessarily a bad thing as far as Black soldiers were concerned.[25]

Peters held his exalted rank for just a quarter of a year before demotion to Private, subsequently snaking and laddering between that and Corporal for the rest of his career. Fortunately, he was discharged at the top of the ladder, retiring in Jamaica on a corporal's pension. His biographer John Ellis thinks his up and down ranking in the 2nd WIR may have been the result of being assumed a musician because he had served in a White regiment. Once his musical abilities were exposed he was put back to square one! Whatever the reason, it was not his inadequate soldiering. His Army reference speaks of a 'good and efficient soldier, seldom in hospital, trustworthy and sober'.[26]

Ellis points out that Peters had the company of another Black veteran of Waterloo resident in Jamaica, the Reverend George Rose. Finishing his days as a Sergeant with the Black Watch, he had transferred from the 73rd Foot (Highland Light Infantry) Regiment. Born to slaves in Jamaica in 1787, Rose became the highest-ranking non-commissioned officer in the British Army. He fled from the island to the UK as an 18-year-old, determined not to give up his life to planters. Volunteering for the Army during the Napoleonic Wars, he battled with his regiment in Germany and the Netherlands – where he was wounded – and Belgium (Quatre Bas and Waterloo) where the 73rds suffered 135 wounded or killed out of 558, including Rose whose right arm was badly damaged with gunshot.

The 73rds were disbanded in 1817, Rose joining the 42nd (Highland) Foot (Black Watch), 'a regiment fiercely proud of its tradition of martial prowess'.[27] By 1831 he had been promoted to Sergeant. This was highly unusual for a Black soldier at a time when other regiments were both becoming more reluctant to accept men of colour and actively shedding them. This oasis of enlightenment within the Scots regiment may have been a consequence of progressive leadership by Lieutenant Colonel Munro, who created a library for his men and was instrumental in promoting Rose.

Between 1837 and 1849, when he re-settled in slave-free Jamaica, Rose lived in Glasgow earning a living as a preacher for the Primitive Methodists, proselytising on Glasgow Green.

The attraction of the Army for free Blacks was equality of pay with White peers. This would have been unobtainable in most other sectors of the economy, where any kind of living would be hard to come by. However, it should also be remembered that the West India Regiment of the late 18th century was manned by slaves and press-ganged Africans. It was not until the momentous year of 1807 that, with the enactment of legislation abolishing slave trading by British ships (on 1 January 1808), a revised Mutiny Act forbade enslaved soldiers within the forces: 'All Negroes purchased by or on account of His Majesty, His Heirs and Successors and serving in any of His Majesty's Forces, shall be taken to be free'.[28]

After the Napoleonic Wars, with the gradual enlargement of Britain's overseas interests and the concomitant racialisation of British culture and politics, growing opposition to men of colour in the British Army, at all levels, saw the numbers of Black musicians decline. Indeed, 'Henry Martin of Santa Cruz was discharged from the 77th Foot in 1822 on account of being a man of colour'.[29] This chromatic development of the armed forces to a whiter shade of pale can be first identified in Imperial India where, in the 1790s, Anglo-Indians – commonly known as Eurasians – were collectively discharged. By 1808 they had disappeared from the British Army stationed on the sub-continent. This was, in large part, a response by the military and political elites to the success of the slave revolt led by Toussaint L'Ouverture in San Domingo and the massacre of Whites that followed. Having brown-skinned, Eurasian officers in charge of darker-skinned Indians did not sit easily in the minds of India's British rulers once the potential social ramifications of events in the erstwhile French colony were absorbed.

There are exceptions to this increasing imposition of the colour bar, such as Africans Private Lenox Simpson of the 41st Foot and James Durham, who was born in Sudan. Simpson saw action in one of the bloodiest campaigns of the 19th century, in Afghanistan in the early 1840s. It was an imperial venture characterised by hand-to-hand fighting, heavy casualties, ineptitude and disarray. Marx argued that history repeats itself, first as tragedy, second as farce. The present invasion of Afghanistan, instigated and led by the USA's Bush administration assisted by the Blair–Brown government in the UK, in an attempt to fulfil the former's quest of 'full spectrum dominance' – global economic and military supremacy – confirms the truth of the German revolutionary's maxim. Afghanistan proved to be unconquerable in the 19th century and may well prove the same today. It did for Private Simpson, being invalided to the Royal Hospital, Chelsea, on his return to the UK, and it will probably do for the USA elites' vision of world military domination.

After the Battle of Ginnis in 1885, as a 5-year-old (orphan?), Durham was found on the banks of the Nile by the Durham Light Infantry (DLI). Collectively adopted by the sergeants of the 1st Battalion, he was made mascot and taken to India in 1887. Given the name of two of his guardians and the regiment, James Francis Durham, he enrolled in 1899. Trained as a musician, he played clarinet and violin in the regimental orchestra. His first visit to the British Isles with the DLI was in 1902, to Aldershot, and then Cork in 1905. He did spend some time in the provenance of his regiment, the north-east of England, making an indelible impression upon one local, Jane Green, from Darlington, whom he married in 1908. Durham died from pneumonia two years later, 8 August, in Fermoy, Co. Cork with the compensatory knowledge that Jane was due to give birth to their child, Frances, delivered safely a matter of weeks later.

Durham was buried with a military ceremony, his headstone paid for by officers and men of his battalion. The reason for his adoption may have been a simple outpouring of human compassion by the men of the north-east regiment. Yet, at the time of his capture, a fellow African was making a name for himself in Darlington and Newcastle as a footballer and athlete of special talent. Did Arthur Wharton's exploits argue with 'common-sense' notions of Black inferiority, thereby increasing the cultural value, and human worth, of 'the Black' in the minds of these men from north-east England?

Overlaying 19th-century mind and practice was an ideological explanation of past events that highlighted, deleted, re-coloured and projected. Simply, the past was rewritten, the present 'understood' according to the 'correct' political template and an imagined monochrome future planned for through policy, law, practice and regulation. This worldview envisaged a White army.

The 'vanilla-isation' of the British armed forces during the 19th century reversed a trend. While British elites at home, and abroad in their colonies, could not accept a rainbow army, the Imperial Romans, 1,600 years earlier, accepted such as the vital muscle of their empire. During the 2nd century there is evidence that 'a division of Moors'[30] was stationed at Hadrian's Wall. Britain, as part of the Roman Empire between AD 43 and 476, had been ruled by Governor Septimius Severus during the latter part of the second and first decade of the 3rd centuries of the first millennium. A North African born at Leptis Magna in what is now Libya, Severus died at York in 211.

The practical demands of the First World War for healthy, fit, young men pulled the military back in the direction it had been taking in the 18th century with regard to recruitment. Black Britons and Black British subjects from the colonies enlisted in the Army, Air Force and Navy. Richard Smith discusses their commitment to the cause of the 'Mother Country' and the reward some of them received for their loyalty.

> In May 1915, nine men from Barbados stowed away on the SS *Danube* in order to come to Britain and volunteer. When they were discovered on board ship, they were arrested and appeared at West Ham Police Court and were subjected to taunts from the magistrate.[31]

Tull's brother William was a sapper in the Royal Engineers, the same regiment as Charles Augustus Williams, the Bajan father of comedian Charlie Williams who played centre-half for Doncaster Rovers in the 1950s. In January 1916, as Lance Sergeant Walter Tull was sent to the Front around Givenchy, Jamaican leatherworker Egbert Watson, living in Camden Town, enlisted as a gunner in the Royal Garrison Artillery. His tour of duty in France lasted just two months before he was shipped home unwell in 1917 suffering from myalgia – muscle pain, often caused by chronic fatigue – and epilepsy. Eugene and John Brown, the Nigerian father and uncle of Roy Brown, a club colleague of Stanley Matthews at Stoke City in the late 1930s, served in the 5th North Staffordshire Regiment while attending college in Britain. Eugene was killed in action, while John ended his war days in hospital. Boxer Charlie Cooper, a local celebrity in the north-west of England, joined the Manchester Regiment, his enlistment recorded with a photograph by the *Daily Dispatch* on 30 May 1917. A battalion of the Manchesters served in the 41st Division, alongside the 23rd Middlesex.

David Killingray lists a number of men of African origin who served in the British Army in the First World War, including the Brighton-born son of a Ghanaian lawyer, Frank S. Dove, who enlisted in 1915 in the Royal Tank

Corps as Private 91658. For bravery in the field during the Battle of Cambrai he was awarded the Military Medal. Others mentioned by Killingray are J. Egerton Shyngle, Patrick Freeman, Bob Collier, Henry Solomon, George Williams and Frederick Njilima. The latter signed his attestation as Frederick Graham and joined the 150th Battalion, Machine Gun Corps. Wounded on the first day of the German Aisne offensive, 27 May 1918, he was hospitalised in Cambridge and had the Military Medal pinned on his breast before being repatriated to Nyasaland with a one-fifth disability pension. Entertainer Bata Kindai Amgoza ibn LoBagola, the 'African Savage', born Joseph Howard Lee in Baltimore, Maryland, USA, in 1887, enlisted at the British Army recruiting office in New York as a Black Jew from West Africa. Posted to the 38th Royal Fusiliers, an overwhelmingly Jewish battalion, he served in Palestine and Egypt, complaining: '[They] taunted me. I was the only Black among them. They were not willing to accept me as a Jew, because of their prejudice against my colour'.[32]

Of these Black British Army soldiers, Norman Manley of the Royal Artillery probably made the greatest post-war impact, forming and leading the People's National Party in Jamaica. Studying at Oxford on a Rhodes scholarship, he joined the Field Artillery with his brother Roy and served in France. Rising through the ranks, he did not get the customary respect due an NCO from ordinary soldiers, though being light skinned (of Irish and African-Caribbean heritage).

> When I joined, I joined a mounted unit and I was part of the most mobile part of it. I had grown up with horses and horse drawn vehicles, and knew more about them than miners and town bred Londoners, so naturally within a month I was a Lance Corporal or Bombardier as they were called in the Artillery, and by the time we left for France I was promoted Corporal. Here I came up against violent colour prejudice. The rank and file disliked taking orders from a coloured NCO and their attitude was mild by comparison with that of my fellow NCOs. Corporals and sergeants resented my sharing status with them. They were more spiteful and later conspired to get me into trouble.[33]

In disgust, frustration and irritation Manley gave up his stripes and joined another regiment as a gunner, eventually winning a Military Medal.

As well as 'Negroes' the *Manual of Military Law* also categorised men of colour as 'aliens', despite their legal status as British subjects, restricting their proportion per regiment to two in every hundred.

> Any person who is for the time being an alien may, if His Majesty think fit to signify his consent through a Secretary of State, be enlisted in His Majesty's regular forces, so, however, that the number of aliens serving together at any one time in any corps of the regular forces shall not exceed the proportion of one alien to every fifty British subjects, and that an alien so enlisted shall not be capable of holding any higher rank in His Majesty's regular forces than that of a warrant officer or non-commissioned officer.[34]

The numbers of men of colour attempting to enlist in the BEF was worrying the Establishment. Indeed, Secretary of State for War and recruitment sergeant for the BEF, Lord Kitchener, believed 'Blacks' colour makes them too conspicuous in the field . . . Black soldiers [are] a greater source of danger to friends than enemy'.[35] The success of Blacks in enlisting pre-conscription often depended upon degree of colour and the whim of the recruiting officer. In December 1914, on the very day Tull signed his Short Service Attestation form B 2505, a principal clerk at the Colonial Office, Gilbert Grindle, commented 'I hear privately that some recruiting officers will pass coloureds. Others, however, will not, and we must discourage coloured volunteers'.[36]

Perhaps we would be attributing too much importance to Tull's enlistment if we connect Grindle's statement with his registration. Yet Tull joined up in London, he was a well-known figure – the only Black footballer to have played outfield in the first division – a face on cigarette cards and in sporting newspapers. Did news filter through to Whitehall that a prominent Black Briton had entered the ranks of the Middlesex Regiment? Did officers at the recruitment office seek advice from their superiors, who in turn sought advice from their political superiors? In the sometimes surreal, Kafkaesque world of Westminster, Downing Street and the higher echelons of the Civil Service, it would not be surprising if Tull's enlistment caused vexed beads of perspiration to drip from the foreheads of old sweats now witnessing the playing out of Wolseley's 1886 prophecy.

One particular recruitment poster made explicit the type of men the BEF was seeking: 'If you are a Whiteman prove your colour and courage now. Help [us] to wipe out this Black spot in Europe'. Worried about order in the ranks, stirred by 'common-sense' notions of the superiority of the White race, in October 1915 the government created the British West Indies Regiment (BWIR) for soldiers of colour, irrespective of whether they enlisted in Britain or the Caribbean. Jamaican Alonzo Nathan was a case in point. A sailor from Cardiff before the war, he enlisted in the first instance in the Army Service Corps before, in May 1916, being transferred to the BWIR.

Fellow Jamaican James Slim joined the Coldstream Guards, an elite regiment. His enlistment did not meet the approval of the War Office who discharged him after less than two months, despite the excellence of his physical condition and behaviour. Historically, men of colour had been commissioned medical officers, including Sierra Leoneans James Africanus Horton and William Broughton Davies. In 1859 Horton, the first Black graduate of the University of Edinburgh, joined the British Army Medical Service, eventually reaching the position of Surgeon Major, a previously unscaled height for a man of colour. (He added Africanus to his name to emphasise his African heritage.)

Attending to the medical requirements of British soldiers in the same decade that Horton and Davies were diagnosing and treating their wounds and ailments was Jamaican Mary Seacole. Initially rejected for nursing duties by the War Office, the military and Florence Nightingale's organisation, she made her own way to the Crimea to fulfil her vocation of caring for those she called her 'sons', the British soldiers on active service. On her return from the Crimea and subsequent bankruptcy in 1856, the following year she published her autobiography, the *Wonderful Adventures of Mary Seacole in Many Lands*. The book eventually brought deserved recognition for her tenacity, perseverance and devotion to her profession in dangerous circumstances.

Richard Smith has uncovered the application of G. O. Rushdie-Gray for a commission in the Army Veterinary Corps as a medical officer. Rushdie-Gray, a veterinary officer for the Jamaican government, was recommended for his commission by the Governor of Jamaica, William Manning, yet the Army could not accept him because he was 'too Black'![37] Dr James Jackson Brown, a GP from Lauriston Road, Bethnal Green, applied for a commission in the Royal Army Medical Corps. He was offered instead the post of Warrant Officer, which he declined.

A mixed-heritage East Ender who did serve was Ikey Bogard. A gang leader from the working-class Commercial Road area of Shoreditch, he won a Military Medal in 1918 as Private 263049 of the Monmouth Regiment. Despite also being known as Darkey the Coon, his ethnic origins are uncertain. He has been labelled Jewish and a man of colour. It's quite possible he was both. Another gang leader, Arthur Harding, active in the East End underworld of the early 1900s, recalls his feared rival.

> We were involved in a feud with the Coons. They were the biggest villains the East End had, they were all 'shundicknicks' – ponces . . . usually the man who lives on a woman is a coward . . . but Darkey was a big man and a fighter – he'd think nothing of giving somebody a rip, and he could be very vicious. He was gaffer over all the Jewish chaps up Whitechapel and Aldgate . . . He was very flamboyant, he dressed like a cowboy. He used to wear a big open shirt, like a woman's blouse, and a flash belt with something stuck in the case. It wasn't illegal to carry a gun at that time; weapon stuck down his belt; a big panama hat on – he was quite a character in that way.[38]

Harding's view that many aristocrats acquired their titles and landed estates through the slave trade defies Marx's notion that working-class criminals are apolitical members of the lumpenproletariat. This commerce in people overshadowed virtually all other types of crime, commented the East End villain in interviews with historian Ralph Samuel, thus providing the reader with a clue, maybe, as to why Bogard and he drifted into alternative life-styles.

The introduction of conscription early in 1916 allowed greater bureaucratic control over the colour of men walking through the doors of the Recruiting Office. Yet, for many in the military and political Establishment, the prospect of polychrome regiments in the British Army was still causing sleepless nights. Many British subjects – and US citizens like LoBagola/Joseph Howard Lee masquerading as a French colonial subject – offered themselves at British Army recruiting offices in the United States. In September 1917 16 Black men were accepted in Chicago 'owing to a misunderstanding'.[39] The case caused friction within the War Office. Though Parliament had recently passed the Military Services Convention Act which allowed the United States military to accept British subjects prohibited entry to the British Army, if the Chicagoans' enlistments were cancelled it would quite probably, if publicised, have a negative effect on colonial recruitment into the war effort generally. Rather than allow a propaganda victory for the US military – 'we accept Blacks you reject' – it delayed the deployment of Black British subjects recruited in the USA 'until it is found possible to enlist them in the British Army'.[40]

While the men of Whitehall were trench digging against men of colour they were also prosecuting those men of colour not heeding their conscription. Robert Reubens, a South Asian from Singapore, was tried at Brighton Magistrates Court in 1917 for failing to report for military service. His defence was that he was in the UK to study, thus exempted. Even though the Ministry of National Service argued he should not have been served with a conscription notice he was convicted. A case of damned if you do, damned if you don't.

In the summer of 1918, four years into the war and desperate for fighting men, the Army Council officially sanctioned 'British subjects of colour' in the British Army as long as they blended in culturally in terms of diet and language.

> The intention of the Army Council was, and is, to provide a place
> in the combatant arms of the British Army for British subjects of
> colour resident in Great Britain and the United States and also for
> the better class British subject of colour or half caste resident in the
> Colonies for whom no appropriate combatant unit exists in the
> colony in which he resides.[41]

The prohibition against commissioning men of colour as combat officers into regular British units remained. In a letter to Edward written from France on 10 August 1917, Tull ends with a postscript 'am applying for a transfer to the BWI when the Batt. Come out tomorrow'. Its place as a footnoted afterthought belies its significance: why would the recently commissioned 2nd Lieutenant want to switch regiments after serving two and a half years with soldier comrades with whom he also shared a vocational affinity? It suggests that he was acutely conscious of his 'otherness' as a Black officer in a White battalion; that he did indeed face a residue of hostility even among his brother footballers; and that he would have felt more at ease in a force that had as its uniting element the common experience of racism. He may have also thought his chances of promotion to Captain and posting to a less intense theatre of war would be enhanced by the transfer. Culturally, the British West Indies Regiment would be a varied mixture. Recruits could, in theory, come from any part of the British Empire. It speaks to Tull's emerging political awakening that he felt his presence would be of more use and better received among those with whom he shared an ethnic and political affinity rather than a cultural and professional commonality.

Had his request for a transfer been granted, the development of his political conscience might have quickened if the actions of soldiers of the BWIR during 1918 and 1919 are a guide. After the signing of the Armistice, 11 November 1918, in preparation for their demobilisation, battalions of the BWIR were encamped at Taranto, Italy. They included Clifford Powell, Gershom Brown and Eugent Clarke who, in 1999, at the age of 105, received France's Légion d'Honneur for meritorious service in the First World War. Disqualified from a pay rise because of their colour and ordered to perform what rank-and-file soldiers deemed as menial and humiliating tasks – including cleaning the toilets of the Italian Labour Corps – a generalised rebellion developed into a mutiny. On 6 December 1918, soldiers of the 9th Battalion attacked their officers. That day also, 180 sergeants sent a petition to the Secretary of State stating their grievances over a number of issues, including pay, separation allowances and internal discrimination that militated against promotion – in short, how the practical operation of the colour bar affected their working, living, emotional and mental condition. So worried were the colonial authorities by the radicalisation of the BWIR troops that they encouraged many to take agricultural work in Cuba. Over 30 per cent of the veterans, some 4,000, including Clifford Powell, took up the offer and remained there for the rest of their lives. A Colonial Office memo of 1919 stated 'nothing we can do will alter the fact that the black man has begun to think and feel himself as good as the white'.[42]

Mutinies in the armies of the First World War were not unusual. Russian soldiers, after the February Revolution of 1917, turned on their officers; British, French and Canadian troops revolted on the Western Front in the same year. The war saw increasing numbers of British soldiers being court-martialled and sentenced, often to death, for indiscipline, refusal to obey orders and mutiny. According to one source the figures were 528 in 1914; 10,488 in 1915; 12,689 in 1916; 13,165 in 1917; and 1,035 in 1918.[43] The decrease in sentences for 1918 is interesting because mutinies and general indiscipline increased, continuing after the 11 November Armistice.

The politically conscious elements of the ruling classes of Europe, formerly divided by economic competition and war, now united against the Bolshevik threat from the revolutionary Russian republics. Field Marshall Sir Henry Wilson, Chief of the Imperial General Staff, and Winston Churchill, a member of the War Cabinet, were the most vocal anti-communist warriors within the Establishment, stridently arguing for troops to fight alongside the 'White', anti-Bolshevik forces. As Lloyd George attended the peace talks in Paris, they advocated compulsorily retaining over a million men in khaki to sanitise the virus of democracy-from-below spreading from the East.

In fact, Britain had signalled its intentions before the Armistice. After Russia's effective exit from the war in December 1917, British troops occupied Archangel on the White Sea in August 1918, just ten months after Lenin's Bolsheviks came to power. However, the refusal of many demob-expectant troops to be sent to fight Slavic communism resulted in the eventual withdrawal of British forces by late 1920. The Tommies' rejection was based not only on war fatigue but a feeling among many that what had occurred in Russia – working-class Soviets replacing a feudal aristocracy as the forum of political power – wouldn't be a bad thing in Salford, Limehouse and Aston. The level of unrest, not just in the Army but also in society, has led many historians to argue that Britain in 1919 was close to social revolution. On occasion this working-class anger at the glaring economic and social inequality in society imploded, culminating in racist attacks. More widespread, popular and positive, though, were the organised assaults on class privilege coming from increased membership of, and action by, trade unions. These, by the early years of the 1920s, incorporated all sections of the workforce, skilled and unskilled. The election of the first Labour government in 1923, too, reflected the mood of the people.

Between 3 and 12 May 1926, over five million trade unionists withdrew their labour in support of the locked-out miners fighting 'not a penny off the pay, not a second on the day'. Despite the defeat suffered by the

Miners' Federation and the working class in general after the nine days of May, socialist ideas and revolutionary action continued. Communists were elected to parliament, councils, trade unions posts, and membership of the Communist Party increased.

Many war veterans who were promised 'a land fit for heroes' by Lloyd George in the 'khaki election' of 1918 wondered why, after they and their comrades had arrived back to homes fit for pigs, the ruling elites, who had spent an estimated seven million pounds per day on the war, could do nothing to prevent the mass unemployment of the 1930s. The issue of substandard working-class housing didn't go away. Through the funding of slum removal and house-building programmes inter-war governments recognised that millions lived in houses without baths or lavatories. Between 1919 and 1939 over 340,000 unfit houses were demolished and one and a quarter million council houses built. Yet in 1943, 90 per cent of houses in Stepney still had no baths. The problem was structural, a question of tenure: there was an over-supply of large, luxury and second homes and a severe shortage of low-rent housing. In 1938 over 360,000 houses were unoccupied; two years earlier it was estimated that 350,000 houses were overcrowded.

Alan Bleasdale wrote an astute and evocative drama, *The Monocled Mutineer*, based upon a book of the same name by William Allison and John Fairley. The series graphically portrayed the issues and themes surrounding the British rebellion at Étaples in 1917 through the eyes of a deserter, Percy Topliss. Produced by Ruth Caleb, executive producer of BBC4's 2008 Tull drama *Walter's War*, it was a controversial, popular success on BBC1, providing valuable ammunition to those wanting a political cleansing of the 'Marxist' BBC by, in the first instance, ridding the corporation of its Director-General Alasdair Milne. They were successful. Milne went and the programme has not been repeated. Many left-leaning political activists and media workers believed pressure from the MoD was instrumental in its suppression.

The mutineers of the BWIR were not the only men of colour to refuse orders. On 5 September 1917, two companies of South East Asian soldiers went on strike at Boulogne. Unarmed, the next day they tried to desert their barracks. For their insubordination 47 were gunned down, 23 dying of their wounds. Less than a week later, another group, No. 74 Labour Company, responded with an act of solidarity and also went on strike. This time 19 were wounded by those ordered to restore military discipline; four were killed. These instances of rebellion among mainly Chinese members of the Labour Corps were not unique. Others did occur, such as the event at Fontinettes in which four were killed and nine wounded.

Although mutinies on the Western Front and at Taranto were quelled, the anger of the participants was not. It found new articulation in the formation of the Chinese Wartime Labourers Corp in Shanghai; 26 unions created by veteran Labour Corps soldiers in Canton; and the Caribbean League, an organisation dedicated to furthering the self-determination of the Caribbean peoples. These radicalised soldiers returned to their awakening regions and islands, changed forever by their experiences in the First World War; they were determined not to go back to the status quo ante.

Until June 1918, when the Army Council created an opening in the colour bar, men of colour resident in Britain, or who had travelled to Britain to enlist, often at great personal cost, were 'encouraged' instead to work in munitions, engineering and other, similar, industries crucial to the war effort. Yet even in these industries they caused offence to some national institutions. A Salvation Army report spoke of a 'coloured invasion' in Manchester; three leading unions, the Miners' Federation, the National Union of Railwaymen and the National Transport Federation, shamefully approved a combined resolution condemning 'the sinister movement to import coloured labour into this country'. [44]

It wasn't only their legal status and experience as civilians in the UK that may have confused and irritated people of colour. Their compatriots who had enlisted in the Caribbean and Africa and travelled to Britain with their regiments were complimented on their superior physique compared to the sunken chests and stunted development of the working-class Tommy from a grime-ridden back-to-back in smokestack, industrial inner-city Britain. West Indies soldiers in the 1915 Lord Mayor's show were depicted in the print media as 'huge and mighty men of valour'. [45]

Continually being unearthed, literally, is evidence adding to, enlarging and giving greater depth to our understanding of the ethnic composition of Britain's armed forces. In April 2006 the remains of 8372 Private William Lancaster of the 2nd Battalion Royal Lancashire Fusiliers were discovered by amateur archaeologists in Ypres. The *Mail on Sunday*, 23 April 2006, carried a photo of the young, bowler-hatted Edwardian with his infant son, Richard, on page 54. A former regular soldier, born in Preston in 1882, Lancaster lived in Burnley with his wife Phoebe and their four children at Napier Street. He was called up as a reservist in August 1914. In that year he died during the First Battle of Ypres on 10 November, aged 32. No mention in the article is made of his ethnicity, though the image suggests he is of mixed heritage.

Royal Flying Corps/Air Force

The Air Force (Constitution) Act of 1917 restricted entry into the Royal Air Force to men of pure European descent. Although sections of the act permitted voluntary enlistment of 'any inhabitant of any British protectorate and any negro or person of colour' in exceptional circumstances, no such 'aliens' were to be promoted above the rank of Non-Commissioned or Warrant Officer

writes former World War Two RAF Navigator Cy Grant from Guyana in his memoir, 'A Member of the RAF of Indeterminate Race' (2006). Trained as a barrister but unable to find chambers that would accept him, he became a stage and screen actor and British television's first regular Black entertainer on shows in the 1950s and 60s, such as *Tonight*. Yet, for a brief period in the summer of 1943, Grant achieved notoriety throughout Germany. Shot down in Holland and captured, his photo was featured in the official newspaper of the Nazi party, the *Völkischer Beobachter*. Underneath the illustration of a squinting, weary, young, African-Caribbean officer was printed 'Ein Mitglied der Royal Air Force von unbestimmbarer Rasse ('A Member of the RAF of Indeterminate Race'). His ethnic categorisation was proudly displayed as propaganda by the Nazis to illustrate the miscegenation tendencies of the British in the 'race' war. We are the only people fighting to protect the purity of the Whites, was the message. In fact, as Grant points out, there were but a 'black few' in the RAF even though he was commissioned an officer and 'personally never experienced any racism'.[46]

This statement by Grant was more a testament to the decency of ordinary airmen than a comment on the progressive thinking and behaviour of his superiors. Roger Lambo, in a letter to Grant, cites Air Chief Marshal Sir John C. Slessor who, in a memo of 16 August 1945, argues men with names such as 'U-ba or Ah Wong, looking as though [they] had just dropped out of a tree' were not desired in the RAF. A week later, for diplo-matic, publicity and propaganda reasons, the Air Ministry decided to lift the colour bar. Instead it would rely on medical and administrative staff to weed out those with brown skin. 'On Paper coloured troops (would) be eligible for entry to the service, but the process of selection (would) elimi-nate them'.[47]

The National Army Museum pamphlet *We Were There*, an accompany-ing document to their 2008 exhibition of the same name, states that there were, from 1917, five pilots of colour serving in the Royal Flying Corps (RFC, later the Royal Air Force) in the First World War. These included William Robinson Clarke, Sardar Hardit Singh Malik and Flight Lieuten-ant Indra Lal – Laddie – Roy.

Jamaican William Robinson Clarke, working on barrage balloons then RE8 fighter planes, was shot down and wounded over enemy territory in France in 1917. Incredibly, he survived for many decades despite the shrap-nel – piercing shards of metal – remaining within his stomach.

Sardar Hardit Singh Malik was born into an elite Sikh family from Rawal-pindi in the Punjab on 23 November 1894. After graduating from Balliol College, Oxford, he joined the RFC as a cadet in 1917, becoming the first Sikh in the RFC. In an attempt to accommodate his ethnic custom, a larger than normal flying hat was designed to be worn over his turban. He was nicknamed the Flying Hobgoblin.

> Hardit Singh was posted to Filton, near Bristol, eventually flying the Sopwith Camel, the most advanced fighter at this time. He got his wings in under a month. Posted to 28 Squadron the formation soon flew out to St Omer in France, then to an airfield in Flanders near the village of Droglandt . . . In one major dogfight, with over a hundred British and German fighters scrapping over the battle lines, Hardit Singh shot down his first German Fokkerand. He went on to notch another eight aerial victories in the weeks ahead, before he himself was wounded in action, but survived in amazing circumstances. After months in hospital, Hardit Singh rejoined the service, now renamed as the Royal Air Force, flying the Bristol Fighter, probably the best fighter of the war, with 141 Squadron at Biggin Hill, a specialist unit created for defending London from raiding Zeppelins and Botha bombers.[48]

Despite his primary sporting passion being golf, Hardit Singh Malik played first-class cricket for the University of Oxford and Sussex, among other teams, in a career that spanned 16 years. (For those interested his averages were, batting, 19.87 runs per innings; bowling, 50.33 per wicket.) After leaving the RAF, as expected of a man from his class and caste, he had prestigious careers as a diplomat and politician, including ambassador to France and prime minister of Patiala State. Passing many hours in the autumn of his life on the golfing green, he died in India in November 1985, aged 91.

Flight Lieutenant Indra Lal – Laddie – Roy enlisted in April 1917, aged 18, having been, since 1911, a pupil at St Paul's School, Hammersmith, London. Born in Calcutta, he was gazetted a couple of months after Tull on 5 July 1917. Part of his Officer Cadet training was at Turnberry in Scotland, the site of Edward Tull's golf club. It is not known if they met. Indra was posted to 56 Squadron, 30 October 1917. Beginner's luck an absent friend, within a couple of months he was hospitalised after a crash landing. However, if the start to his career was unfortunate, his return to flying and posting to 40 Squadron in June 1918 marked a heroic chapter in the early history of the RAF. He was credited with nine victories in less than two weeks during July before being shot down in flames in a dogfight and killed at Carvin, France, on 22 July 1918. Aged just 19, he was buried at Estevelles Communal Cemetery in the Pas de Calais. In September 1918 he was posthumously awarded the Distinguished Flying Cross for his contribution to the war in the skies. His citation in the *London Gazette*, 21 September 1918, read:

> A very gallant and determined officer, who in thirteen days accounted for nine enemy machines. In these several engagements he has displayed remarkable skill and daring, on more than one occasion accounting for two machines in one patrol.

The Royal Navy

Historically, the Navy has employed many people of colour over generations. During the 18th century, at the height of the slave trade, British ships of the Royal and Merchant Navies sailed to Africa, India and the

Caribbean, returning with goods and people. Marika Sherwood, in her excellent discussion of Black workers and their relationship with the British armed forces during the Second World War, points out that the Navigation Laws of 1660 dictated three-quarters of sailors on English ships be English (i.e., White). By 1794 an increase in shipping trade as a result of the industrial revolution occasioned a dearth of seamen, leading to an amendment in the Laws officially sanctioning Black sailors.

> 'Negroes in the seas of America, belonging to any Person being His Majesty's Subject' were permitted to crew British ships. Though originally confined to the trade between the West Indies and North America, West Indian seamen made their way to Britain, settling and sailing from Liverpool, Cardiff, Barry, North and South Shields and London.[49]

Note the unqualified assumption of ownership of the 'Negro'! Blacks did serve in the Royal Navy in the 18th century, where the official and cultural attitude was less prohibitive and hostile than the Army. Olaudah Equiano was one, having been sold to an officer who renamed him Gustavas Vassa. While slaves were used on ships, usually when a British officer had taken his slave to sea with him,

> the Admiralty inclined to regard a man-of-war as a little piece of British territory in which slavery was improper . . . In rare cases when owners claimed back from the Navy slaves whose ownership was beyond dispute, the Admiralty was prepared to release them, as it did in the case of some slaves impressed . . . (But) the Admiralty felt that volunteers deserved protection . . . The same line was taken with slaves fleeing from enemy plantations and even those of the East India Company.[50]

African-American Briton Hammon also served with the Royal Navy in the 18th century. While it is not known if he was a slave he did write of his experiences in *Narrative of the Uncommon Sufferings and Surprising Deliverance of Briton Hammon, a Negro Man*,[51] published in 1760. Injured in 1759 while fighting the French in the Seven Years War, he was hospitalised at Greenwich Naval Hospital.

Peter Fryer notes that 47 African-Americans made claims for compensation upon the British government for wartime losses as a consequence of fighting for the king in the American War of Independence. Twelve of these served in the Navy, including Benjamin Whitecuff, hanged by the Americans as a spy only to be rescued by British cavalry three minutes after the drop.[52]

An example of the Georgian Navy's relatively enlightened attitude toward people of colour is their contrasting use and status within the judicial process. In British colonies practising slavery, Blacks could not act as witnesses or give testimony against Whites.

In some colonies such as the Gold Coast, a separate, ethnically exclusive legal system evolved. Fair and just practice was not a quality of government characteristic of this part of British West Africa. Indeed, during the 19th century, between 1878 and 1882, the Gold Coast colonial administration put in place a legal system in which local custom and practice informed the code of law for Africans while Europeans came under a separate code based upon English law. This dual structure formally differentiated and categorised the population by ethnicity. Different strokes for different folks; the strokes reserved for aberrant Africans.

Yet, in the Navy, in 1761, two White men were hung for sodomy by a court-martial, relying on the testimony given by the prosecution's star witness, a Black sailor. It also promoted Black sailors to positions of responsibility: John Perkins, commissioned Lieutenant in 1782, was one of the officers commanding the brig *Endeavour*. Within a couple of years he was entrusted with full command. In 1797 he was officially elevated to the status of commander. Seven years before retiring to Jamaica in 1812, Perkins was handed the responsibility for the frigates *Arab* and *Tartar*.

Another character in this triangular Black Atlantic transmission was Thomas Brown, a Guianan Petty Officer in the Royal Navy of the mid-19th century, whom we have discussed already. A contemporary of Thomas Brown's was William Hall, the first Black sailor awarded the highest British military honour of the Victoria Cross. The son of former American slaves, Hall began his working days at shipyards at Hantsport, Nova Scotia, Canada, building wooden ships for the merchant marine. Unsurprisingly, before reaching the age of maturity, he was lured away by imagination, wanderlust, seafarers' tales and the romance of the craft he helped build, joining the crew of a merchant ship. Later, in 1852, aged 31, he enlisted in the Royal Navy at Liverpool. Soon in action in the Crimea – did he come across Mary Seacole? – he was assigned to the naval brigade in which sailors joined their infantry comrades in battle.

After returning from Russia to England Hall worked on both HMS *Victory* and HMS *Shannon*, in the role of captain of the foretop. In further action in India at the siege of the British Residency of Lucknow, November 1857, he was tested to the limits of his bravery. All his *Shannon* shipmates having been killed fighting to lift the siege, except for a Lieutenant James Young, Hall held his nerve, continuing to fire his cannon until the dual walls of the Shah Najaf mosque had been holed, enabling British soldiers to enter. For his bravery he received the Victoria Cross at Queenstown, Ireland on 28 October 1859, while serving with HMS *Donegal*. Seventeen years later, in 1876, he retired with the rank of First Class Petty Officer, re-settling in Nova Scotia.

Like many working-class heroes his exploits were quickly forgotten, and he was buried unceremoniously, in 1904, in an unmarked grave. After a long public campaign, 41 years later he was given a burial service in Hantsport Baptist Church befitting his deeds.

> The monument at the Hantsport Baptist Church bears an enlarged replica of the Victoria Cross and a plaque describing Hall's courage and devotion to duty. A branch of the Canadian Legion in Halifax was renamed in his honour; also, a gym in Cornwallis, the DaCosta-Hall in Montreal (an education program for Black students), and the annual gun run of the Halifax International Tattoo carry on his name. In 1967, Hall's medals were returned to Canada from England to be shown at the 1967 Expo in Montreal. Later, as property of Nova Scotia, the medals were transferred to the Nova Scotia Museum.[53]

A practice of the 19th-century Navy was to use local personnel for their particular skills in regional operations: Somali sailors in the Persian Gulf and Red Sea because of their expertise in handling small boats, a quality particularly suited to work on survey ships; Goans as cooks and stewards (who, against the rules, were allowed moustaches!). In the First World War West Africans were used to navigate the inland waterways of Mesopotamia (historically, the land between the Tigris and Euphrates rivers).

The National Army Museum's *We Were There* exhibition also records the First World War service of Albert Marshall from Ceylon (Sri Lanka). A fireman with African and Maltese convoys, he sailed the Arctic route. Dick Lawless, in his research of the Arab community of Tyneside, found 'during the First World War Arab seamen were in demand in the Merchant Marine'[54] because large numbers of British seamen had joined the Royal Navy. Yet, after the war, the Aliens Order, 1920, and the Special Restriction (Coloured Alien Seamen) Order, 1925, resulted in many Arab seamen being re-classified as 'coloured aliens', reducing their liberties in Britain, making employment harder and deportation easier. Given the racist attacks on, and deaths of, sailors of colour in British ports such as Liverpool, South Shields and Cardiff immediately after the First World War, the inner-voice question of 'why did I fight?' may well have taunted these brown seamen.

In all three armed services, Army, Navy and Air Force, during the First World War there were people of colour. The Army and Air Force had brown-skinned officers. This was not because the Establishment, in particular the military chiefs of staff and the political elite in the War Office and Colonial Office, deemed Black equal to White. It was a consequence of practical considerations, or what Marx would have termed 'social being determining consciousness': the war effort needing men and these, through their actions, proving up to the task. (The RFC/RAF officers were both upper-middle class and public schoolboys.)

Unfortunately, the return of peace also witnessed a reoccurrence of ideological notions of race supremacy whereby nonsensical ideas clouded wartime experience with irrational prejudice. A strict colour bar was, once more, ruthlessly imposed. This will be discussed further in the last chapter.

10

Here and now

In 1918 Private T. Billingham, in the face of a mass advance by grey-suited German troops, tried to recover the body of his fellow soldier and commanding officer. Though his heroic action did not succeed, the subsequent recovery of Walter Tull, begun some 85 years later, has truly been a journey of discovery for an army of inquisitive people. He has brought profound change to the lives of many descendants of his brothers and sisters. He has captured my imagination, time and energy. He brought my children and me to France one blustery, cool autumn day in 1994 to find him. Thirteen years later, in August 2008, I returned with Dan Snow and his BBC *One Show* crew. Underneath Tull's name on the memorial wall at Faubourg d'Amiens cemetery was a small wooden cross laid anonymously by a pupil from Impington Village College. A suburb of Cambridge, Impington is a place I know well, having played for its local football team, Histon FC. I don't know the current ethnic composition of the comprehensive but I'd guess it is still overwhelmingly White. Yet someone representing the school had made a trip to France to pay homage to their Black hero.

Indeed, following my children's 1994 footsteps have been hundreds of other youngsters, including history teacher Dan Lyndon's pupils from Fulham who filmed their visit and scattered poppies at the site of his death. Tales from his life have been animated by Tom Hillebrand assisted by children from Tull's former elementary (primary) school in Folkestone and the National Children's Home in London. The footage of both can be seen on YouTube. At present, apart from writing this biography, I am editing a play about Tull, with scenes written by children from schools around the country. It is a part of the *Crossing the White Line* project managed by Peter Daniel, education officer of Westminster Archives. Funded by the people of this country through a Heritage Lottery grant, the project includes an exhibition, teaching pack and mural highlighting the obstacles and achievements in Tull's life.

Northamptonshire Black History Association (NBHA) has already produced detailed and extensive teaching packs for primary and secondary pupils. Written by Dan Lyndon, the NBHA teaching packs, aimed at Key Stages 2 and 3, may be used by the Walter Tull Association (WTA) in Bristol, a sports and arts social enterprise organisation managed by Beresford Lee and Lloyd Russell in their supplementary schools. These evening and weekend classroom-based initiatives are part of a programme of activities and interventions designed to better the quality of life for Bristol's working-class young, Black and White, by using Tull as a role model.

In October 2007, I attended a prize-giving dinner at Bristol's imposing Council House hosted by the WTA at which awards were presented to local people who had achieved beyond the ordinary, such as athletes, community volunteers and foster parents. There was one 'outsider' who was handed a prize: Edward Finlayson was given a posthumous award on Walter's behalf. The most moving moment of the evening was not watching England's defeat by South Africa in the rugby World Cup final on a pull-down screen at one end of the Council House, but the surprised response of award recipients whose hard work is not usually recognised by people and organisations outside their immediate circle.

It was at the launch of these packs in December 2006 that the widening and formal launch of the campaign to win back Tull's Military Cross took place. After making a plea to the audience for help in what had largely, up to then, been a limp one-man-band effort, I was approached by Nikki Taylor of NBHA who introduced me to Northampton South MP, Brian Binley. He offered to help in any way possible. I have written about the results of this collaboration between a Tory and a Marxist below. Northampton Borough Council has also given its formal support to the campaign. Since that December I have received bundles of brown packages with letters inside from Northampton schoolchildren addressed to the Ministry of Defence, demanding they give Tull his MC; and in July 2008, Northampton pupils took to the streets with their demands, making a public noise about the injustice. Moving into a more abstract realm, a feature film is in development with a script, actors, a director, producer, members of the crew already in place. It has the active support of Brian Binley MP, a great-nephew of

'Fanny' Walden, a team-mate of Tull's at Northampton, whose grandfather also fought in the 23rds Middlesex. Apart from facilitating meetings about the film project with government ministers and potential financial backers, Binley has tabled an Early Day Motion (EDM) asking

> That this house remembers Walter Tull for his contribution to British sport as a professional footballer for Tottenham Hotspur and Northampton Town football clubs; expresses its sincere gratitude for his lesser known role as a soldier who fought in the 17th Middlesex Regiment during the First World War; notes that he was accepted for Officer Training and appointed to a Commission in the Special Reserve of Officers in 1917; remembers that he sadly lost his life as an officer of the 23rd Middlesex Regiment in 1918; notes that his Commanding Officer mentioned him in despatches for his 'gallantry and coolness' on the Italian Front and recommended him for a Military Cross; regrets that he was not awarded the Cross because, as a British citizen of non-European descent, he should not have been commissioned at all and calls upon the Government to right this sizeable injustice by posthumously awarding him the Military Cross for his gallantry.[1]

The EDM had the signatures of over 50 MPs at the recess of Parliament in July 2008. This wasn't the first EDM concerning Tull. In April 2007, Keith Vaz MP sponsored one requesting

> That this House fully supports the campaign to recognise the achievements of Walter Tull with a statue in his honour; notes that Walter Tull was the first black British officer to lead white soldiers into battle; recognises his strong record of bravery and gallantry in wartime, being posthumously awarded the British War and Victory Medal; further notes his prior accomplishments as a successful professional footballer for a number of clubs, often in the face of vocal racial abuse; and believes that Walter Tull is a timeless role model for every generation.[2]

As I write this, over 90 years after his death, Tull has not (posthumously) received the Military Cross. Providing the 2nd Lieutenant with *his* medal would repay a debt owed to him and many other Black soldiers, for so long written out of British military history. In their letters to Edward Tull informing him of his brother's medal recommendation, both 2nd Lieutenant Pickard and Major D. S. Poole broke military rules.

> The subject of recommendations for honours and rewards is to be treated as strictly confidential and officers are forbidden to divulge at any time the nature of the recommendations they have made.
>
> In no case should the relatives or friends of an officer or soldier be informed that he has been recommended for reward.[3]

This quote is from *Instructions Regarding Recommendations for Honours and Rewards*, a detailed and comprehensive booklet laying out the regulations and procedures for military awards. Major Poole, one of the highest-ranking officers in the battalion, responsible for submitting medal recommendations, would have known the protocol and that his disclosure to Edward was officially prohibited. He still chose to inform him. It could be argued that Pickard, as a junior officer, may not have been aware of the restriction, but this is unlikely given his status as Company commander. What is certain is that Pickard had first-hand experience of Tull's soldiering skills, trusting his life and that of his men to their Black comrade. It is highly significant that both took the time and trouble to let Walter's next of kin know that he had been put forward for a medal. It begs the question: did they know a little more, especially Poole? He would have been informed of any decision regarding the recommendation. If told that Tull was not to receive a medal, did his frustration spur him to let Edward know a recommendation had been made? If the rule had been followed, only Tull, the officer who submitted the application on Army Form w 3121 and the personnel at the Military Secretary's Office and General Headquarters who received the original and copy would have known. (An example of profound irony is a letter to Edward from the Military Secretary, dated 12 April 1918, stating 'The Military Secretary is desired by the Secretary of State for War to express his deepest sympathy with Mr Tull-Warnock in the loss of his *gallant* [my emphasis] brother'.)[4]

Poole and Pickard ensured Tull's family would know. Did either or both hope Edward would pursue the matter? Major General Sidney Lawford, as commander of the 41st Division, would also have been involved in the recommendation process. Is it likely that, having personally cited Tull for his 'gallantry and coolness', he would have then rejected a call for a Military Cross? What were the odds of an officer mentioned in his battalion's War Diary for a leading part in a much publicised and applauded raid, formally congratulated by his Brigade commander, not receiving any medal or award? Admittedly, I don't have the statistics – I don't know if they exist – but I guess the probability would be very low. We do know officers were decorated for their persistent valour rather than a single act of bravery. Yet Tull was not decorated as an officer despite having 'certainly earned it' by being 'brave and conscientious; popular; liked by his men'; leading a raiding party that did 'excellent work'; being 'true and faithful'; 'a great player of "both games"'; and having 'a very high reputation for courage and devotion to duty'. These qualities, recognised by Pickard and Poole, men working closely with him, did not merit *any* special award or decoration *whatsoever*.

In May 2008 I was sent the copy of an email in which Major Robin Wheeler of the Army Legal Services admitted there had been a colour bar in the British Army during the First World War in spite of his parent employers, the Ministry of Defence, consistently denying its existence. Wheeler ended his confession with the mitigation that he and his legal department didn't have as much time as 'Mr Vasili' to trawl through the public archives. It was pathetic closure to what could have been a cathartic admittance. His reluctant climbdown was based upon a re-examination of the *Manual of Military Law* (1914) which I had quoted personally to people within the MoD. The *Manual* is a government publication. It sits on their shelves.

With the MoD having belatedly accepted the existence of a colour bar, it strengthened the argument that Tull was not decorated because of his colour. I decided to act upon Wheeler's mistaken supposition and trawled through the *London Gazette* MC awards for the Manchester and Middlesex Regiments during the first half of 1918 (the Manchesters served in Italy as part of 123 Brigade). I wanted to compare the citations for successful MC awards with Tull's. All began with 'for conspicuous gallantry and devotion to duty', qualities identified in Tull by Majors Lawford and Poole: 2nd Lieutenant Alec Booth of the Manchester Regiment was given his medal for 'coolness under machine gun fire';[5] Lawford's citation referred to Tull's 'coolness . . . in spite of heavy fire'. Captain Edward Redfern Thompson of the Manchester Regiment was decorated for 'penetrating enemy lines to a depth of 350 yards';[6] Tull led his covering party to a depth of 300 yards, according to Haig Brown's report of the 1 January raid written for General Headquarters. 2nd Lieutenant Herbert Fisher of the Middlesex Regiment had his recommendation accepted for being 'in charge of an observation party attached to an assaulting battalion'.[7] The most convincing example of unequal treatment is the award of a Military Cross to 2nd Lieutenant A. J. Acarnley

> for conspicuous gallantry and devotion to duty. When he was in command of a patrol reconnoitring the farther side of the river his position was discovered, but owing to his good leadership and initiative, he succeeded in withdrawing his patrol without loss. His patrol work at all times has been most conspicuous and during numerous crossings of the river he has displayed great courage and skill.[8]

It is important to emphasise that I'm not questioning the validity of any of these men's awards – far from it – but I am querying why someone who carried out similar acts was not decorated at all. Acarnley obviously merited his award. But the citation could have been written for Tull. He had also led men across the river more than once; he had also come under fire and led his men back to safety, without casualties. He had also been commended for his courage.

Throughout the war a system of quotas per medal operated. Awards and honours caused much friction and controversy, especially between front-line troops and non-combatants, such as staff officers in the rear. Exacerbating this tension was the perception that elite regiments such as the Guards and Household Cavalry were allotted a higher number. There is also the word-of-mouth suggestion that it was harder for working-class officers to be decorated and promoted. I have not seen any (research) evidence to support this other than Tull himself who, though embodying a contradiction as a Black officer, did not achieve either decoration or promotion. (Lack of, or apparently undeserved, promotion did generate irritable and fractious relations between senior and junior officers.)

Military Cross awards constituted nearly 18 per cent of all awards given for action in the field. Inaugurated in December 1914 as a medal for junior commissioned ranks – captain and below – many of its early recipients were officers well away from the firing line. A little under two years after its inception, the Army Council decided to clarify the criteria for nomination.

In consideration of the selection of officers, &c., for honours and decorations a clear distinction should be drawn between those serving in formations in direct contact with the enemy, such as divisions and lower formations, and those officers and men who are employed in the more distant areas of the Armies and Lines of Communication, or who are training and administering the forces of the Crown elsewhere.[9]

As a result, from 1917, the MC was intended for those who had distinguished themselves in the field. Further, the number of awards reserved for officers in France was increased to 500 each month. The rules were refined again in 1918 with the Army Council stressing the award should be for 'services in action only'.[10] 'Rewards were to be recommended . . . as immediate rewards for "acts of gallantry" in the presence of an enemy'.[11]

Changboo Kang, in his study of the British infantry soldier during the First World War, found that nearly 41 per cent of officers in the Royal Warwickshire Regiment were awarded MCs in 1918. The number of honours increased as the war continued, with the 1918 figure of 115 comprising 47.5 per cent of the total given during the conflict. He argues that the role of the platoon commander – invariably a 2nd Lieutenant – as a specialist in the field, became more important. Attacks and counter attacks on enemy positions by raiding parties led by subalterns increased in the latter stages of the conflict, providing the opportunity for individual acts of bravery and exemplars of extraordinary leadership.

It can be concluded . . . in cases of regimental officers on the company and platoon levels, performing acts of gallantry in operations of an offensive nature was the best way to . . . win a military honour.[12]

In written correspondence regarding the medal, Parliamentary Under-Secretary of State for Defence and Minister for Veterans, Derek Twigg, has argued that the Military Cross cannot be awarded posthumously. He has been backed up by some old sweats who have been posting messages on the Great War Forum website. Yet Section 46 of the *Instructions* (1918) booklet states

All orders, decorations and medals may be granted to officers or other ranks who are killed in action or who die of wounds, provided the officer initiating the original recommendation signed it before their death.[13]

To award Tull his medal will have a practical and symbolic significance: it will right an historic injustice to an individual; serve as a belated recognition of the collective acts of bravery and gallantry by Black soldiers; and act as an apology for their second-rate treatment as combatants during the war and veterans after when they were overlooked and ignored in the London victory parades. It will, most importantly, do something all politicians are keen to do when they have committed a breach of the rules, caught lying or violated rules: draw a line under the injustice caused by the colour bar. It will allow the military to shake off the lingering odour of past sins and move forward with a clear conscience.

The National Army Museum, in 2008, attempted to recover the contribution of people of colour in their exhibition *We Were There*. This theme is being repeated on a pan-European scale in Ypres with the In Flanders Fields Museum's exhibition *Multicultural Aspects of the First World War*.

Unfortunately, the Ministry of Defence are not moved enough by Tull's achievements and the mystery surrounding the rejection of his nomination to posthumously award his Military Cross. The most recent correspondence received on behalf of the campaign by Binley sees the MoD sticking stubbornly to their line that a special case cannot be made for Tull. This has been the standard response to previous appeals made by MPs I have coerced on this issue, David Lammy (Tottenham) and Glenda Jackson (my local representative). To award Tull his MC after so long, argue the MoD, with no supporting documents other than the letters of Major Poole and 2nd Lieutenant Pickard, would set an unwelcome and door-opening precedent leading to a rush of similar pleas from many others. Like two stubborn people crossing a narrow bridge in opposite directions, we're at an impasse. The argument in support of Tull is that it suited the Army and the War Office to appoint him an officer in the Special Reserve in 1917 despite this being against the rules, thereby setting a precedent in their favour. To rebalance the scales of justice by giving him the medal for which he was *recommended* and which he *deserved* would acknowledge the unique nature of his case and cause. This would not be unprecedented. In 2006 Maori Sergeant

Haane Manahi was posthumously recognised for his bravery 63 years after his Victoria Cross recommendation was '"inexplicably" countermanded by an anonymous Whitehall official during the Second World War'.[14]

As the years accumulate since Tull's death in action so does his significance. It is almost a symbiotic relationship. His stature as a figure of national importance is confirmed by his entries in the *Oxford Dictionary of National Biography* and the *Oxford Companion to Black British History*; his inclusion in an exhibition by the Imperial War Museum entitled *Sport and War*; the BBC4 drama *Walter's War* and documentary *Walter Tull: Forgotten Hero* broadcast on 9 and 13 November 2008, respectively; his Memorial Garden and eponymous road at Sixfields Stadium in Northampton; the Radio 4 afternoon play dramatising his life, aired in 2003; the BBC4 documentary *Black Flash* featuring Tull, transmitted in 2003; the biography by Rod Wickens published in 2003; the *Guardian* feature article by Richard Askwith in 1998; the Radio 5 documentary *Across the White Line* featuring Walter, broadcast in 1996. This list is not comprehensive.

Perhaps it is only at death that a full appraisal of one's contribution to the greater good is made. Major General T. D. Pilcher, commander of the 17th Division (New Army) at the (first) Battle of the Somme, in a letter to his officer son in June 1916, warned him about the misguided allure of pursuing honours.

> The only reward worth having is knowledge that you have done your duty, and whether your work be recognised, or whether you be blamed and others get the credit for what you have done, should not worry you as long as you have this knowledge in your heart. Your motive must be to do the best you can for your country and not to play to the gallery in order to obtain a reward. Do not give way to selfish vanity; it is not the acquisition of honours and rewards, but the abnegation of self that has wrought out all that is noble, all that is good, and nearly all that is useful in the world.[15]

This could also have been written for Tull. It reflects the ethos by which he lived his life – not just as a soldier; the philosophy that governed his actions. Neither he, nor brother Edward, nor his living descendents have grieved over the non-award of his MC. They have the satisfaction that he died doing his best for his men in a conflict that had both disillusioned him and brought out those qualities one only discovers in times of extreme crisis. The war was a hellish burden. Yet the knowledge it revealed about Tull the man has been a gift, both to him and us. His deeds created a man bigger than the world in which he lived. He acted, ad-libbed, achieved, strove with an obstinate tenacity that defined his character and took him way beyond the fence. The heartfelt obituaries and letters of condolence written after his death, though glowing and effusive, do not fully measure the man. 'An officer and a gentleman every inch of him', said the *Rushden Echo*, 12 April; the *Northampton Independent* on 13 July said 'he was a thorough gentleman, and beloved by all'; 'allow me to say how popular he was throughout the battalion', wrote 2nd Lieutenant Pickard; Northampton Town secretary, A. Jones, who provided a reference for his commission, informed Edward Walter was 'a great player of "both games" & a gentleman'; 'your brother bore a very high reputation for courage and devotion to duty', stated Major D. S. Poole.

The passing of time has infused a moral calibration and historical context to his achievements, revealing his worth and stature in a less grainy, more visible light. As tragic as his death was the disappearance of his deeds as a Black working-class Briton from popular culture and consciousness. The obstacles he surmounted in life, such as the colour bar in the Army, remained after death defiant and rigid in blocking his memory. Though he cleared ground for himself beyond the boundary fence, the real, the lasting gain of his legacy lies in the population of this clearing by similar others. Had the full significance of his accomplishments on the fields of Battle and Play – in 'both games' – been seared into contemporary memory perhaps the contribution of Black Britons to the history of the UK would have been more widely, generously and speedily recognised.

It is said by some that the nature of a society's moral character can be found in its treatment of minorities, such as prisoners, children, elderly, ethnic and religious groups. Societies consider themselves democratic, free and equal. The litmus test of that claim is the social status and well-being of those who have little political and economic power. Early 20th-century Britain's Black population was small compared to the early 21st century, with their lives subject to harsher turns of misfortune and discrimination. Jamaican author Theophilus Scholes, writing in 1905, recounted the unsolicited comment made to a Black man on a London street:

> One of the company . . . called the attention of his comrades to
> the presence of the coloured man, and then said: 'Look at that
> thing' . . . This laceration of the feeling, which has now become
> a practice in England, is due partly to the fact that Englishmen,
> having adopted the notion that they are superior to coloured men,
> have found rudeness and incivility to be the best supports of the
> imposture.[16]

Despite the degradation and humiliation suffered by people of colour in
the opening decades of last century, Walter Tull still swapped his shin-pads
for puttees. Judged by this action, Britain does not seem to have been a hell
on earth for this particular Black man.

Pulled along by his abilities, aptitude and talent, he did not seek fame
and glory. Had there not been a war, he would not have joined the military.
He was, in 1914, enjoying life as a professional footballer – a working-class
man playing for a working-class club in a working-class town looked-up
to by working-class people. He brought kudos and recognition to those
around him. He had that most precious and elusive commodity for a Black
Briton: respect from the community in which he lived. Compared to the
daily toil of the shoe worker in one of Northampton's numerous footwear
factories he had the life of Reilly. Yet he was prepared to give it all up, for
the time being at least, for khaki.

As an orphan, professional footballer and soldier/officer, Tull navi-
gated divergent extremities: calm waters and boat-breaking storms. As a
mixed-heritage boy in a loving family in Imperial Britain at the height of
its modernity, day-to-day simplicities were contextualised by the imposed
burden of hostility to his colour. Yet, as the reporter *DD* said of his dignity
as a young adult in the face of racist hostility, his behaviour was a lesson to
the White men on the pitch. Perhaps he should have said 'to all men' and
left it at that. His death in battle was poignantly poetic in the sense that it
encapsulated those two opposite but entwined essences of life, heroism and
tragedy: 'killed [on the battlefield] instantaneously with a bullet through
the head'.[17] Billingham, who tried to rescue him, says he lived for two
minutes. Walter had soldiered virtually the duration of his war; a veteran
of numerous campaigns; awarded the 1914–15 Star and British War and
Victory medals; cited for gallantry and recommended for a Military Cross.

It could be argued that Tull was politically naïve. He served in an army that didn't want him; whose chiefs of staff argued Black soldiers were a threat to discipline; that accepted the findings of 'science' that he and his kind were throwbacks. That Charles Arundel Moody was the next Black officer, during the Second World War, suggests that the colour bar was relaxed in times of war for practical reasons and returned in peacetime for ideological reasons. Marika Sherwood, a historian of the Black Diaspora, outlines how the barriers of prejudice operated.

> Army Order 89 of 1938 passed by the Army Council, restricted entry to men of pure European descent. The amendment was made 'to regularise a semi-official ruling because of the difficulty of placing a coloured British subject who had enlisted in this country in 1936. Until the amendment was made, the only way of excluding undesirable non-Europeans was by telling the Examining Medical Officer to find them unfit or by some other equally undesirable subterfuge . . . The Military Colleges . . . only accepted men of pure European descent who were the British-born sons of British-born parents . . . Section 95 of the Air Force Act stated that enlistment was only open to men of pure European descent, though aliens could be accepted. The Navy's officers were also limited to British subjects of pure European descent. Ratings could be 'Maltese and men of Colour who are the sons of British-born subjects'.[18]

After the Second World War, debate continued within the War Office as to the suitability of Black soldiers in the forces, in particular whether 'coloureds' should be accepted for the 'gazetting of officers to regular commissions'.[19] At a cabinet meeting on 3 June 1947, the (Labour) Secretary of State for War argued 'British soldiers would not take kindly to serving under coloured officers and discipline would be undermined'. Some within government wanted to see recruitment become even more ethnically exclusive.

> 'Anglo-Saxon' should be substituted for 'European'. We should like gentlemen of North American, Australian and New Zealandic (sic) descent, but do not want those descended from various types of European parents, even if they themselves were British subjects.[20]

National Service, introduced in 1947, entailed compulsory military training for Britain's youth. This exacerbated the colour question for the forces'
ethnic gatekeepers as 'male British subjects of non-European descent ordinarily resident in Britain will become liable'.[21] In keeping with past practice
a bureaucratic deception was suggested by the Army Council Secretariat.

> By administrative action it might be possible to refrain from
> calling up persons who are coloured. But the anomaly of admitting
> coloured men for compulsory service and rejecting them as profes-
> sional soldiers is one which cannot be defended without difficulty.[22]

Tull fought for a country that, once the war had ended, responded to race
riots in Liverpool, Cardiff, Newport and London by setting up repatriation
committees in Hull, South Shields, Glasgow, Cardiff, Liverpool, London
and Salford. Black people who had been involved in the war effort were *for-
cibly* repatriated by William Joynson-Hicks, co-founder of the Footballers'
Battalion, who as Home Secretary, 1924–9, ordered that 'coloured' seamen
who could not prove their British nationality must register with the police
as 'aliens', thereby entering a legal and bureaucratic process that often ended
in deportation – some British-born 'aliens' to countries they had never seen.

The war changed the world. It damaged individuals, matured political
movements and quickened revolution. In a letter from the Front in which
Tull writes to Edward that he has asked for a posting to the British West
Indies Regiment, the 2nd Lieutenant indicates his developing political
awareness, forged by the contrast of his day-to-day practice of leading men
on the front line and his surreal status as a Black combat officer, a contradiction that he would have been aware of given his training at Gailes. As
an 'alien/Negro' the rules stated he could only be commissioned into an
'honorary rank', barred from 'exercising any actual command or power'[23]
and that he was an illegal officer in the Special Reserve of Officers because
he was not of 'pure European descent.'[24]

In consequence of, and despite, the carnage Tull became more acutely
aware of who and what he was. Had he been granted his request for a
posting to the BWI Regiment – kept away from much front-line action
because of the political unease about how this experience would be used
after the war – he would have officered radicalised soldiers who eventually mutinied while in Italy in 1918 and who would return to an awakening

Caribbean working class shaking off its shackles through strikes, demonstrations and riots that swelled in the wake of peace, a loud and unmistakable testament to the growing self-confidence of the anti-colonial movement.

In 1919, working-class Britain was in a rebellious state. Whether the war created the mood of revolt among workers – sometimes taking a horribly distorted and misguided form as we saw above with the race riots – or merely speeded up a process that had been years in fermentation, is not for debate here. The fact is it happened. Families, individuals, veterans were changed by the war, including Tull, his eagerness to enlist souring to a hatred for the carnage.

Tull's days at Tottenham and Northampton brought pressures unknown to his White team-mates. As a soldier he was the only Black combat officer in the British Army until the Second World War. (It wasn't until the 1990s that the elite Guards Regiment inducted its first Black recruit.) His dogged persistence in not accepting the pre-determined roles reserved for people of his class and ethnicity has left a solid and inspiring legacy.

Late in the morning of Sunday 11 July 1999 on a hot, sunny day in front of a sizeable crowd at their Sixfields Stadium, Northampton Town FC unveiled a memorial standing within a Garden of Remembrance. The sculptured wall of achievement, designed by Paul Mason, was funded by donations from the public and organisations such as the Professional Footballers' Association and Kick It Out. Since, the road leading into Sixfields Stadium has been renamed Walter Tull Way. The trend set by the football club caught on. The headquarters of Northampton Probation Service is now Walter Tull House.

The memorial was the culmination of years of hard work and persistence by Brian Lomax, an elected supporter director of the club, and Northampton South MP Tony Clarke. In his speech Brian Lomax told how the club's project to install a physical memorial to Walter Tull had reached people far and wide. In his hand, Chamberlain style, he held a letter he'd received from a junior football club in Accra, Ghana, praising the Cobblers for their progressive action. It ended by asking if the club could send some much needed and very scarce football kit and equipment. I smiled. I had received the same letter; so had Howard Holmes at Football Unites, Racism Divides and various others. Like Brian I had sent some surplus shirts and shorts. I hope they did go to those who needed them but I've a suspicion that they may have been set out for sale on an Accra market stall or roadside!

Edward Finlayson, representing Tull, spoke about his surprise at the rapid acknowledgement his great-uncle was now receiving. Artist Colin Yates displayed his evocative exhibition of Black footballers, *Black Looks*. A steel band entertained between speakers. After the speeches and the ceremonial removal of the curtain covering the sculpture, the West Indian Ex-Servicemen's Association played the Last Post. It was an emotional day that rippled with love. At last the soldier with no grave was laid to rest with a show of affection and gratitude that befitted his accomplishments. It was my humbling honour to write the epitaph inscribed upon the memorial.

> Through his actions, Tull ridiculed the barriers of ignorance that tried to deny people of colour equality with their contemporaries. His life stands testament to a determination to confront those people and those obstacles that sought to diminish him and the world in which he lived. It reveals a man, though rendered breathless in his prime, whose strong heart still beats loudly.

Postscript

As the manuscript was being prepared for production the 1911 Census became available. On the morning of Monday 3 April 1911 – when the household details were, for the first time, entered onto the information sheet by the head of the household – Walter was to be found at the home of widow Mrs Theresa W. Cove, aged 54, 6 Kymberley Road, Harrow. Also residing were Theresa's single daughters, Winifred Eva, 19, Grace Elizabeth, 17, Dorothy Durrett, 14, and her son David Owen, 13.

This collection of names, ages, gender and marital status throws up all sorts of questions and possibilities, given that Walter was unmarried and supposed to be living in Tottenham around this time. A friendship with David seems unlikely, given his adolescence, which suggests there may have been a romantic reason for the Spurs footballer's visit (via the Metropolitan Line?), to Middlesex.

The appealing ambiguity of this census entry further propels a momentum that rarely fails to slow and has become a motif of the Tull's story. As I save and exit this file I know his tale is unfinished.

Notes

1 Finding the Tulls

1 'Tales of Grandfathers', handwritten memoir of Jean Finlayson, n.d., in Finlayson Family Collection.

2 'Tales of Grandfathers'.

3 Interview with Jean Finlayson (née Tull-Warnock) and Rev. Duncan Finlayson, Appin, Argyll, 20 February 1995.

4 Interview with Rev. Duncan Finlayson, 2 June 2008.

5 Interview with Rev. Duncan Finlayson.

6 Interview with Rev. Duncan Finlayson. As a featherweight boxer, Duncan used to train with Harold Moody junior while the latter, 'a fine specimen', was studying in Glasgow. 'He would lie on a mat and say "hold me down". We would jump on his back and finish up with the life squashed out of us'. Duncan first met Harold at Edward Tull-Warnock's apartment in St Vincent's Street, Glasgow.

7 Quoted from *Pleasure, Profit and Proselytism: British Culture and Sport at Home and Abroad, 1700–1914*, J. A. Mangan (ed.) (London, 1982), ch. 5 'Catalyst of Change: John Guthrie Kerr and the Adaptation of an Indigenous Scottish Tradition', p. 101.

8 Obituary, *Carrick Herald* (Girvan), 15 December 1950.

9 Obituary, *Carrick Herald*.

10 Interview, *Carrick Herald*.

11 Interview, *Carrick Herald*.

12 'Tales of Grandfathers'.

13 Finlayson Family Collection.

14 David Dabydeen and Shivani Sivagurunathan in the *Oxford Companion to Black British History*, David Dabydeen, John Gilmore and Cecily Jones (eds) (Oxford, 2007), p. 417.

15 *Oxford Companion to Black British History.*
16 Quoted from Jeffrey Green, *Black Edwardians, Black People in Britain 1901–1914* (London, 1998), p. 178.

2 A mixed-heritage family in 19th-century Folkestone

1 Baptism Book, no. 557. This information was kindly provided by Graham Humphrey, the great-great-grandson of Daniel Tull.
2 'Daniel Tull: A Short Journal', Finlayson Family Collection.
3 'A Short Journal'.
4 'A Short Journal'.
5 Hilary Beckles, *A History of Barbados* (Cambridge, 1990), pp. 112–14, 129.
6 *A History of Barbados*, p. 90.
7 *A History of Barbados*, p. 113.
8 According to her mother in a letter written to Daniel on 26 April 1880 in the Finlayson Family Collection.
9 Finlayson Family Collection. My thanks to Marilyn Stephenson-Knight of the Dover War Memorial Project for information on the Palmer and Coombe families. Descendants of both are still living in the Dover area.
10 Finlayson Family Collection.
11 Finlayson Family Collection.
12 Finlayson Family Collection.
13 Finlayson Family Collection.
14 National Archives (NA), London, 1891 Census, Folkestone north, column 1, schedule 50. Living in the street nearby were a harness maker, three general labourers and two gardeners.
15 *Blackwood's Edinburgh Magazine*, no. 943 (May 1894), vol. 155, p. 660.
16 *Blackwood's Edinburgh Magazine*, no. 943 (May 1894), vol. 155, pp. 660–73.
17 Finlayson Family Collection.
18 Edward Tull, 'The Film that Will Never Be Screened', Finlayson Family Collection.
19 Application form for the admission of a child to the Children's Home and Orphanage.

3 Tull, the 'many' and the 'few'

1 These terms are borrowed from Percy Bysshe Shelley's poem, *Mask of Anarchy*, written after the Peterloo Massacre of 1819 in Manchester. The last verse reads:
    Rise like Lions after slumber
    In unvanquishable number –
    Shake your chains to earth like dew

Which in sleep had fallen on you –
Ye are many – they are few.

2   L. Harlan, *Booker T. Washington: The Making of a Black Leader, 1856–1901* (New York, 1972), p. 241 quoted from *Black Edwardians*, p. 238.

3   'Mr Spurgeon' quoted in J. Salter, *The East in the West or Work among the Asiatics and Africans in London* (London, 1895), pp. 70–1.

4   Henry Fielding, *Tom Jones* quoted from Peter Ackroyd, *London: The Biography* (London, 2001), p. 578.

5   *London*, p. 711.

6   Though the writer is unknown, I have a suspicion, based upon writing style and biographical circumstance, it could be William Cowper.

7   Martin Hoyles, *The Axe Laid to Root* (London, 2004).

8   *The Axe Laid to Root, or a Fatal Blow to Oppressors, Being an Address to the Planters and Negroes of the Island of Jamaica*, no. 1 [1817], cols. 12–13 quoted from Peter Fryer, *Staying Power: The History of Black People in Britain* (London, 1984), p. 221.

9   *Staying Power*, p. 239.

10 *Staying Power*, p. 262.

11 *The Encore*, 14 September 1905, quoted from *Black Edwardians*, p. 81.

12 H. Sampson, *The Ghost Walks: A Chronological History of Blacks in Show Business, 1865–1910* (London, 1988), pp. 351–2 quoted from *Black Edwardians*, p. 88.

13 John Cameron, *Association Football and How to Play It* (London, 1909).

14 A. B. C. Merriman-Labor, *Britons through Negro Spectacles* (London, 1909), p. 105.

15 *Britons through Negro Spectacles*, p. 115.

16 *Britons through Negro Spectacles*, pp. 175–6.

4   The Children's Home and Orphanage

1   NCH online history, www.theirhistory.co.uk/70001/info.php?p=13&pno=0.

2   Uncle Jonathan, *Walks in and around London* (1895) in Lee Jackson, *The Victorian Dictionary* at www.victorianlondon.org/searchframe.html.

3   'The Story of Forty Years, 1869–1909 for the Children of Sorrow', *Highways and Hedges*, July and August 1909, p. 104.

4   NCH archive, Tull file 'Epitome of Correspondence' (hereafter Epitome). Letters between Adcock and Stephenson, January–February 1898.

5   Application form, section 13.

6   Epitome.

7   22 January 1898, Epitome.

8   22 January 1898.

9 William Bradfield, *The Life of the Reverend Thomas Bowman Stephenson* (London, 1913), p. 153.

10 Gordon E. Barritt, *Thomas Bowman Stephenson* (Peterborough, 1996), p. 22.

11 *The Life of the Reverend Thomas Bowman Stephenson*, p. 250.

12 *The Life of the Reverend Thomas Bowman Stephenson*, p. 321.

13 Reverend Thomas Bowman Stephenson quoted from *The Life of the Reverend Thomas Bowman Stephenson*, William Bradfield (London, 1913) in Terry Philpot, *Action for Children: The Story of Britain's Foremost Children's Charity* (Oxford, 1994), p. 20. Thanks to Sarah Metcalfe for alerting me to this quote.

14 Medical report in the application form.

15 Epitome.

16 Epitome. The allegorical irony of this statement from a Christian institution points to frictions between ideology and practice which permeated all imperial, metropolitan social relations when the dimension of ethnicity was introduced.

17 Epitome.

18 Eptome.

19 Edward Tull, 'The Film that Will Never Be Screened', Finlayson Family Collection.

20 'The Story of Forty Years', p. 108.

21 Thomas Bowman Stephenson, *Concerning Sisterhoods* (London, 1890), pp. 73–4.

22 *Concerning Sisterhoods*, pp. 17–18.

23 From Sergeant W. D. Tull, no. 55, A Coy., 17th Middlesex Regiment, British Expeditionary Force, c/o GPO, *c.* February 1917 in Finlayson Family Collection.

24 *East London Observer*, 29 August 1914, p. 3, in Ralph Samuel, *East End Underworld* (London, 1981), p. 321.

25 'The Film that Will Never Be Screened'.

26 Letter from Clara to CHO, 8 December 1898, in Epitome.

27 Cyril Davey, *A Man for All Children: The Story of Thomas Bowman Stephenson* (London, 1968), p. 91.

28 *A Man for All Children*, pp. 195–6.

29 Butcher to Gregory, 11 October 1900 in Epitome.

30 Butcher to Gregory.

31 'The Story of Forty Years', p. 98.

32 Mr and Mrs Warnock to Mr Pendlebury, principal of Bonner Road, undated (*c.* October 1900) in Epitome.

33 Letter from Edward to Walter, 15 November 1900, in Epitome.

34 Letter from Edward to CHO, 27 May 1903, in Epitome.

35 Interview with Jean and Rev. Duncan Finlayson.

36 Reg Ferm, *Ice Cold Charity* (Sussex, 1990), p. 9, an autobiography of orphanage life in the 1920s.

37 *Ice Cold Charity*, p. 128.

38 16 May 1903 in Epitome.

39 Profile, *Football Star*, 20 March 1909.

40 Correspondence in Epitome, 23 October 1907.

5 Football

1 *Football Star*, 20 March 1909.

2 *Illustrated Sporting and Dramatic News*, 17 April 1909, p. 271.

3 *The Weekly Herald* (Tottenham and Edmonton), 12 March 1909.

4 Letter written from RMSP *Araguaya*, 26 May 1909, to Mr Morgan at NCH in London, NCH Archives, Highbury, London.

5 Letter written from RMSP *Araguaya*.

6 Letter written from RMSP *Araguaya*.

7 *The Weekly Herald* (Tottenham and Edmonton), 16 June 1909.

8 John Harding, *For the Good of the Game: The Official History of the Professional Footballers' Association* (London, 1991), p. 29.

9 *Buenos Aires Herald* (*BAH*), 8 June 1909.

10 *BAH*, 17 June 1909, p. 9.

11 *BAH*, 17 June 1909, p. 9.

12 *BAH*, 17 June 1909, p. 9.

13 *BAH*, 8 June 1909, p. 9.

14 *BAH*, 20 June 1909, p. 9.

15 Action by players over wage capping and unionisation meant the tourists had left behind a highly charged political environment. Yet the industrial climate in Argentina was far more turbulent and volatile. Two hundred thousand workers had been on strike for ten days in May, eventually crushed with brute force by the army.

16 *BAH*, 6 June 1909, p. 3. 'Wednesday next' refers to Liga Argentina v. Tottenham Hotspur. Spurs won 4–1, with Tull at centre-forward.

17 *BAH*, 23 May 1909, p. 9; see also 15, 17, 25, 26, 27, 29 June.

18 *BAH*, 23 May 1909, p. 9.

19 *The Weekly Herald* (Tottenham and Edmonton), 16 June 1909.

20 *A Romance of Football: The History of Tottenham Hotspur FC* www.purshistory.com/pages/38.htm.

21 Adam Powley and Martin Cloake, *The Spurs Miscellany: The Ultimate Book of Tottenham Trivia* (London, 2006), p. 7.

22 John Cameron, *Association Football and How to Play It* (London, 1909), p. 76.

23 *Association Football and How to Play It*, p. 34.

24 *Association Football and How to Play It*, pp. 35, 40.

25 *The Wednesday Herald* (Tottenham and Edmonton), 8 September 1909.

26 *Daily Chronicle*, 2 September 1909.

27 *Newcastle Daily Chronicle*, 2 September 1909.

28 Both *Newcastle Journal*, 2 September 1909. Thanks to Mark Metcalf for providing these Newcastle reports.

29 *Daily Chronicle*, 6 September 1909.

30 *The Wednesday Herald*, 15 September 1909.

31 *Daily Chronicle*, 13 September 1909.

32 *Athletic News*, 13 September 1909.

33 *Tottenham and Wood Green Advertiser*, 25 September 1909.

34 *The Wednesday Herald*, 29 September 1909.

35 *Tottenham and Wood Green Advertiser*, 9 October 1909.

36 *Daily Chronicle*, 4 October 1909.

37 *Tottenham and Wood Green Advertiser*, 16 October 1909.

38 *The Wednesday Herald*, 20 October 1909.

39 *Football Star*, 9 October 1909.

40 *Bristol Evening News*, 2 October 1909.

41 *Bristol Evening News*, 2 October 1909.

42 *Bristol Evening News*, 2 October 1909.

43 *Bristol Evening News*, 2 October 1909

44 C. L. R. James, *Beyond a Boundary* (London, 1996), p. 214.

45 Jeffrey Green, 'Brown, James Jackson' in *Oxford Dictionary of National Biography* (Oxford, 2004).

46 G. Wagstaffe-Simmons, *Tottenham Hotspur Football Club: Its Birth and Progress 1882–1946* (Tottenham, 1947).

47 Ulrich Hesse-Lichtenberger, *Tor! The Story of German Football* (London, 2002), p. 42.

48 *Tor!*, p. 99.

49 *Northampton Daily Chronicle*, 18 October 1911.

50 *Northampton Daily Chronicle*, 18 October 1911.

51 *Football Echo* (Northampton), 4 March 1911.

52 In Rod Wickens, *From Claret to Khaki* (Liverpool, 2003), p. 33.

53 *Northampton Daily Chronicle*, 21 October 1911.

54 *Football Echo* (Northampton), 15 March 1913.

55 *Football Echo*, 13 September 1913.

56 *Football Echo*, 5 April 1913.

57 *From Claret to Khaki*, p. 45.

58 *From Claret to Khaki*, p. 46.

6 Other pioneer Black footballers in the UK, 1872–1918

1   Information supplied to author by email from Richard McBrearty, curator, Scottish Football Museum, 6 March 2008.

2   Email from Richard McBrearty.

3   Chronicle World – Changing Black Britain, June 2002, www.chronicle-world.org.

4   Douglas Lamming, *A Scottish Soccer Internationalists' Who's Who 1872–1986* (London, 1987), p. 219.

5   CO 96/238/2044.

6   *Leith Observer*, 19 March 1898.

7   *Leith Observer*, 8 October 1898.

8   *Edinburgh Evening Dispatch*, 9 September 1899.

9   *West Herts and Watford Observer*, 12 October 1907.

10 *Carrick Herald* (Girvan), 15 December 1950.

11 *Sports Special The Green 'Un*, Sheffield, 9 November 1918.

12 *Newcastle Evening Chronicle*, 2 September 1899.

13 *Sporting Man* (Newcastle), 5, 6 September 1899.

14 *African Review*, 9 September, 1899 vol. xx, no. 355; *Sporting Man* (Newcastle), 7 September 1899; 8 September.

15 *Football Echo and Sports Gazette*, 2 September 1899.

16 *Athletic News*, 18 September 1899.

17 *Sporting Man*, 6 September 1899.

7 Bloods, sweat and fears: other Black sports people

1   *The Illustrated Sporting and Dramatic News*, November 1899, p. 319.

2   An honorary title, See jaiarjun.blogspot.com/2004/11/ranji-maharajah-of-connemara.html.

3   *The Sporting Chronicle*, Wednesday 17 December 1930, p. 4.

4   *Black Edwardians*, p. 164.

5   In Arthur Ashe Jnr, *A Hard Road to Glory*, vol. 1 (London, 1993), p. 27.

6   *A Hard Road to Glory*, p. 27.

7   Jeffrey P. Green, 'Boxing and the "Colour Question" in Edwardian Britain: The "White Problem" of 1911', *International Journal of the History of Sport*, vol. 5, no. 118 (1988).

8   www.pbs.org/race/000_About/002_03_a-godeeper.htm.

9   *Black Edwardians*, p. 173.

10 Peter Lovesey, *The Official Centenary of the AAA* (London, 1979), p. 75.

11 *Beyond a Boundary*, p. 214.

12 A fuller version of this debate regarding Meyer, Edward, Liddle, Abrahams

and *Chariots of Fire* can be found in Phil Vasili, *The First Black Footballer – Arthur Wharton, 1865–1930: An Absence of Memory* (London, 1998), pp. 183–90.

8 War

1   Eric Hobsbawm, *The Age of Empire 1875–1914* (London, 1995), p. 318.
2   Coulson Kernahan, *The Experience of a Recruiting Officer* (London, 1915), ch. XVIII.
3   Andrew Riddoch and John Kemp, *When the Whistle Blows: The Story of the Footballers' Battalion in the Great War* (Yeovil, 2008), p. 42.
4   *When the Whistle Blows*, p. 44.
5   John Terrain (ed.), *General Jack's War Diary: War on the Western Front 1914–18* (London, 1993), p. 91, cited by James Roberts, '"The Best Football Team, the Best Platoon": The Role of Football in the Proletarianization of the British Expeditionary Force, 1914–1918', *Sport in History*, vol. 26, 1 April 2006, p. 31.
6   Lieutenant General R. S. S. Baden-Powell, *Scouting for Boys: A Handbook for Instruction in Good Citizenship* (London, 1908) in '"The Best Football Team, the Best Platoon"', p. 9.
7   *The Socialist Pioneer*, 16 December 1914.
8   A. F. Pollard in a letter to *The Times*, 7 November 1914 in Tony Mason, *Association Football and English Society 1863–1915* (Brighton, 1980), p. 251.
9   Stephen Jenkins, *They Took the Lead: The Story of Clapton Orient's Major Contribution to the Footballers' Battalion in the Great War* (London, 2005), p. 42.
10 7 December 1914, in *Association Football and English Society 1863–1915*, p. 254.
11 *They Took the Lead*, pp. 44–5.
12 Sergeant Stanley A. Lane, 'The Great War 1914–18: Personal Experiences of a Front Line Infantryman', Imperial War Museum, London, 97/10/1, p. 1.
13 *The Great War 1914–18*, p. 2.
14 C. Clark, *The Tin Trunk: Letters and Drawings* (London, 2000) in *When the Whistle Blows*, pp. 58–9.
15 *The Tin Trunk*, p. 70.
16 Benjamin Disraeli, *Sybil* (London, 1845).
17 C. Clark (London, 2000), p. 26, in *When the Whistle Blows*, p. 71.
18 Everard Wyrall, *The Die-Hards in the Great War, vol. 1 1914–16* (London, 1926), p. 238.
19 To Mr Hodgson-Smith, exact date unclear, 1916, in Finlayson Family Collection.
20 *When the Whistle Blows*, p. 89 quoting H. Taylor, *Jix: Viscount Brentford* (London, 1933), p. 138.
21 *When the Whistle Blows*, p. 89 quoting H. Taylor, p. 138.
22 Military Service Record, WO 339/90293/175466, NA, Kew, London.

23   Quoting from *Berkshire Chronicle*, 18 August 1916 in *When the Whistle Blows*, p. 97.

24   *First World War Diary of Bdr Charles Bertram Spires*, myweb.tiscali.co.uk/ tedspires/Diary.htm.

25   War Office, *Instructions for the Training of Platoons for Offensive Action* (London, 1917), p. 13, in Changboo Kang, 'The British Infantry Officer on the Western Front in the First World War. With Special Reference to the Royal Warwickshire Regiment' (unpublished), Centre for First World War Studies, University of Birmingham (2002), p. 245.

26   Private papers of C. H. Cox, Imperial War Museum, London, 88/11/1, p. 2.

27   A synopsis of Ben Shephard, *A War of Nerves* (London, 2002) at www.rbooks. co.uk/product.aspx?id=0712667830.

28   War Diary, 17th Battalion Middlesex Regiment) WO 95/1361, entry for 13 November 1916

29   *The Die-Hards in the Great War, vol. 1 1914–16*, p. 243.

30   Siegfried Sassoon, *Memoirs of an Infantry Officer* (London, 2001), p. 151, in '"The Best Football Team, the Best Platoon"', p. 31.

31   Written 4 July 1916, quoted in the *Journey's End* programme for the production at the Cambridge Arts Theatre, 24–29 January 2005.

32   C. R. M. F. Crutwell, *A History of the Great War* (Oxford, 1934), p. 154.

33   F. P. Crozier, *A Brass Hat in No Man's Land* (London, 1950), p. 42, in *Mutinies* by David Lamb (geocities.com/cordobakaf/mutinies.html), p. 3.

34   *Manual of Military Law*, War Office (London, 1914), p. 471.

35   A. R. Haig Brown, *My Game Book* (London, 1903).

36   'The Football Player', A. R. Haig Brown, *Sporting Sonnets* (London, 1903).

37   A. R. Haig Brown, *The OTC and Great War* (London, 1915), p. 89.

38   *Alan Roderick Haig Brown: Writings and Reflections*, Valerie Haig Brown (ed.) (Toronto, 1982).

39   Private papers of 2nd Lieutenant W. Paterson, Imperial War Museum, London.

40   Thanks to Heather Hurst for this information and the obituary quotations.

41   Private papers of 2nd Lieutenant W. Paterson, Imperial War Museum, London, 89/7/1, p. 78.

42   Private papers of 2nd Lieutenant W. Paterson, p. 79.

43   Private papers of 2nd Lieutenant W. Paterson, p. 80.

44   CN (Alec John Dawson), *A 'Temporary Gentleman' in France: Home Letters from an Officer in the New Army* (London, 1916), pp. 43–4, in 'The British Infantry Officer on the Western Front in the First World War', p. 265.

45   War Office, *Instructions for the Training of Platoons for Offensive Action*, 1917, p. 13, in 'The British Infantry Officer on the Western Front in the First World War', p. 245.

46   War Office, *Instructions for the Training of Platoons for Offensive Action.*

47   I. Fletcher (ed.), *Letters from the Front: The Great War Correspondence of Lieutenant Brian Lawrence 1916–17* (Tunbridge Wells, 1993), p. 35, in 'The British Infantry Officer on the Western Front in the First World War', p. 307.

48   Alan Sillitoe, *Raw Material* (London, 1978), p. 105.

49   *Raw Material*, p. 105.

50   12 April 1918, Finlayson Family Collection.

51   *The Die-Hards in the Great War, vol. 2 1916–19*, p. 118.

52   Private papers of Captain L. N. Phillips, Imperial War Museum, London, 77/103/1.

53   Private papers of C. H. Cox.

54   Arthur Nugent Floyer-Acland, 'The Journal of Arthur Nugent Acland. The Duke of Cornwall's Light Infantry. The Great War 1914–18', Imperial War Museum, London, 03/29/1, p. 72.

55   'The Journal of Arthur Nugent Acland', pp. 76, 80.

56   WO 95/2639.

57   Francis Mackay, *Battleground Europe: Touring the Italian Front 1917–1919* (South Yorkshire, 2002), p. 53.

58   *Battleground Europe*, pp. 60–1, quoted from Norman Gladden, *Across the Piave* (London, 1959).

59   War Diary, 23rd Middlesex Regiment WO 95/4243.

60   *First World War Diary of Bdr Charles Bertram Spires.*

61   Finlayson Family Collection.

62   *Manual of Military Law* (1914), p. 471.

63   Diary of Major General Pope-Hennessy, Imperial War Museum, London, 03/35/1, pp. 80–1.

64   Patricia Seaton Lawford, *The Peter Lawford Story* (New York, 1988).

65   WO 95/157/633 War Diary 123 Brigade 'Report on raid carried out by the 23rd Middlesex Regiment on the night of 1st/2nd Jan. 1918', Alan R. Haig Brown.

66   WO 95/157/633 'Italy, GHQ, Intelligence Summaries, January 1918'.

67   *The Die-Hards in the Great War, vol. 2 1916–19*, p. 191.

68   John Bourne, *Britain and the Great War 1914–1918* (London, 1989), in '"The Best Football Team, the Best Platoon"', p. 218.

69   Captain Desmond Allhusen, 8/King's Royal Rifles, quoted from Malcolm Brown, *1918: Year of Victory* (London, 1998), p. 4, in '"The Best Football Team, the Best Platoon"', p. 33.

70   'The Journal of Arthur Nugent Acland', p. 88.

71   *Raw Material*, p. 93.

72   Interview with Jean and the Rev. Duncan Finlayson, 1995.

9 'Not of pure European descent'

1   G. Arthur, *The Letters of Lord and Lady Wolseley* (London, 1922), p. 10, in Robert B. Edgerton, *The Fall of the Asante Empire* (London, 1995), p. 110.

2   WO 32/6889 'Enlistment of Eurasians into British Regiments', 29 December 1886, in David Killingray, 'All the King's Men? Blacks in the British Army in the First World War, 1914–1918' in Rainer Lotz and Ian Pegg (eds), *Under the Imperial Carpet: Essays in Black History* (Crawley, 1986), p. 170.

3   'All the King's Men?', pp. 167–9.

4   John D. Ellis, 'Drummers for the Devil? The Black Soldiers of the 29th (Worcestershire) Regiment of Foot, 1759–1843', *Journal of the Society for Army Historical Research*, vol. 80, autumn 2002, no. 323, p. 196.

5   Ronald Hyam, *Empire and Sexuality: The British Experience* (Manchester, 1991), p. 118.

6   Reverend William Moister, *Memoir of the Rev. H. Wharton* (London, 1875), p. 205.

7   *Short Guide to Obtaining a Commission in the Special Reserve of Officers* (London, 1912), p. 8.

8   *Glasgow Evening Times*, 12 February 1940. The sub-heading ran: 'Glasgow Man Who Signed for Rangers FC', *League of Coloured Peoples Newsletter*, no. 6, March 1940.

9   *Manual of Military Law*, p. 471.

10 Richard Smith in *The Oxford Companion to Black British History*, p. 176.

11 The *Manual of Military Law* (1914) defines the Special Reserve of Officers as 'a branch of the Reserve of Officers . . . designed to ensure that all units, services and departments of the regular forces shall be complete in officers on mobilization; to make good wastage which will occur in the regular forces in war, and to provide officers for special reserve units', p. 198. Immediately underneath is the paragraph which states all officers must be of pure European descent.

12 Charles Messenger, *Call to Arms: The British Army 1914–18* (London, 2005), pp. 322–3.

13 WO 339/62717.

14 CO 318/336/57983.

15 For Mitchell see Glenford Howe, *Race, War and Nationalism: A Social History of West Indians in the First World War* (Oxford, 2002), p. 52; and CO 321/282/40055, CO 321/286/47950; for Allwood, CO 351/21/25411, minute, 31 May 1915, CO 351/21/140468, 31 August 1915.

16 Walter Tull's death certificate, *Army Officers Records of War Deaths 1914–21*, SA 048397.

17 CO 272/477/15080.

18 CO 318/333/46453.

19   CO 318/333/46453.

20   CO 318/333/50043.

21   Paragraph 385 of Navy Regulations in Marika Sherwood, *Many Struggles: West Indian Workers and Service Personnel in Britain (1939–45)* (London, 1985), p. 1.

22   Sir Walter Scott, *Old Mortality* (1816), ch. 12, in *Staying Power*, p. 81.

23   John D. Ellis, 'Drummers for the Devil? The Black Soldiers of the 29th (Worcestershire) Regiment of Foot, 1759–1843', *Journal of the Society for Army Historical Research*, 80, autumn 2002, no. 323, p. 194.

24   *Staying Power*, p. 88.

25   John D. Ellis, 'A Natural Light Infantryman', *The Journal of The Royal Highland Fusiliers*, winter 2001, vol. xxvi, no. 2, p. 106.

26   'A Natural Light Infantryman'.

27   John D. Ellis, 'An Exemplary Soldier: The Reverend George Rose', *Black and Asian Studies Association Newsletter*, 31 September 2001, p. 9.

28   Brian Dyde, *The Empty Sleeve: The Story of the West India Regiments*, p. 29, in 'Drummers for the Devil?', p. 190.

29   WO 25/473 in 'Drummers for the Devil?', p. 197.

30   WO 25/473 in 'Drummers for the Devil?', pp. 1–2.

31   Richard Smith, *Moving Here*, www.movinghere.org.uk/galleries/histories/caribbean/settling/ww2.htm#.

32   Quoted by David Killingray, 'All the King's Men?', p. 177. His claim to be a Black Jew is not without precedence. See www.freemaninstitute.com/Gallery/lemba.htm for information on the chromosomal links of the Lemba people of southern Africa with the Judaic population of Israel. A Black soldier with the French Army West African, Kande Kamara, fought on the Western Front, hating it: 'You couldn't hold your teeth because of all your trembling, because during those days everything was going boom! It was disgusting . . . [a] white man's war . . . we were black and we were nothing . . . the Germans called us boots. This hurt every black man, because they actually underestimated us, and disgraced and dishonoured us.' Like many, he returned home, politicised by his experience, questioning the 'benefits' of western civilisation.

33   Norman Manley in Glenford Howe, *Race, War and Nationalism: A Social History of West Indians in the First World War* (Oxford, 2002), p. 131.

34   *Manual of Military Law* (London, 1914), p. 471.

35   www.channel4.com/history/microsites/U/untold/programs/war/page2.html.

36   CO 318/333/50043, West Indian Contingent, minute by Grindle, 21 December 1914, quoted by David Killingray in 'All the King's Men?', p. 170.

37   Richard Smith, *Jamaican Volunteers in the First World War* (Manchester, 2004), p. 65.

38   *East End Underworld*, p. 152.

39   'All the King's Men?', p. 178.

40   'All the King's Men?', p. 179.

41   CO 323/782/41475, War Office to Under-Secretary of State, Colonial Office, 24 August 1918 in Richard Smith, *Jamaican Volunteers in the First World War* (Manchester, 2004), p. 68.

42   www.channel4.com/history/microsites/U/untold/programs/war/page2.html.

43   Figures compiled by H. V. Clarke and quoted in *The Workers' Dreadnought* in Dave Lamb, *Mutinies* (2005) geocities.com/cordobakaf/mutinies.html, p. 37.

44   Richard Smith, *Oxford Companion to Black British History* (2004), pp. 176–7.

45   *Oxford Companion to Black British History*.

46   Cy Grant, *'A Member of the RAF of Indeterminate Race'* (Bognor Regis, 2006), pp. 54, 27.

47   AIR 2/13437 quoted by Lambo in *'A Member of the RAF of Indeterminate Race'*, pp. 49–50.

48   Mr Pushpinder Singh, www.bharat-rakshak.com/IAF/History/1940s/Sikhs. html excerpt from *History of the Indian Airforce* (forthcoming).

49   *Many Struggles*, p. 133.

50   N. A. M. Rodgers, 'The Wooden Wall', pp. 159–61, in *Black and Asian Studies Association Newsletter*, 26 January 2000, p. 9.

51   *Staying Power*, p. 192.

52   See entry for Hammon, Briton, in *The Oxford Companion to Black British History*, pp. 205–6. The editors write it is not known conclusively if Hammon alone penned his *Narrative*.

53   B. Pachai, *William Hall: Winner of the Victoria Cross* (Nova Scotia, 1995), pp. 5–39. Courtesy of Nova Scotia Museum, Halifax, Nova Scotia.

54   'The Arabs of Tyneside: a disappearing community' in *Black and Asian Studies Association Newsletter*, 21 April 1998, p. 7.

10   Here and now

1   EDM 1851, 20 June 2008.

2   EDM 1295, 18 April 2007.

3   General Staff, *Instructions Regarding Recommendations for Honours and Awards* (London, 1918).

4   Finlayson Family Collection.

5   Supplement to *London Gazette*, 6 April 1918, p. 4,207.

6   Supplement to *London Gazette*, 18 March 1918, p. 3,432.

7   Supplement to *London Gazette*, 18 February 1918, p. 2,914.

8   This citation from the *London Gazette* is quoted in *Battleground Europe*, p. 64.

9   WO 163/21, minutes of the proceedings of, and précis prepared for, the Army Council for the Years of 1915 and 1916, pp. 33–4, in 'The British Infantry Officer on the Western Front in the First World War', p. 362.

10   WO 163/22, minutes of the proceedings of, and précis prepared for, the Army Council for the Year 1917, p. 92, in 'The British Infantry Officer on the Western Front in the First World War', p. 363.

11   *Instructions Regarding Recommendations for Honours and Rewards*, p. 4, in 'The British Infantry Officer on the Western Front in the First World War', p. 363.

12   'The British Infantry Officer on the Western Front in the First World War', p. 375.

13   My thanks go to Andrew Riddoch for bringing this booklet to my attention.

14   Paul Chapman, Telegraph.co.uk at www.telegraph.co.uk/global/main.jhtml?view=DETAILS&grid=&xml=/global/2006/10/09/nmarois09.xml.

15   T. D. Pilcher, *A General's Letters to His Son on Obtaining His Commission* (London, 1917), p. 108, in 'The British Infantry Officer on the Western Front', p. 353.

16   Theophilus E. Samuel Scholes, *Glimpses of the Ages*, vol. 2 (London, 1908) in Fryer, *Staying Power*, p. 439.

17   Letter from Major B. S. Poole, Middlesex Regiment to Edward Tull, 12 April 1918 in Finlayson Family Collection.

18   Personal email correspondence.

19   WO 32/10592.

20   WO 32/10592.

21   WO 32/10592.

22   WO 32/10592.

23   *Manual of Military Law*, p. 471.

24   *Manual of Military Law*, p. 198.

Bibliography

Ackroyd, Peter, *London: The Biography* (London, 2001).

Ashe Jnr, Arthur, *A Hard Road to Glory*, vol. 1 (London, 1993).

Baden-Powell, Lieutenant General R. S. S., *Scouting for Boys: A Handbook for Instruction in Good Citizenship* (London, 1908).

Barritt, Gordon E., *Thomas Bowman Stephenson* (Peterborough, 1996).

Beckles, Hilary, *A History of Barbados* (Cambridge, 1990).

Bourne, John, *Britain and the Great War 1914–1918* (London, 1989).

Bradfield, William, *The Life of the Reverend Thomas Bowman Stephenson* (London, 1913).

Brown, Malcolm, *1918: Year of Victory* (London, 1998).

Cameron, John, *Association Football and How to Play It* (London, 1909).

Clark, C., *The Tin Trunk: Letters and Drawings* (London, 2000).

Crozier, F. P., *A Brass Hat in No Man's Land* (London, 1950).

Crutwell, C. R. M. F., *A History of the Great War* (Oxford, 1934).

Dabydeen, David and Sivagurunathan, Shivani (eds), *Oxford Companion to Black British History* (Oxford, 2007).

Davey, Cyril, *A Man for All Children: The Story of Thomas Bowman Stephenson* (London, 1968).

Dawson, Alec John (CN), *A 'Temporary Gentleman' in France: Home Letters from an Officer in the New Army* (London, 1916).

Disraeli, Benjamin, *Sybil* (London, 1845).

Edgerton, Robert B., *The Fall of the Asante Empire* (London, 1995).

Ferm, Reg, *Ice Cold Charity* (Sussex, 1990).

Fletcher, I. (ed.), *Letters from the Front: The Great War Correspondence of Lieutenant Brian Lawrence 1916–17* (Tunbridge Wells, 1993).

Folkestone, Sandgate and Hythe Pictorial (Folkestone, 1890).

Fryer, Peter, *Staying Power: The History of Black People in Britain* (London, 1984).

Gladden, Norman, *Across the Piave* (London, 1959).

Golesworthy, Maurice, *The Encyclopaedia of Association Football* (London, 1973, 11th edition).

Grant, Cy, *'A Member of the RAF of Indeterminate Race'* (Bognor Regis, 2006).

Green, Jeffrey, *Black Edwardians: Black People in Britain 1901–1914* (London, 1998).

Green, Jeffrey, 'Brown, James Jackson' in *Oxford Dictionary of National Biography* (Oxford, 2004).

Haig Brown, A. R., 'The Football Player' in *Sporting Sonnets* (London, 1903).

Haig Brown, A. R., *My Game Book* (London, 1903).

Haig Brown, A. R., *The OTC and Great War* (London, 1915).

Haig Brown, Valerie (ed.), *Alan Roderick Haig Brown: Writings and Reflections* (Toronto, 1982).

Harding, John, *For the Good of the Game: The Official History of the Professional Footballers' Association* (London, 1991).

Hesse-Lichtenberger, Ulrich, *Tor! The Story of German Football* (London, 2002).

Hobsbawm, Eric, *The Age of Empire 1875–1914* (London, 1995).

Howe, Glenford, *Race, War and Nationalism: A Social History of West Indians in the First World War* (Oxford, 2002).

Hoyles, Martin, *The Axe Laid to Root* (London, 2004).

Hyam, Ronald, *Empire and Sexuality: The British Experience* (Manchester, 1991).

James, C. L. R., *Beyond a Boundary* (London, 1996).

Jenkins, Stephen, *They Took the Lead. The Story of Clapton Orient's Major Contribution to the Footballers' Battalion in the Great War* (London, 2005).

Kernahan, Coulson, *The Experiences of a Recruiting Officer* (London, 1915).

Killingray, David (ed.), *Africans in Britain* (London, 1994).

Killingray, David, 'All the King's Men? Blacks in the British Army in the First World War, 1914–1918' in Rainer Lotz and Ian Pegg (eds), *Under the Imperial Carpet: Essays in Black History* (Crawley, 1986).

Lamming, Douglas, *A Scottish Soccer Internationalists' Who's Who 1872–1986* (London, 1987).

Lawford, Patricia Seaton, *The Peter Lawford Story* (New York, 1988).

Lovesey, Peter, *The Official Centenary of the AAA* (London, 1979).

Mackay, Francis, *Battleground Europe: Touring the Italian Front 1917–1919* (South Yorkshire, 2002).

Mangan, J. A. (ed.), *Pleasure, Profit and Proselytism: British Culture and Sport at Home and Abroad, 1700–1914* (London, 1982).

Mason, Tony, *Association Football and English Society 1863–1915* (Brighton, 1980).

Merriman-Labor, A. B. C., *Britons through Negro Spectacles* (London, 1909).

Messenger, Charles, *Call to Arms: The British Army 1914–18* (London, 2005).

Moister, Reverend William, *Memoir of the Rev. H. Wharton* (London, 1875).

Pachai, B., *William Hall: Winner of the Victoria Cross* (Nova Scotia, 1995).

Philpot, Terry, *Action for Children: The Story of Britain's Foremost Children's Charity* (Oxford, 1994).

Pilcher, T. D., *A General's Letters to His Son on Obtaining His Commission* (London, 1917).

Powley, Adam and Cloake, Martin, *The Spurs Miscellany: The Ultimate Book of Tottenham Trivia* (London, 2006).

Riddoch, Andrew and Kemp, John, *When the Whistle Blows: The Story of the Footballers' Battalion in the Great War* (Yeovil, 2008).

Salter, J., *The East in the West or Work among the Asiatics and Africans in London* (London, 1895).

Samuel, Ralph, *East End Underworld* (London, 1981).

Sassoon, Siegfried, *Memoirs of an Infantry Officer* (London, 2001).

Scholes, Theophilus E. Samuel, *Glimpses of the Ages*, vol. 2 (London, 1908).

Sherwood, Marika, *Many Struggles: West Indian Workers and Service Personnel in Britain (1939–45)* (London, 1985).

Short Guide to Obtaining a Commission in the Special Reserve of Officers (London, 1912).

Sillitoe, Alan, *Raw Material* (London, 1978).

Smith, Richard, *Jamaican Volunteers in the First World War* (Manchester, 2004).

Stephenson, Thomas Bowman, *Concerning Sisterhoods* (London, 1890).

Taylor, H., *Jix: Viscount Brentford* (London, 1933).

Terrain, John (ed.), *General Jack's War Diary: War on the Western Front 1914–18* (London, 1993).

Vasili, Phil, *Colouring over the White Line: The History of Black Footballers in Britain* (Edinburgh, 2000).

Vasili, Phil, *The First Black Footballer – Arthur Wharton, 1865–1930: An Absence of Memory* (London, 1998).

Wagstaffe-Simmons, G., *Tottenham Hotspur Football Club: Its Birth and Progress 1882–1946* (Tottenham, 1947).

War Office, *Instructions for the Training of Platoons for Offensive Action* (London, 1917).

War Office, *Manual of Military Law* (London, 1914).

Wickens, Rod, *From Claret to Khaki* (Liverpool, 2003).

Wyrall, Everard, *The Die-Hards in the Great War*, vol. 1 *1914–16* and vol. 2 *1916–19* (London, 1926).

Newspapers

Athletic News (Manchester)
Buenos Aires Herald
Carrick Herald (Girvan)

Daily Chronicle
Edinburgh Herald and Post
Football Echo (Northampton)
Football Star
Glasgow Evening Times
Guardian
Illustrated Sporting and Dramatic News
Leith Observer
London Gazette
Newcastle Evening Chronicle
The New York Times
Northampton Daily Chronicle
The Socialist Pioneer
The Sporting Chronicle
Sporting Man (Newcastle)
Sports Special The Green 'Un (Sheffield)
The Times
Tottenham and Wood Green Advertiser
The Wednesday Herald (Tottenham and Edmonton)
The Weekly Herald (Tottenham and Edmonton)
Wesleyan Methodist Magazine

Journals and articles

African Review, 9 September, vol. xx, no. 355.
Black and Asian Studies Association Newsletter.
Blackwood's Edinburgh Magazine, 943 (May 1894) vol. 155.
Ellis, John D., 'Drummers for the Devil? The Black Soldiers of the 29th (Worcestershire) Regiment of Foot, 1759–1843', *Journal of the Society for Army Historical Research*, vol. 80, autumn 2002, no. 323.
Ellis, John D., 'An Exemplary Soldier: The Reverend George Rose', *Black and Asian Studies Association Newsletter*, 31 September 2001.
Ellis, John D., 'A Natural Light Infantryman', *Journal of the Royal Highland Fusiliers*, winter 2001, vol. xxvi.
Green, Jeffrey P., 'Boxing and the "Colour Question" in Edwardian Britain: The "White Problem" of 1911', *International Journal of the History of Sport*, 5, 118 (1988).
Highways and Hedges, newsletter of the National Children's Home.
League of Coloured Peoples Newsletter, 6 March 1940.
London Gazette, 18 February 1918, 18 March 1918, 6 April 1918.
Roberts, James, '"The Best Football Team, the Best Platoon": The Role of

Football in the Proletarianization of the British Expeditionary Force, 1914–1918', *Sport in History*, vol. 26, 1 April 2006.

Sandhu, Sukhdev, 'A League of His Own', *Guardian*, 3 April 1999.

The Socialist Pioneer, 16 December 1914.

Vasili, Phil, 'Walter Daniel Tull, 1888–1918: Soldier, Footballer, Black', *Race and Class*, 38, October–December 1996, no. 2.

Public documents

Census, Folkestone, 1891.

Colonial Office files: 96/238/2044, 272/477/15080, 318/333/46453, 318/333/50043, 318/336/57983, 321/282/40055, 321/286/47950, 323/782/41475, 351/21/140468, 351/21/25411.

Early Day Motions: 1295, 18 April 2007; 1851, 20 June 2008.

National Archives, London.

Walter Tull's death certificate, *Army Officers Records of War Deaths 1914–21*, SA 048397.

War Diary, 17th Middlesex Regiment.

War Diary, 23rd Middlesex Regiment.

War Office files: 25/473, 32/10592, 95/2639, 95/1361, 95/157/633, 95/4243, 163/21; 163/22, 339/90293/175466, 339/62717.

Theses

Kang, Changboo, 'The British Infantry Officer on the Western Front in the First World War. With Special Reference to the Royal Warwickshire Regiment' (unpublished), Centre for First World War Studies, University of Birmingham (2002).

Private and archive collections

Cox, C. H., private papers, Imperial War Museum, London, 88/11/1.

Epitome of Correspondence, Tull file, NCH Action for Children.

Finlayson Family Collection, Strathpeffer, Scotland.

Finlayson, Jean, *Tales of Grandfathers*, n.d. (unpublished), Finlayson Family Collection.

Floyer-Acland, Arthur Nugent, 'The Journal of Arthur Nugent Acland', Imperial War Museum, London, 03/29/1.

Lane, Sergeant Stanley A., 'The Great War 1914–18: Personal Experiences of a Front Line Infantryman', Imperial War Museum, London, 97/10/1.

Paterson, 2nd Lieutenant W., private papers, Imperial War Museum, London, 89/7/1.

Phillips, Captain L. N., private papers, Imperial War Museum, London, 77/103/1.

Pope-Hennessy, Major General, *Diary of Major General Pope-Hennessy*, Imperial War Museum, London, 03/35/1.

Interviews

Jean Finlayson (née Tull-Warnock) and Reverend Duncan Finlayson, Appin, Argyll, 20 February 1995.

Reverend Duncan Finlayson, Edward Finlayson and Pat Justad, Strathpeffer, 2 June 2008.

Stephen Coombe, Folkestone, 18 June 2008.

Rita Humphrey, Maidstone, 22 June 2008.

Websites

www.bharat-rakshak.com/IAF/History/1940s/Sikhs.html   Mr Pushpinder Singh, *History of the Indian Airforce* (forthcoming).

www.channel4.com/history/microsites/U/untold/programs/war/page2.html   A discussion of the role of the British West Indies Regiment in the First World War.

w.w.w.chronicleworld.org   *Chronicle World – Changing Black Britain.*

geocities.com/cordobakaf/mutinies.html   *Mutinies* by David Lamb.

jaiarjun.blogspot.com/2004/11/ranji-maharajah-of-connemara.html   A discussion of the life of Ranjitsinhji.

www.movinghere.org.uk/galleries/histories/caribbean/settling/ww2.htm#   Richard Smith, *Moving Here.*

myweb.tiscali.co.uk/tedspires/Diary.htm   *First World War Diary of Bdr Charles Bertram Spires 1917–1918.*

www.pbs.org/race/000_About/002_03_a-godeeper.htm   An exploration of the connection between 'race', science and social policy.

www.rbooks.co.uk/product.aspx?id=0712667830   A synopsis of Ben Shephard, *A War of Nerves* (London, 2002).

www.spurshistory.com   *A Romance of Football: The History of Tottenham 1882–1921.*

www.telegraph.co.uk/global/main.jhtml?view=DETAILS&grid=&xml=/global/2006/10/09/nmarois09.xml   An article on Sergeant Haane Manahi.

www.theirhistory.co.uk   NCH online history.

www.victorianlondon.org   Lee Jackson, *The Victorian Dictionary.*

Index

Page numbers in *italic* at the end of index entries refer to photographs in the picture section.

17th Middlesex 139, 141–2, 144, 146–8, 149–51, 152, 153, 154, 155, 159, 160–1, 167, 194, 218
23rd Middlesex 149, 152, 159, 161, 166, 167, 170, 172–6, 179, 181, 182, 183, 184, 199, 218
Abbott, Diane 18
Abomah (African giantess) 53
Abrahams, Harold 134, 135, 136
Adcock, Rev. George 35, 56–7, 60
Afghanistan 197–8
Alcindor, Dr John 128
Aldridge, Ira 48
Aldridge, Luranah 48
Allwood, Dr A. J. 192, 203
Amateur Football Association 80, 144
amateur/professional debate 78–81
anti-communism 206
anti-Semitism 135, 136
Archer, John 48
Ardiles, Osvaldo 98
Argentina 82–6, 87
armed forces, ethnic composition of 208–15
Armstrong, Bob 133
the arts, Black people in 48–53
Ashe, Arthur 130, 131
Aston Villa 77, 104, 122, 125
athletics 121, 128, 134–6

Baden-Powell, Lieutenant General 143
Baptist, John 195
Barbados 27–8, 29, 30
Barber, Tom 141
Basuto football team 121–4, 125–6
Beer, Bill 20, 23, 24, 168
Beer, Clara (stepmother) 20, 23, 24, 26, 33–4, 35, 56, 57, 59, 60, 67, 69–70, 168
Bennett, Louis 128
Bhownagree, Sir Mancherje Merwnajee 48
Billingham, T. 184–5, 216, 226
Binley, Brian 217–18, 223
Black radicalism 40, 42–3, 45–6, 47, 208, 228–9
Blackburn Rovers 111–12, 120
Blunden, Edward 153
Blyden, Edward Wilmot 51
Boer War 90, 123, 124, 125
Bogard, Ikey 67, 203
Bowfrey, Benjamin 42
Bowie, Jimmy 16, 19
boxing 129–33
Bridgetower, George Augustus 49
Bristol City 93, 94, 95–6, 119
British West Indies Regiment (BWIR) 178, 191, 192, 194, 202, 205, 228
Brown, David 90
Brown, Eugene 199
Brown, Gershom 205

Brown, Dr James Jackson 73, 97, 128, 202
Brown, John 199
Brown, Roy 199
Brown, Thomas 32, 213
Bruce, Lewis 51
Buckley, Frank 141–2, 150
Bull, Walter 79, 106

Cameron, John 88–90
Caribbean League 208
Cato Street Conspiracy 45
Catton, J. A. H. 114
Chapman, Herbert 102–4, 167
Chariots of Fire 134–7
Charrington, Frederick N. 144
Chartists 46–7
Chelsea FC 84, 88, 99
Children's Home and Orphanage
    (CHO) 19, 23, 35, 54–6, 58, 59–66,
    67–8, 69, 70–2, 73, 148; *4, 5*
Christian Brotherhood Movement 132
Christmas Day matches (1914) 143
Churchill, Winston 132, 206
Clapton FC 12, 73, 75, 76, 78; *7, 8*
Clapton Orient 77, 104, 146, 164
Clark, Lieutenant John 149, 151, 152
Clarke, Eugent 205
Clarke, William Robinson 210
Clough, Joe 51
Coleridge-Taylor, Samuel 48–9
Collier, Bob 200
Collins, Reginald Emmanuel 191–2
commercialisation of football 79
Constantine, Learie 96
Coombe, Stephen 25–6
Cooper, Charlie 199
Corbett, Fred 119
Corbett, James 130
Costa (Asian footballer) 120–1
Cother, Edwin 24, 117, 118
Cother, John 117–18, 119
cricket 72, 73, 80, 88, 96, 107, 127, 128,
    136, 211
Cuffay, William 46, 47
cycling 129

Dana, Charles 130–1
Darnell, A. J. 168
Davidson, William 45
Davies, William Broughton 202
Davis, Belle 50
Dhingra, Madan Lal 97
Dobbs, Bobby 129
Dove, Frank S. 199–200
Duffy, David Anthony 47
Durham, James 197, 198

Edward, Harry 134, 136
Edwards, Samuel Jules Celestine 51
Equiano, Olaudah 40, 43–4, 45, 212
Everton FC 75, 78, 81, 82, 84, 86, 91, 144

female suffrage 40
Ferm, Reg 71
Finlayson, Edward (great-nephew) 217,
    230
Finlayson, Jean (niece) 13, 14, 15–16, 17,
    18, 19, 20–1, 22, 71, 174, 186; *24*
Finlayson, Rev. Duncan 13, 14, 15, 16, 17,
    21, 22; *24*
First World War 25, 26, 39–40, 138–86;
    Black servicemen 178, 191, 192, 194,
    199–200, 202, 205, 208–11, 215;
    casualties 152, 161, 162, 167–8, 185;
    cessation of professional football
    144, 145–6, 147; medal quota system
    221; mutinies 40, 163, 182, 205–6,
    207–8; origins of conflict 138–9;
    racist commissioning practices 163–4,
    169, 180, 190–2, 194, 204–5; racist
    recruitment practices 139–40, 187, 190,
    192–3, 201, 203–4, 209–10; Treaty of
    Versailles 100
Folkestone 23–4, 25, 29, 31–2, 41, 155
Football Association 26, 76, 82, 145
Football Controversy 144–7
football grounds, wartime requisitioning
    of 144–5
Football League 145
Footballers' Battalions *see* 17th
    Middlesex; 23rd Middlesex

Foster, Allen 155
Foulke, Billy 89, 126
Freeman, Patrick 200

Gardiner, Charlotte 42–3
Gee, Rex 162
George V 194
Germany 99–100, *see also* First World War
Gerrish, Walter 141
Glover, John 42
Goodall, John 117
Gordon Riots (1780) 42–3
Grace Hill Wesleyan Chapel 54, 56
Grant, Cy 209
Grantham, Colonel 141, 144, 150
Graves, Robert 153–4, 164
Gregory, Dr A. E. 59, 69

Haig, Sir Douglas 143, 160, 176, 185
Haig Brown, Lieutenant Colonel Alan 152, 163–6, 167, 181, 183, 221
Hall, William 213–14
Hammon, Briton 212
Harder, Otto 'Tull' 99, 100, 101
Harding, Arthur 66–7, 203
Hardy, Thomas 45
Harrison, Frederic 143
Hayes-Fisher, William 143, 144, 145, 146
Heanor Town 101, 106
Hegazi, Hassan 120
Horton, James Africanus 51, 202
Humphrey, Graham 22
Humphrey, Rita (great-niece) 22; *23*

imperial campaigns, Black soldiers serving in 187, 188, 189, 195–6
Iraq war 124
Isaac, Billy 128
Italy 40, 158, 176–82, 205

Jackson, Peter 130
James, C. L. R. 96, 127, 136
James, Joseph Barbour 137
Jeptha, Andrew 129, 133

Johnson, Albert 129
Johnson, Jack 24, 131, 132–3
Johnson, Len 129
Johnson, William 129
Jonas, William 141
Joynson-Hicks, William 143, 144, 145, 146, 149, 150, 153, 228

Keenor, Fred 141
Kerr, John Guthrie 19
Kett, Robert 43
Kinnaird, Lord 144, 145
Kitchener, Lord 145, 194, 201

Lancaster, William 208–9
Lane, Stanley 148–9
Langford, Sam 133
Lawford, Peter 180–1
Lawford, Major General Sidney 166, 172, 180, 181, 219–20
League of Coloured Peoples 11, 17, 190
League of Universal Brotherhood 132
Liddle, Eric 134, 135–6
Lloyd George, David 125, 206, 207
LoBagola (Joseph Howard Lee) 200, 203
Lomax, Brian 229
London, Black community in 41–2, 43
London Combination League 150
London, John Edward 'Jack' 134, 136
London Corresponding Society 45

McClain, Billy 50
McCrae, Lieutenant-Colonel Sir George 145
Macdonald, Bobby 128
Malik, Sardar Hardit Singh 210–11
Manahi, Haane 224
Manchester City 98, 145
Manchester United 92, 142
Manley, Norman 200
Maori football team 126
Marshall, Albert 215
Massaquoi, Hans-Jürgen 100
Mercer, Mabel 49
Meredith, Billy 79

Merriman-Labor, A. B. C. 51–2
Methodism 28, 33, 54, 56, 59, 66, 78, 81,
    104–5, 143, 197
Meyer, Rev. F. B. 131–2, 133
Military Cross: criteria for nomination
    221–2; posthumous awards 222–3; Tull
    and 175, 181, 184, 217–24; 25
Mitchell, Dr W. S. 192
Mohamed, Duse 49, 51
Moody, Charles Arundel 11, 190, 227
Moody, Harold 11, 190
Morrison, Arthur 66
Muscular Christianity 78, 81, 136, 165,
    166
Mussabini, Sam 134

Naoroji, Dadabhai 47, 48
Nathan, Alonzo 202
National Service 228
Nazism 99–100, 101
Needham, Archie 141, 150
Newcastle United 78, 103, 122
Njilima, Frederick 200
Norris, Henry 143–4, 145, 146, 150
North Board School 31, 32–3, 57; 3
Northampon Town 11, 99, 101–7, 168,
    229; 13

Oehler, Kenneth 192
Offiah, Martin 134
officer corps 167–8
officer privileges 171–2
officer training 169–70, 171
Ollivierre, Charles Augustus 128
Orange Free State Football Association
    (OFSFA) 121–2
Orme, Joe 141
Owens, Jesse 49

Palmer, Ernest (cousin) 26
Palmer, George Thomas (cousin) 26
Palmer, Harriet (aunt) 26
Palmer, John Alexander (uncle) 26
Palmer, Robert (cousin) 30
Palmer, Sarah-Ann (grandmother) 29–30

Palmer, Stephen John Alexander (cousin)
    26
Palmer, Walter Henry (cousin) 26
Palmer, William (cousin) 26, 30
'pals' battalions 139, 142
Pan-African Conference (1900) 42, 48, 132
Passchendaele 26, 157–8, 162, 172, 175,
    176
Patch, Harry 157–8
Perkins, John 213
Peters, James 129
Peters, Samuel 195–6
Pickard, 2nd Lieutenant 57, 179, 181, 184,
    219, 225
Pilcher, Major General T. D. 224
political and social role of sport 125,
    127–8, 142–3
politics, Black people and 39–48
Poole, Major D. S. 57, 175, 181, 219, 225
poor relief system 34–5, 57, 59, 72
Powell, Clifford 205
Preston North End 94, 104, 114–15
Pretyman-Newman, Major John 152
Prophitt, Benjamin 47

Queen's Park 110–12, 113, 114

race riots 42, 228, 229
racism 17–18, 21, 40, 52, 94, 96–7, 98,
    99–100, 108, 116–17, 129–34, 160, 188,
    200, 215, 226; in the armed forces
    139–40, 163–4, 169, 180, 187, 190–3,
    194, 197, 198, 201, 203–5, 209–10,
    226–8; in journalism 116, 123–4, 125,
    130–1; scientific racism 98, 99–100,
    117, 131, 132, 133, 159, 188, 189, 196, 209
Rance, Charles 76, 99
Rangers FC 16, 86, 168
Ranjitsinhji, K. S. 127, 128, 164, 188
regimental musicians, Black 194–5, 197,
    198
repatriation 228
Reubens, Robert 204
Rivers, W. H. R. 159
Roberts, Charlie 79

Robeson, Paul 17, 21–2
Roman army, men of colour in 198–9
Ronaldo, Cristiano 89
Rose, Revd George 196–7
Roy, Indra Lal 210, 211
Royal Air Force 194
Royal Army Medical Corps 192, 202
Royal Flying Corps/Air Force 209–11
Royal Navy 194, 211–15
rugby 80, 103, 129
Rushden 107, 108, 186
Rushdie-Gray, G. O. 202

St Lucia 28, 29
Saklatvala, Shapurji 48
Sassoon, Siegfried 153, 159, 162
Scanlon, Bob 129
Scholes, Theophilus 51, 225–6
Seacole, Mary 202
'shamateur' clubs 81, 115
Sheffield United 77, 90, 104, 126
shell shock 155–6, 157, 158–9, 160
Shyngle, J. Egerton 200
Simpson, Lenox 197, 198
slavery and abolition 27, 28, 29, 42, 43–4,
    45, 46, 89, 97, 98, 116, 194, 197, 203,
    211–12, 213
Slessor, Air Chief Marshal Sir John C.
    209–10
Slim, James 202
Smith, Connie and Augustus 50
social class 42, 79, 80, 128, 136, 140, 145,
    147, 152, 162, 167, 170, 186, 206, 221
Solomon, Henry 200
Somme 26, 158, 159, 160–2, 167, 183, 185
Spires, Bertram 155–7, 179–80
sports science 89–90
Stephenson, Dr Thomas Bowman 54–5,
    56, 57, 58–9, 64–5, 66, 68, 166
Sunderland 90, 91, 94, 122–3

Taylor, Marshall 129
Tennant, Harold 144
Tickler, Lieutenant Arthur 146–7
Tomkins, Eric 'Wassie' 107

Tottenham Hotspur 11, 12, 77–8, 80,
    81–9, 106, 119, 126; 10, 11
Toussaint L'Ouverture, François
    Dominique 40, 43, 48, 197
trade unionism 42, 45, 79, 182, 206–7
Tull, Alice (mother) 22, 26, 29, 30, 31, 33
Tull, Anna (grandmother) 27, 28, 30–1
Tull, Bertha (sister) 30
Tull, Cecilia (Cissie) (sister) 13–14, 20,
    23–4, 31, 56, 67; 1; 16
Tull, Daniel (father) 22, 27–8, 29–30, 31,
    32, 33–4, 44, 74, 108, 121; 1
Tull-Warnock, Edward (brother) 11,
    12–13, 16, 17–21, 22, 23, 31, 33, 57, 60,
    61–4, 66, 67–71, 119, 148, 168, 169, 186,
    190; 1, 5, 16
Tull-Warnock, Elizabeth (sister-in-law)
    19–20
Tull, Elsie (sister) 20, 24, 26, 31, 56; 1
Tull, Gertrude (sister-in-law) 24, 25, 168
Tull, Gladys (niece) 24, 168
Tull, Mildred (niece) 22, 24–5
Tull, Miriam (sister) 20, 24, 34, 35
Tull, Walter: army officer 163–4, 167,
    168, 169, 170, 171, 173–4, 179, 191, 228,
    229; 15, 16; 17, 18; 19, 20; birth and early
    life 31, 32–3; 1; character and qualities
    41, 57, 67, 72–3, 166, 175, 225; in the
    Children's Home 23, 60, 67–8, 70–1,
    71–3, 75, 148; 5; 6; cricket player 72, 73,
    88, 107; death of 20, 183–5, 226; ethical
    difficulties over professionalism 78–9,
    80, 81; football career 75–107, 168; 7,
    8, 10, 11, 12, 13; letters from the front
    173–4; love life 107, 108–9, 168, 230;
    memorials to 25, 186; 21, 22; and the
    Military Cross 175, 181, 184, 217–24;
    25; military service 139–40, 141, 148,
    152–3, 154–5, 159–60, 163–4, 168–9,
    172–5, 179–80, 181, 201, 204–5, 226–7;
    posthumous stature of 216–17, 224–5,
    229; printing apprenticeship 59, 71, 72,
    73–4, 78, 107; racial abuse of 94, 96;
    shell shock, treated for 155–6, 159, 160;
    South American tour 78, 81–8; 9

Tull, William (grandfather) 27
Tull, William Stephen (brother) 22,
    23–4, 25, 30, 34, 56, 67, 119–20, 155,
    168, 199; *1*
Turnbull, Sandy 141
Turpin, Randolph 130
Twaji, Joseph 122
Twigg, Derek 222

Universal Races Congress (1911) 132
Uruguay 83, 86

Vassa, Anna Maria 44
Vassa, Joanna 44, 45
Vaz, Keith 218

Walker, John 96, 115–16, 117
Walker, Robert 110–11, 112, 113, 121
Wall, Fred 139
Walter Tull Association (WTA) 217
Warnock, James 16, 20, 68–9, 70, 72
Warnock, Jean 20, 68, 70, 168; *16*
Washington, Booker T. 41
Watford FC 117, 118
Watson, Andrew 110, 111, 112–13, 114, 115,
    121

Watson, Egbert 199
Wedderburn, Robert 40, 45, 46
Wells, 'Bombardier Billy' 131
Wells-Holland, Captain Henry 146
West Ham United 119
Wharton, Arthur 48, 90, 96, 97, 104,
    105, 112, 113, 114–15, 121, 126, 128, 136,
    188, 198
Wharton, Henry 187, 189
White supremacism 130–1, 132–4,
    159
Whitecuff, Benjamin 213
Willard, Jess 133
Williams, Annie 107, 168
Williams, Charlie 199
Williams, George 200
Wilson, Field Marshal Sir Henry 206
Wolseley, General Garnet 187, 188–9
Wolverhampton Wanderers 142
Woodward, Vivien 40, 75, 77, 86, 88, 89,
    141, 153
Woolwich Arsenal 84, 94, 98, 102, 103
Wrigglesworth, Fred 71
Wylie, Sir William Hutt Curzon 97

Young Leaguers Union (YLU) 69, 71